PROMISES BROKEN
Courtship, Class, and Gender
in Victorian England

VICTORIAN LITERATURE AND CULTURE SERIES
Karen Chase, Jerome J. McGann, *and* Herbert Tucker, *General Editors*

PROMISES BROKEN
Courtship, Class, and Gender
in Victorian England

Ginger S. Frost

UNIVERSITY PRESS OF VIRGINIA
Charlottesville and London

THE UNIVERSITY PRESS OF VIRGINIA
Copyright © 1995 by the Rector and Visitors
of the University of Virginia

First published 1995

Library of Congress Cataloging-in-Publication Data

Frost, Ginger Suzanne, 1962–
    Promises broken : courtship, class, and gender in Victorian
England / Ginger S. Frost.
        p.   cm.—(Victorian literature and culture series)
    Includes bibliographical references and index.
    ISBN 0–8139-1610-0 (alk. paper)
    1. Breach of promise—Great Britain—History—19th century.
    2. Man-woman relationships—England—History—19th century.
    3. Courtship—England—History—19th century.   I. Title.
    II. Series.
    KD754.F76   1995
    346.42'022—dc20
    [344.20622   95–7637
                                                          CIP

Printed in the United States of America

Contents

Acknowledgments

I could never have written this book without the financial support of numerous organizations. First, I would like to thank the History Department at Rice University for their unswerving support. I also owe a debt of gratitude to the Graduate Council of Rice for awarding me the Lodieski Stockbridge Vaughn Fellowship in 1990, which freed me to begin my writing. Most of all, I would like to thank the North American Conference on British Studies for giving me their Dissertation Year Fellowship in 1989, and the British Council for their gift of a travel award. Without their help I would not have been able to travel to Great Britain and complete my research.

Any number of patient archivists and their staff members aided me in my work in London. I am grateful to the staffs of the Public Record Office at Chancery Lane, the Institute of Advanced Legal Studies, and the British Library for their hard work on my behalf. I was welcomed and received much encouragement at the Institute of Historical Research, particularly from Alice Prochaska and the Women's History Seminar, for which I am grateful. I particularly feel indebted to Guy Holborn, who allowed me to use the Lincoln's Inn Library free of supervision, and his kind and helpful staff. And I warmly thank David Doughan for his support and advice in using the Fawcett Library. Finally, I owe my biggest thanks to the staff of the British Library's Newspaper Annex at Colindale, a group who cheerfully delivered a score of volumes of provincial newspapers to me every day for over a month. Without them I would not have been able to develop such a comprehensive study.

The Interlibrary Loan Department at Fondren Library at Rice managed to uncover a number of valuable sources for me while I worked in the United States, some of which were not even in the British Library. For that I appreciate their help. I also would like to thank the History Department of Northwestern University for their timely offer of a department associateship in 1993–94. I was able to use their libraries and other resources to make much needed revisions. I have been fortunate to have worked at several libraries in different institutions across the country, and I thank the staffs of the following: the University of Houston Law Library, University of Michigan Law Library, University of Georgia Library, Northern Illinois University Library, and New York Public Library. I also appreciate the support and encouragement of my colleagues for two years at Wesleyan College in Macon, Georgia.

Thomas Haskell and Helena Michie read the manuscript and suggested many improvements while it was at the dissertation stage. In addition, any number of historians throughout the last few years have read portions or all of the manuscript and given excellent advice, including Gale Stokes, Lawrence Stone, David Sugarman, Philippa Levine, Ellen Ross, Nancy Grey Osterud, Roderick Phillips, Judith Blackwelder, Nancy Fix Anderson, Martha Vicinus, and the twelve members of the NEH seminar that she led at the University of Michigan in the summer of 1992. Despite their immense assistance, however, I owe the most intellectual debt to two fine mentors. First, I am grateful to Professor Martin Wiener, who not only read the manuscript and vastly improved it, but gave me the topic in the first place. Second, I want to thank John Gillis, who first recommended the book for publication and acted as a second adviser from that time on. My debt to both men is immeasurable.

I also want to thank *Gender and History* for their permission to reprint materials already published by them in 6 (Summer 1994): 224–45, under the title "'I Shall Not Sit Down and Crie': Feminism, Class and Breach of Promise Plaintiffs in England, 1850–1900." Part of this manuscript has also appeared as "'Improper Intimacies': Illicit Sex in Victorian England," in *Marriage and the Family in History: Papers from the First Carleton Conference on the History of the Family* (Canadian Scholars' Press, forthcoming). I appreciate their permission to republish the work.

The editors and staff at the University Press of Virginia also deserve my thanks, particularly Cathie Brettschneider and Gerald Trett, who oversaw the process of turning my overlong manuscript into this book. I also owe a debt of gratitude to Enid Hickingbotham, my copyeditor. She kept my work from having numerous inconsistencies. And a special thanks to Peggy Wogan for her cheerful, intelligent help in proofing the manuscript.

Naturally, I also have had support closer to home. I want to thank my mother, Marillyn Rheay Frost, for being the fiercely partisan supporter that all writers need. I also feel gratitude to my sister, Jackie Jackson, and my niece, Elizabeth Rheay Dixon, who provided much-needed breaks from history. Finally, I owe the most to Jim Schmidt, who read the manuscript several times and vastly improved it. Despite all this assistance, though, any mistakes in this work are entirely my own.

Parts of this manuscript have been published before. A précis of my research appeared in *Gender and History* in volume 6 (Summer 1994) under the title "'I Shall Not Sit Down and Crie': Feminism, Class and Breach of Promise Plaintiffs in England, 1850–1900." Another section of this manuscript appeared as "'Improper Intimacies': Illicit Sex in Victorian England," in *Marriage and the Family in History: Papers from the First Carleton Conference on the History of the Family* (Canadian Scholars' Press, 1994, forthcoming). I appreciate their permission to republish the work.

PROMISES BROKEN

Courtship, Class, and Gender
in Victorian England

Introduction

The Myth of Breach of Promise

SUITS FOR BREACH OF PROMISE of marriage were well known to the public in Victorian England. From at least the 1830s a variety of writers recognized the inherent humor and drama of the action and began to fictionalize the cases as they were then brought. The depictions of the trials during the century gave a strangely uniform representation of the people who brought such litigation and the outcome of their conflicts. This interpretation built up an idealized myth of breach of promise, one which influenced the perception of the suit far more than actual cases did. This myth can be best seen in five fictional accounts of trials between the 1830s and the 1890s.

In 1836 Charles Dickens published *The Pickwick Papers,* an early work that was instantly popular.[1] Part of the appeal of the novel was its comically apt depiction of a breach of promise of marriage case. The defendant in Dickens's version was Samuel Pickwick, and the plaintiff was his widowed landlady, Martha Bardell. Pickwick had lodged with Bardell for two years when he approached her about hiring a manservant. He went about it in a circuitous way, asking, "Do you think it a much greater expense to keep two people than to keep one?" and commenting on how nice it would be for her young son to have a companion (Dickens, 170). Consequently, Bardell got the wrong impression. Thinking he was proposing, she threw herself in his arms, and before he could disentangle himself, she fainted. Three of his friends entered the room at that moment and witnessed the awkward embrace.

Pickwick went on to hire Sam Weller as his manservant, but he never corrected his landlady's mistaken impression. Bardell soon realized that he had no intention of fulfilling his promise, so she went to a firm of solicitors, Dodson and Fogg, whom she hired on spec (they would receive their fees from the defendant if the suit succeeded) to sue Pickwick for £1,500 damages. Pickwick was astounded at this turn of events, blaming it on the "grasping attorneys," whom he tried to intimidate into withdrawing the suit (268). Much to his chagrin, however, the case went to trial. His barrister was the inept Sergeant Snubbin, but Dodson and Fogg had retained the renowned Sergeant Buzfuz.[2] Buzfuz knew every trick in the book: he brought the widow in, weeping, with her child at her feet; he masterfully dealt with his mostly reluctant witnesses; and he made a great deal of the bits of correspondence that Bardell could offer as evidence.

(520–21)[3]

> *Two letters have passed between these parties. . . . Let me read the first:—* "*Garraway's, twelve o'clock.—Dear Mrs. B.—Chops and Tomata sauce. Yours, PICKWICK.*" *Gentlemen, what does this mean? Chops and Tomata sauce. . . . Gentlemen, is the happiness of a sensitive and confiding female to be trifled away, by such shallow artifices as these? The next has no date whatever, which is in itself suspicious.—* "*Dear Mrs. B., I shall not be at home till tomorrow. Slow coach.*" *And then follows this very remarkable expression—* "*Dont trouble yourself about the warming-pan.*" *The warming-pan! . . . Why is Mrs. Bardell so earnestly entreated not to agitate herself about this warming-pan, unless . . . it is a mere cover for hidden fire?*

Pickwick's barrister confined himself to an inadequate speech, and Justice Stareleigh slept through most of the trial, only confusing everyone in his summation.[4] Unsurprisingly, the jury found for Bardell, with damages of £750.

Already this scenario was an amusing parody of the class of suit and the legal process. But Dickens did not leave the story there. Pickwick refused to pay the award or the costs of the action, and he was thrown into the Fleet Prison for debt. Eventually, Dodson and Fogg grew impatient of getting their fees. Bardell had signed a *cognovit* to the effect that if Pickwick did not pay, she would do so. Unfortunately, she had too little money to pay the fees, and she, too, was thrown into prison. After several of Pickwick's friends appealed to him on her behalf, he agreed to pay the lawyers out of chivalry to a lady in distress, and they both went free.[5] Bardell, in return, agreed to waive her damages, and the ludicrous case came to an end.

Pickwick's ill-fated trip to the High Court was enormously popular with Victorian audiences; at least two plays were based solely on chapter 34 of *Pickwick* in the years after its publication, and a longer play based on the entire book included a dramatization of the trial. According to Percy Fitzgerald in 1902, there was even a French version. A London preacher, a few years after the publication of the work, referred to the trial to illustrate the need for prayer, saying, "In fact, as Sergeant Buzfuz said to Sam Weller, in the trial of Bardell *v.* Pickwick, there is little to do, and plenty to get." An early version of the *Oxford English Dictionary* used Bardell's *cognovit* as an example of its meaning.[6]

Having made such a great impression on the general public, the parody went on to have an even bigger influence on legal writers and practitioners. Two legal volumes used Bardell v. Pickwick as an example in their discussions of the law of hearsay. Barristers sometimes brought up the fictional case in the middle of real ones. Mr. Cole, in *Gregory v. Beach* in 1873, began his closing speech by comparing the plaintiff's barrister to Sergeant Buzfuz. Especially when widows were involved, barristers quoted the numerous sayings of Sam Weller's father about the dangers of courting such experienced women. Newspaper court reporters occasionally added Dickensian touches to their reports. The report of *Jones v. Chapman* in 1889 contained the subheading, "Just what Sergeant Snubbin Did," when the defense barrister confined himself to a closing speech.[7]

In fact, Bardell v. Pickwick came to symbolize most of the alleged abuses of breach-of-promise suits. Ignoring the real villains of the book (Dodson and Fogg), critics of the action concentrated on the fact that the action led to an innocent man being milked for damages. Often, when these men reported a case they disliked, they compared it to the trial in *The Pickwick Papers*. The *Law Times,* in reporting *Haycox v. Bishton,* expounded on the lack of evidence for the plaintiff, concluding that "it was quite the case of *Bardell v. Pickwick.*" The editors also inveighed against *Jones v. Heasman* in 1868 because the correspondence between the couple was scanty. After printing the one short letter Heasman had written to Jones, they complained that "this rivals the famous letter in *Pickwick.*" In 1883 the editors of *Law Notes* made a similar point about a case of which they disapproved.[8]

Furthermore, a great number of people who wrote or spoke about breach of promise discussed the case well into the twentieth century. Charles Mac-Colla, a lawyer who wrote a history of the action, used the case as an example of the abuses of breach of promise. William Blake Odgers, in his work on law reform in 1901, mentioned Bardell v. Pickwick to illustrate the need for the Evidence Amendment Act of 1869. Judge Edward Parry referred to it in his book on women and the laws of England, published in 1916, and F. W. Ashley, who served as a clerk to Justice Avory for over fifty years, mentioned it in his memoirs in 1936, even though Avory primarily dealt with criminal law. Indeed, the popularity of the fictional trial lasted until the suit was abolished. As late as 1956 G. D. Nokes was still using the pseudo-case to explain the law of evidence. And Julius Silverman, in his speech to introduce the bill to abolish the action in 1970, began by referring to Dickens.[9] In short, this fictional case had far more impact on people's perceptions of breach-of-promise suits than any single real case did. By parodying the case, Dickens helped to create a mythical version of the action, which subsequent representations augmented.

Interestingly, Bardell v. Pickwick was not the first dramatization of a breach-of-promise case. In 1832 *Breach of Promise* debuted on the London stage.[10] The two-act play was written by J. B. Buckstone, a hack playwright who wrote dozens of light plays during his long career. *Breach of Promise* was a farcical piece, centering on a widow, Mrs. Trapper, and her three silly daughters. Her friend, Mr. Sudden, was a confirmed bachelor, who had difficulty managing his ward, Mary. Frustrated, he decided on the spur of the moment to ask Trapper to marry him the very next day, thinking that a wife could handle his domestic problems better. At first, Trapper demurred; to prove his sincerity, Sudden wrote out the promise on a piece of paper. Now convinced, she accepted.

Sudden changed his mind quickly when he heard a rumor that Trapper had poisoned her first husband. He hurried back to his fiancée's home and told her that the next day's wedding was off. Her reaction was rage: "*I'm* not to be deceived, sir; *I'm* not to be turned round your finger. I've had too much experience, sir, and I dare you to trifle with me." When Sudden refused to be intimidated, she brought out the written promise, saying, "There's a law to be had— and you shall not make me look little in the eyes of my girls, without dearly paying for it." Sudden realized then that he was going to be sued for breach of promise (Buckstone, 22).

In the second act the trial took place off-stage. Sudden brooded on the day of the trial: "Bless me, how I shall tremble when I take up the paper tomorrow—'Trapper *versus* Sudden. This was an action for breach of promise'" (Buckstone, 23). His gossipy friend Jabber soon arrived with the news that he had lost the case and now owed Trapper £2,000. Sudden resolved to fight her: "I'll resort to every legal shift to avoid paying—I'll harass her, teaze her, kill her, if I can!" He decided to leave the country to avoid both her and his lawyer (Buckstone, 25). Jabber went at once to Trapper's home and warned her; she proceeded to get a judge's warrant and to have Sudden arrested. Just as he was about to be taken away, however, his new tenant, Mr. Hudson, arrived. Hudson, miraculously, turned out to be the long lost husband of Trapper. He had pretended to be dead to escape her bad temper. However, he had repented and had searched for her but had not found her until that moment. The couple was reunited, and the play ended happily for all concerned.

As in *Pickwick,* the trial was played for laughs, but a more serious treatment gave an even less flattering picture of breach of promise. In 1845 an anonymous author published *The Breach of Promise.*[11] Despite the name, most of the book did not concern a breach-of-promise case. The heroine of the novel was Lucilla Temple, a young middle-class woman who fell in love with a penniless artist. Her parents wished her to marry Frank Stanley, a wealthy and honorable gentleman, but she insisted on marrying the man she loved. In the end the two men were revealed to be the same person, for Stanley had pretended to be poor to be sure that Temple loved him truly. As a reward for her fidelity, Temple married the man she adored, pleased her parents, and enjoyed great wealth all at the same time.

The breach-of-promise case was a subplot, a counterpoise to Temple's admirable behavior. The villainess was also named Lucilla, but her last name, significantly, was Undermine. Undermine also loved a poor man, an Irish ne'er-do-well named Rory O'Brien, but she was not satisfied with living on love. Instead, she and her lover plotted to sue the wealthy Sir Felix Archer for damages for breach of promise. Sir Felix had shown an interest in Temple, and Undermine offered to be a go-between for the lovers. She then kept all the love letters, poetry, and tokens for herself. She also arranged to meet Archer on numerous occasions; for example, she made sure that her maid saw him kissing her hand on the day they agreed that she would act as an intermediary. She also told him to pretend to flirt with her at one of his parties, supposedly to make Temple jealous. Finally, she convinced her cousin, who truly loved Archer, that the engagement was a fact. In a short time she built up an impressive array of circumstantial evidence.

After this careful preparation, Undermine brought the case to court, using her unscrupulous brother as her solicitor and O'Brien as her barrister. Before the case came to trial, she played on the sympathies of the public by shamming illness and reluctance to sue. The notes, letters, and poems introduced during the trial hurt Archer's case, "and the plaintiff, robed almost in widow's weeds, and white from watching and fear of detection, won the jury's heart by the vivid contrast her counsel drew of what she had been and what she was" (376). Totally fooled, the jury gave Undermine £20,000. Still, she did not long enjoy her ill-gotten gains. O'Brien promptly gambled and drank the money away, leaving her a beggar. The author intoned in closing that she came to rue the day that she sued for breach of promise.

Trials for breach of promise did not receive extended treatment again until 1875, with the introduction of Gilbert and Sullivan's *Trial by Jury*.[12] This short operetta contained the strongest indictment of breach-of-promise actions up to that date. The curtain rose on the jury, having just been sworn in to hear a breach-of-promise case. The defendant, Edwin, came in first, then the judge, and finally Angelina, the plaintiff. The defendant admitted to having proposed and then abandoned his ex-fiancée for another woman, using as his only defense that he should not marry anyone unless he loved her. Angelina appealed to the chivalry of the men on the jury (and the lasciviousness of the judge), resting her case on her continuing love. Edwin offered to marry both women, which the judge at first felt was an excellent idea. However, when her counsel objected, the judge offered to marry Angelina himself. The plaintiff then cheerfully agreed, and the operetta ended with everyone satisfied.

All of this action was interspersed with Gilbert and Sullivan's witty and ironic verses. The jurors, for example, admitted that they, too, had jilted women when young, concluding, however,

(*Trial by Jury,* 46)

> I'm now a respectable chap
> And shine with a virtue resplendent
> And, therefore, I haven't a scrap
> Of sympathy with the defendant!

The judge related that he got his start at the bar by becoming engaged to a wealthy attorney's "elderly, ugly daughter." As soon as he made his reputation, however, he threw her over:

(48)

> The rich attorney my character high
> Tried vainly to disparage—
> And now, if you please, I'm ready to try
> This Breach of Promise of Marriage!

The hypocrisy of the judge and jury contrasted sharply with the honesty of the defendant. Certainly, Angelina and the judge seemed to be a better match than Edwin and she; this preserved a happy, if bitingly satirical, ending.

A fifth fictional account of a breach-of-promise trial in Victorian England was an odd pamphlet published anonymously in the early 1890s.[13] This pamphlet, *A Strange Case of Breach of Promise of Marriage,* concerned a young man's efforts to extricate himself from an unsuitable engagement, told from the point of view of the man's bachelor uncle. The writer's nephew became engaged to a demanding woman, who expected constant attention, had a bad temper, and sulked when she did not get her way. The nephew tried to reform this objectionable behavior, but he did not succeed and, consequently, stopped loving her. He wrote to her stating that his feelings had changed but that he would remain engaged to her if she insisted. She replied, saying "she could not accept a husband in this way and in effect declined marriage on this understanding." (*Strange Case,* 6) Much relieved, the writer's nephew burned all his correspondence with her, including her letter of release.

The next year he became engaged to another woman, the happy couple made ready to announce their intentions. However, his first fiancée, upon hearing of his good fortune, wrote to him holding him to the original engagement. Since he had destroyed her letter of release, he was open to a breach-of-promise suit. Rather than giving in, he concocted an elaborate plan to avoid the threat of heavy damages. First, he wrote to his former lover, fixing the date and the place of the wedding and peremptorily ordering her to be there. She wrote back saying it was her prerogative to set the date, "but she did not say that she would not, or could not be at the place and upon the date fixed by him" (9). Second, he made arrangements with the parish clerk to publish the banns, bought a ring, and hired a clergyman, making sure that his first fiancée was aware of the arrangements. The young woman in question did not reply to any of his communications. On the day of the wedding he went to the church, but the bride did not appear. If there were any breach, then, it appeared that she had made it, not the groom. Having engineered an alibi, the nephew had only to wait a decent interval to marry the woman he loved.

The vision of breach-of-promise cases given by all of these writers was decidedly negative. In no case did the plaintiff need the award, and in several instances (Bardell, Undermine, and the first fiancée in *Strange Case*) she had no right to one at all. Plaintiffs were represented as vindictive, mercenary, and scheming. Undermine actively planned to defraud Archer; Trapper, an ill-tempered and silly woman, sued out of injured pride; Angelina wanted money; and the final plaintiff threatened out of spite. Only Bardell made an honest mistake. The defendants, on the other hand, were victims (except, perhaps, for Sudden). Pickwick suffered from his unfortunate choice of words; Archer was the target of a plot; Edwin was the only character in *Trial by Jury* who was not a gross hypocrite; and the final defendant suffered with a shrewish ex-fiancée.

Moreover, these fictional plaintiffs did not lose much from their broken engagements. None were engaged for long periods of time (one was not engaged at all), and two of the women had been married before. None had been sexually intimate or compromised in any way by their suitors, nor had any of them lost jobs or set aside schooling in order to marry. Indeed, all of the plaintiffs were comfortable both economically and emotionally, nor were they bereft at the conclusion of their relationships. The implication that breach of promise was unnecessary was hard to miss.

In addition, in none of these depictions did the jury system emerge with dignity intact. The various writers distrusted jury trials, despite the well-known virtues of the system. In *Pickwick* and *The Breach of Promise* juries came to completely wrong conclusions; in *Trial by Jury* they were only saved from doing so by the amorous judge. What all the writers stressed was that the court was not the place to settle private matters; when judges and lawyers got involved in courtship, they were bound to make mistakes and ruin lives. And the men in the jury were certainly not going to be able to overcome these difficulties to find true justice.

Indeed, each portrait of the action became more negative than the last. The steadily growing bitterness of these accounts indicates that male fears of women's power in using breach of promise became increasingly shrill as the century went on. The reason may have been the growing number of cases brought, as well as the publicity they received. It may also have been related to the blossoming women's movement, which asserted itself more and more in the late nineteenth century. Whatever the reason, men assumed that women abused and subverted any legal advantage they had. The women who brought fictional cases were at best wrongheaded and at worst perverse; the men, on the other hand, were gentlemanly and reasonable.

Naturally, numerous pieces of Victorian fiction dealt with broken engagements, though few with actual trials. These works faithfully followed the pattern laid down by the more pointed treatments of the action. Specifically, they had two basic approaches. First, authors often used humor in dealing with this subject, since the juxtaposition of love letters and law courts automatically seemed silly. For instance, in a story published in *Chambers' Journal* in 1860, the engagement was between a grown man and a seven-year-old girl, and the former was jilted for another child in the end.[14] A story with the same title, published in *Bow Bells* in 1867, told of a farcical case in a Native American tribe, a story that was ethnically offensive whilst also effectively belittling the action.[15] Second, most of them preached the value of companionate marriage and romantic love and assumed that losing a betrothed was preferable to an unhappy union. Indeed, the fact of having jilted someone was its own punishment; monetary penalties were slight in comparison to the agony of mind and social stigma that jilters suffered. Writers made this point any number of ways: through portraying the jilter as a thoughtless female, rather than a male; through having the jilter go insane (and thus confirming that the ex-fiancée had had a narrow escape); and through insisting that the breach led to the ultimate happiness of both parties.[16] Whatever the approach, the result was the continued skewed version of breach of promise, one that most middle-class readers probably never went beyond.

Was this unflattering depiction of breach of promise in Victorian popular fiction an accurate portrait? And, whether or not the fictional accounts were reliable, what can breach-of-promise cases tell us about love, marriage, and personal relations in the nineteenth century? The purpose of this study is to answer both these questions in the broadest possible way. The primary bases for the answers are 875 breach-of-promise cases between 1750 and 1970, most of them between 1850 and 1900. These cases were recorded in minute books and pleadings in the Public Record Office. The actual accounts, however, come from the assize reports in provincial newspapers from across England. Breach of promise had a scandalous reputation, and local newspapers often printed every salacious detail when one occurred, including all of the testimony, love letters, and even poetry. The result was a forum in which those beneath the middle class could speak for themselves about courtship and marriage. Their stories gave a different portrait of breaches of promise, one closer to tragedy than comedy. For most plaintiffs the suit was a way to repair lives damaged by unwanted pregnancies, lost careers, and broken dreams.

The majority of plaintiffs and defendants in breach-of-promise cases were of the lower middle and upper working classes. They appealed to the courts to adjudicate their broken engagements, and the female plaintiffs were immensely successful. Breach of promise was an action biased toward women, in part because it allowed them to construct their actions within a melodramatic setting. The plaintiff played the part of the victimized heroine, and the judge and jury usually sympathized; indeed, judgments for the plaintiff, as long as she played the role properly, were almost automatic.

Women plaintiffs succeeded because of several other factors as well. First, expectations of gender were far harder on men than women in courtship. Proper manly behavior demanded honesty, kindness to inferiors, responsibility for sexual immorality, and especially the keeping of promises. Though women also had to pass character tests, theirs were not as strict. In addition, the lower middle and upper working classes had distinct courtship mores, which borrowed both from the upper middle and from the working classes. The nature of their courtship stemmed from their desire for middle-class respectability and their simultaneous lack of economic security. Though most couples wanted to find affection, they also needed good homemakers and providers for a marriage to succeed. They indulged frequently in middle-class sentimentality in their letters and poetry, yet their courtship was informal and largely unsupervised. And although the entire family had a role in courtship, relatives were unable to control the high amount of sexual activity among these couples. In short, lower middle-class and upper working-class lovers had a peculiar set of rules that suited them, but also made broken promises difficult for women to tolerate.

Furthermore, the failure of the engagements was complex; these were not simple losses of affection. Indeed, the value of studying failed courtships, rather than the more usual method of studying successful ones, is that complications of class and gender become clearer. The main problem for lower middle- and upper working-class couples was earning enough money to establish their own homes. The delays, separations, and romantic longings that resulted made a particularly fertile ground for broken engagements, one that affected the genders differently. Often the woman had given the best years of her life, as well as her job and sometimes her chastity, before marriage. Such losses fell more heavily on her than on her fiancé.

Indeed, one of the advantages of these actions was the forum they offered to lower middle- and upper working-class women, one they did not normally have in Victorian England. Because of their disabilities in both class and gender, they could not enter the courtroom as judges, barristers, or even as jurors. Yet as plaintiffs they spoke often and well, usually overshadowing their male opponents. Most plaintiffs in these actions were spinsters; the class of suit was one of the few that they brought as single women, rather than as wives, mothers, or workers. They may have been playing a role that supported patriarchal ideas, but their assertiveness in coming to court belied that performance. Breach of promise allowed women to take the initiative in their lives, and they took the opportunity in large numbers.

In part because of the women's success rate, the breach-of-promise action and the women who brought the suits caused a great deal of controversy. The result was a sustained argument over the action and numerous attempts to abolish it in the late nineteenth century. These arguments throw light on the conflicting Victorian values of romance, individualism, and chivalry toward women. The action is also ideal for exploring the motivations of judges, demonstrating the social values that informed their judgments. What emerges from this debate is the enormous anxieties held by the male debaters on both sides of the issue—about gender, marriage, the common law, and class. Nor were women any less concerned; they too debated the action, and they were also unable to overcome its contradictions. In particular, women involved in the struggle for legal reforms sharply disagreed about the case's value. On the one hand, it treated women as dependents and rewarded them for it; on the other, it granted much needed help to poor women. In this argument of equality versus protection, neither side emerged victorious.

This book is divided into three parts. The first part concentrates on legal issues. Chapter 1 is a brief legal history of the action from its ecclesiastical beginnings to its abolition in 1970. Chapter 2 gives a demand side look at the case, exploring how women brought breach-of-promise actions and the tactics used by both sides to influence the judge and jury. It highlights the theatrical nature of the suit, particularly its conscious similarities to melodrama. The second part delves into the social issues of the action. First, chapter 3 details the gender expectations that strongly influenced the verdicts. Breach of promise focused much more on masculinity than femininity, and the high expectations from the "stronger sex" made for significant disadvantages for them in court. Chapter 4 argues that there was a definite set of courtship practices in the lower middle and upper working classes, based on their desire for respectability and their precarious finances. The details supplied by the newspaper reporters allow a close look at the influence of family and class on courtship as well as the activities of engaged couples and preparations for weddings. Chapter 5 discusses the reasons for broken engagements in these cases—a combination of ideological, structural, and personal difficulties. Chapter 6 deals with premarital sexual intercourse. At least 25 percent of the actions involved sexual contact, allowing us access to the most intimate moments of male-female relations. Chapter 7 is a closer look at four case studies that illustrate the conclusions of chapters 3 through 6. Although these cases were not typical, they do permit the reader to see the details of the many personal stories that the broader chapters might overlook. They also illustrate change and continuity over time, particularly the surprising accessibility of the High Courts in the late Victorian period.

The third part explores various cultural ramifications for the action among the elite. Chapter 8 is an analysis of the (primarily) male arguments over the attempts to abolish breach of promise, arguments that demonstrated the tensions between individualism and support for companionate marriage. This chapter also discusses the peculiar legal problems that breach of promise presented. The case split the legal community; most judges promoted it, while most lawyers did not. It also divided the populace; the lower classes supported it, but the upper classes disapproved. Chapter 9 outlines the reaction of women to the class of suit, exploring their dilemma in confronting an action that protected women and yet placed them in a special category. The elites were mostly uncomprehending about the problems of the plaintiffs, so their attempts at solutions failed. The work concludes with a discussion of the decline and abolition of the action in the twentieth century.

There are obvious limitations to this study. First, I have arbitrarily stopped in 1900 in all but the legal history chapter and the conclusion, and the majority of the studied cases occurred between 1870 and 1900. Thus, my points refer mostly to the late Victorian period. This fact also means that my remarks about change over time are of limited value, since I have in-depth information on only a short period. Second, I am aware that legal sources are problematic, since both sides are concerned with winning the case, not with presenting the unvarnished truth. Plaintiffs and defendants said what they thought would impress the jury; furthermore, many parts of the story were omitted as irrelevant.[17] And, not surprisingly, couples often contradicted each other. When the accounts conflicted, I used my judgment to determine what happened in the courtship, a balancing act that was doubly difficult because women plaintiffs had by far the most say in breach-of-promise trials. I have tried to give both sides whenever I was unsure about the true picture; however, any conclusions I have drawn must be considered tentative.

Finally, in any number of ways breach-of-promise cases are limited as a way to explore courtship. For instance, many cases involved cross-class courtship, which means that their value as a barometer of lower middle-class values is lessened. Second, women tended to sue older, well-established men, since there was little point in suing someone without the means to pay damages.

Therefore, the conclusions about the ages and class of courting couples are of limited value. Third, only a small minority of people who broke up brought their difficulties into the courtroom. The reader must always keep in mind, then, that most instances of this sort of experience were never recorded. Breach-of-promise cases give wonderful details of private lives, but they are only a window to such lives, not an open door.

Despite these limitations, breach-of-promise cases proved to be surprisingly enlightening about courtship, the common law, marriage, and women in late nineteenth-century England. Although not all types of action merit extended treatment, this class of suit lay at a crossroads of legal, social, and cultural values. Furthermore, it reveals the private thoughts of hundreds of previously faceless, nameless, and voiceless people in Victorian society, both men and women. They proved to have quite a different perspective of breach of promise than Dickens, Buckstone, and the other writers. The story of the real actors in the trials, and the upper-class Victorians' misunderstanding of them, is recorded on the following pages.

I

The Legal History of
Breach of Promise

IN MAY 1879 FARRER HERSCHELL introduced a resolution in the House
of Commons to abolish the action of breach of promise of marriage. One of
the arguments he used to gain support for this resolution was that the class of
suit did not have an especially long history: "About two centuries ago it was
established that such an action lay, so that there was no flavour of venerable
antiquity surrounding it."[1] As Herschell went on to explain, he did not mean
there were no breach-of-promise suits before 1679, but that those earlier cases
were of a quite different character than those of the eighteenth and nineteenth
centuries. What he did not explain was that the change, to a large extent, was
due to the slow erosion of the ecclesiastical remedies, a fact that his opponents
pointed out.[2] It would seem, then, that the history of breach of promise could
be used both to criticize and to defend the suit; it was an action both old and
new, a cause of law reform and a result of that reform. Its evolution shows the
adaptability of the common law as well as the difficulties of amending it in the
nineteenth century.

Until 1640 breach of promise of marriage cases were primarily brought in
the ecclesiastical courts. These courts offered two types of remedies because
they recognized two kinds of betrothals. A contract *in presenti* ("I marry you")
amounted to an actual marriage and was treated by the church as such. It required ecclesiastical rites to be complete, and the couple was not to cohabit
before the ceremony. Nevertheless, if a woman or man sued for breach of this
contract, the spiritual courts compelled the reluctant bride or groom to marry.
Even a subsequent marriage to a third person was void once the courts recognized the original betrothal. The second type was a contract *in futuro* ("I will
marry you"). Church courts did allow dissolution of this contract, and a marriage to a third party was not made invalid. The only remedy offered in this case
was an admonition to the unfaithful suitor. However, there was one important
exception to this: if the couple had cohabited, the spiritual courts ruled that the
contract *in futuro* had become a contract *in presenti* and declared the couple married. Ecclesiastical law, therefore, offered a great deal of protection to women.[3]

There were actions for breach of promise brought in the chancery courts before 1640, but they were largely concerned with money and property disputes, often alleging fraud. They did not demand damages for wounded feelings, only for monetary losses. For example, in 1454 Margaret Gardyner and her daughter Alice sued John Keche for refusing to marry Alice. The women had paid him a total of twenty-two "marks" to do so; he had accepted this payment, but married a Jane Bloys instead. He then refused to return the money, so the Gardyners sued him for it and won. As one commentator pointed out, "The plaintiffs in this suit appear to have regarded the matter purely from a business point of view."[4] An example from the sixteenth century was *Palmer v. Wilder*, in which a man sued his fiancée after she married someone else. He claimed that she had deceived him into giving her money and gifts, and he only wanted the return of his investment.[5] Before the seventeenth century, then, litigants used the secular courts to recover pecuniary loss; after all, if they wished to enforce the contract or to vindicate their characters, they could turn to the spiritual tribunals.

The basis of the ecclesiastical action in the Tudor and Stuart periods was the spousal, a much more binding agreement than the modern engagement. Both men and women brought cases before the church authorities in an effort to prove that an informal marriage contract, usually a verbal one, had been made, and the defendant had subsequently broken it. At least until the early seventeenth century, male plaintiffs predominated, and often property considerations were paramount. Mostly bachelors and spinsters brought the action, usually when the plaintiffs were in their twenties or early thirties. All classes were known to bring the suit, but most plaintiffs were tradesmen, yeomen, husbandmen, and craftsmen.[6]

Toward the middle of the seventeenth century the betrothal became less formal; it began to resemble the modern engagement. Binding spousals declined, and church courts retreated from enforcing them. As a result, more and more cases were settled out of court, and the common-law action of breach of promise emerged.[7] The trend away from using the spiritual courts was accelerated by the Civil War and the Interregnum. The church courts were disbanded for almost twenty years, and even after the Restoration they never regained their former authority. Contracts *in presenti* could still be enforced as before, especially after cohabitation, but otherwise religious sanctions were negligible.[8] Plaintiffs, dissatisfied with these results, turned in greater numbers to the common law, bringing the action on a writ of assumpsit, like an ordinary contract action.

From 1660 to 1700 a slow trickle of cases established that the action could lie in secular courts. The decisive case was *Dickison v. Holcroft* in 1674. The plaintiff, Mary Holcroft, alleged that "the defendant by the breach of his promise had 'hindered her preferment to her damage of 100 pounds.'"[9] After a long argument, the court decided that the action did lie, even where only founded on mutual promises.[10] Another important case in the same period was *Harrison v. Cage et uxor* (1698). This suit was brought by a man against the new husband of his wealthy ex-fiancée (as a married woman, Mrs. Cage could not be sued). The jury found for the plaintiff and awarded damages of £400. The defendant appealed, arguing that men should not receive compensation, since they made their living through professions, unlike women, who married to survive. The court refused to countenance a difference between a man's promise and that of a woman and upheld the decision of the lower court.[11] In its early stages at least, breach of promise was not biased in favor of one sex or the other.

Hardwicke's Marriage Act of 1753 accelerated the change in the nature of the action. This law was meant to eliminate clandestine and irregular marriages by taking control of matrimony out of the province of the church. The spiritual courts could no longer enforce contracts *in presenti* (nor those *in futuro* after cohabitation). By abolishing the legality of betrothals, Parliament left jilted lovers with no remedy except the common law. Plaintiffs were not slow to realize this, and the number of actions rose in the last half of the eighteenth century.[12] In addition, the nature of the case began to change. By the 1760s men and women were bringing actions in assize courts for damages for the "non-performance of a marriage-contract," rather than for specific pecuniary loss.[13] In *Horam v. Humphreys* in 1772, Justice Aston used the following terms to explain what the jury should consider for damages: "The injury of fixing a young woman's affections, and then trifling and flying off . . . the prejudice it might be to her in future life: that they should give such damages as the circumstances in evidence, either aggravating or extenuating, should require; and that the rank and condition of the parties would be . . . considered."[14] Other cases in the 1770s continued this trend.[15]

By the end of the eighteenth century breach of promise had evolved into its more modern form, that is, the way it would be brought to court in the nineteenth century. For example, in *Atchinson v. Baker* (1796), a man sued his ex-fiancée for reneging on a promise to marry him when her father died. Her defense was that the plaintiff was too ill to marry her. Here the argument centered on two issues: did a promise to marry after an uncertain future event (her father's death) constitute a general promise to marry, and was a bodily infirmity a good reason for a breach? The court found for the defendant, arguing that her promise had been conditional only and that the state of the plaintiff's health was a valid defense. Even more significantly, the court rejected the plaintiff's later attempt to get a settlement on pecuniary grounds.[16] The most important aspect was the promise and its breach, not monetary arrangements.

Despite similarities to nineteenth-century cases, however, eighteenth-century ones had peculiarities all their own. As in the early modern period, men were quite as willing to bring actions as women and often received substantial awards. A good example was *Schreiber v. Frazer* (1780). Schreiber was a merchant who sued his ex-fiancée, the widow of a general. Both parties were wealthy, and much of the evidence consisted of the plaintiff's many purchases prior to the expected union. Frazer's only defense was that she began to see that they would not get along and therefore decided not to marry. Schreiber was awarded £600 to repay his expenses.[17] The class of people bringing these actions (at least as far as the scanty records indicate) was higher than both before and after the century. Thus, the awards were also high, usually around £500.[18] As could be seen from *Schreiber v. Frazer*, considerations of pecuniary loss could still be a part of breach of promise, although not the main issue. In addition, these cases were rare; reporters referred to them as "remarkable" and worthy of special attention in national publications.[19]

Because breach of promise evolved as part of the common law, the laws governing it in the nineteenth century were worked out through precedent. As Michael Grossberg has pointed out, breach of promise was "a curious legal action, a peculiar combination of contract and tort."[20] Despite this fact, most writers agreed on the nature of the suit and the standard procedures for both the plaintiff and the defense.[21] Indeed, by the Victorian period, the rules of bringing and defending a suit were almost a formula.

The engagement was considered a contract to marry and was legally binding on both parties. However, unlike most contracts, it could not be enforced because the civil courts would not coerce marriage, but the party breaking the contract was liable to damages. The contract had to be mutual and between parties competent to make legal contracts—for example, those who were old enough and sane. Of course, the man had to have made and the woman to have accepted a definite promise, but it was not necessary that all the terms of the betrothal should be settled at once. The court assumed that the marriage would take place within a reasonable time, whether or not the pair had actually set a date. The definition of a reasonable time varied with the general circumstances of the couple. The court also accepted the validity of conditional promises if the agreement was "suitable." For instance, a man could promise to marry when a business venture had ended, or a woman could agree to marry upon attaining a dowry. However, should the man or woman definitely repudiate the promise before the condition had been met, the jilted party could still sue.[22] On the other hand, judges deemed conditions in "restraint of marriage" (that is, ones that made marriage impossible or uncertain for either party) as void.

If no specific time had been set, the plaintiff must first have requested fulfillment of the promise and demonstrated his or her readiness to marry for a breach to have occurred. If the plaintiff were female, this request could be made by a third party or without witnesses, in deference to a woman's modesty. Normally, a breach happened when the defendant married another person, when the plaintiff discovered that the defendant was already married, or when the defendant broke off the engagement. Even if the defendant later retracted the repudiation, the plaintiff could still sue.

Breach of promise was a personal action, and only the injured party was entitled to sue (not parents or guardians). A person under twenty-one could sue but not be sued for a promise made before his or her majority. Furthermore, the action ended with the death of either the defendant or the plaintiff. The only exception was if the plaintiff could prove "special damages," as, for instance, if his or her estate had suffered on account of the engagement. In actual practice, no damages were deemed special enough to warrant an award after the defendant's death. This handicap on plaintiffs was not changed until the twentieth century.

The burden of proof was on the plaintiff, but because of the private nature of courtship and marriage, judges accepted circumstantial evidence and hearsay. Proof of a proposal could be inferred from visits, "walking out" together, stating intentions to third parties, wedding preparations, gifts, or the expectations of relatives and friends. The woman's acceptance could be inferred simply by her lack of objection to the offer, or by a number of other factors: her apparent attachment to the man, declarations of intent to marry either to him or to others in his presence, or distress at the subsequent rejection. However, mere courtship and politeness were not sufficient to prove an engagement.

The defendant could choose between a variety of defenses, the most popular of which was to accuse the plaintiff of unchastity (if a woman) or cruelty or inability to provide (if a man). However, the defendant had to prove that he or she was unaware of the misconduct when he or she got engaged. A related defense was to claim to be the victim of fraud. A woman, for instance, was expected to reveal information like unchaste behavior or unfitness for sexual intercourse. In these cases, however, the plaintiff must have misled her or his lover deliberately; otherwise, the court expected the defendant to have discovered all relevant information before proposing or accepting a marriage proposal.

Until 1859 a plaintiff could try to plead illness. In that year the Court of Exchequer handed down a decision in *Hall v. Wright,* in which the male defendant had pleaded that he was too ill to marry. The barons reversed the lower court decision in favor of the defendant on the grounds that "the delicacy of health, alleged as an excuse, is the man's misfortune, not to be visited, beyond what is inevitable, upon the woman." Even if he could not marry her, he should make some restitution.[23] Thus, the plea of ill health was no longer good, although the defendant could still use the illness of the plaintiff to good effect if it incapacitated him or her from fulfilling marital duties. But the illness had to be current; even the former insanity of the plaintiff did not constitute a good defense if he or she were sane at the time of the promise.[24]

Some circumstances or conditions of the contract could render it void. First, contracts in restraint of marriage were not valid, nor were those made under duress. Second, those made in return for sexual favors were considered "illicit commerce"—that is, prostitution—which automatically canceled the obligation. In a similar way, a promise given in order to induce a woman to remain a man's mistress did not stand; such promises "tended to immorality" and were therefore "against public policy." However, if the proposal of marriage were made independently of sexual intercourse, the fact that the couple had engaged in premarital sex could not be held against the plaintiff. Third, the fact that the marriage, when consummated, would be illegal made a good defense. For example, if the parties were too closely related by blood or if the defendant was divorced (and unable to remarry by law), these defenses held. In addition, if the defendant was already married and the plaintiff was aware of the fact, the promise was not enforced, but this defense did not succeed if the plaintiff was ignorant of the marriage. A final possible defense was to claim mutual consent to the breach.

The amount of damages remained entirely up to the jury. If the award seemed excessive, the defendant could appeal for a reduction or a new trial. However, the higher courts seldom interfered with the juries' awards. Damages included compensation for wedding preparations, the loss of the benefits of marriage, and punitive damages for "wounded feelings." The jury considered the social standing and wealth of the defendant, particularly if he or she was of higher station than the plaintiff. Also the length of time the plaintiff had been engaged, and thus "on the shelf" was a factor, especially if the plaintiff were female, since a woman of thirty hardly had the same chances of marriage as a woman of twenty. Finally, juries also considered the plaintiff's loss of virtue, if applicable.

The plaintiff could bring up numerous circumstances in aggravation of damages. For example, although seduction was a separate action, it could still aggravate a female plaintiff's distress, and juries often gave awards to compensate for loss of marriageability. However, the sexual intercourse had to have happened after the promise and on the faith of that promise. Aggravation could also be claimed if the defendant unsuccessfully attacked the plaintiff's character during the court battle, especially with insinuations of unchastity. In other words, the defense of unchastity was a dangerous one; it could work, but it could also backfire.

On the other hand, the defendant could offer some circumstances in mitigation of damages. The bad conduct of the plaintiff, either before or after the engagement, could lessen the award. Juries also took into consideration the disapproval of either set of parents. However, the defendant could not successfully argue that he or she had saved the plaintiff from an unhappy marriage, nor, in the case of a male defendant, could he claim unchastity if the plaintiff's disgrace was the result of his actions. Finally, the defendant could plead lack of means; juries considered how much a man or woman could pay before they awarded huge amounts.

Though many of the changes in breach of promise came from case law, several statutes in the nineteenth century also affected the action. As early as 1840 William Miles attempted to widen its use: he introduced a bill to grant a remedy for seduction under a promise of marriage at the summary level so that poor women could use the petty sessions. This was, in effect, a reform of the bastardy clause of the New Poor Law of 1834, which had placed total responsibility for illegitimate children on women. Since most working-class women could not afford the costs of the High Court, Miles hoped to give them a cheaper alternative. According to this proposal, a woman could not simply sue for breach of promise; only if the promise had been followed by a pregnancy could she bring the action. If the seduction were accomplished after a promise of marriage, the woman herself could sue, but if there were no promise, her parents (or guardian) could sue for loss of service. Awards were limited to £30, the magistrate would decide whether the case should be brought, and there would be "no judgement against the man on the unsupported evidence of the woman."[25]

This attempt to soften the severe aspects of the bastardy clause of the New Poor Law was roundly criticized, both in Parliament and out. The journal *Justice of the Peace,* although admitting the "necessity of some enactment of some kind" to help seduced women, criticized almost every provision of the bill.[26] Most of the other commentators refused to admit the need for any change at all, believing new enactments would bring back the worst abuses of the Old Poor Law. For example, the editor of *Jurist* insisted that "any young woman, providing she select a man of some little property, may assure to all the bastards she chooses to bring into the world, a much better provision, than she, supposing her to be in an humble condition of life, could by marrying a respectable man of her own station. Can any person be in doubt as to the tendency of such a law?"[27] Similarly, Sir Edmund Head, a minor scholar and future poor-law commissioner, wrote that such laws encouraged vice and increased poor rates. Lower-class men had no money to pay damages, so they would be forced to marry, bringing about more unhappy and poverty-stricken marriages.[28] Many of the men in Parliament agreed; though the bill passed its second reading in the House of Commons by one vote, it never got a third reading. Some change in the harsh provisions of the bastardy clause had already occurred in 1839, and a further, more substantial revision came in 1844. In this instance, though, the desire to protect women did not overcome reservations about aiding "vice." Many of these arguments would be replayed in later debates about breach of promise itself.[29]

The next legislative issue to affect the action dealt with the law of evidence. Until the late nineteenth century neither the plaintiff nor the defendant could testify in breach cases. In 1851 the Evidence Amendment Act changed the rules of evidence to admit more parties to the witness box, but breach-of-promise cases were expressly excluded. The authors of the bill felt that in such cases the temptation to perjury would be too great if the plaintiff and defendant were allowed to testify.[30] However, feeling about this issue slowly changed over the next fifteen years, and this transformation coincided with a wide-ranging desire to reform the antiquated aspects of the common law. Alfred Waddilove, for example, pointed out in a paper for the Society for the Promotion of Social Science how ludicrous it was that the two people most closely involved in a promise were the sole people excluded as witnesses. Furthermore, he offered several other arguments for reform: "In an action for damages by reason of a breach of contract, the evidence of the plaintiff is received, and why not in an action for breach of promise of marriage, which is, in fact, a breach of contract? On the other hand, the defendant might explain away all or much that was adduced to fix him with the promise."[31] Waddilove ridiculed opponents' worries that "designing" women would fool credulous juries with frivolous accusations. He argued that cross-examination would expose most frauds on both sides of the dispute.

Many people came to agree with Waddilove, although some still had reservations. Robert Wilson, for instance, who commented on Waddilove's paper, agreed that parties should be competent as witnesses but felt that plaintiffs should be required to corroborate their stories in some way. A Mr. Forsythe, who was a barrister, even suggested requiring written proof of the promise.[32] These arguments and suggestions were echoed in the House of Commons when George (later Lord) Denman introduced a bill to change the law of evidence in 1869.

Denman emphasized that he sponsored the Evidence Amendment Bill to help courts arrive at the truth by allowing cross-examination of both parties.[33]

He also highlighted the bill's additional provision: that no breach-of-promise plaintiff "shall recover a verdict unless his or her testimony shall be corroborated by some other material evidence in support of such promise."[34] The legislators left vague what they meant by material evidence, but this was clearly an attempt to reduce the number of cases where a plaintiff succeeded through perjury (requiring written proof was supported but not adopted).[35] Though opponents continued to warn that the bill would increase suspect actions, it passed by a substantial majority and went immediately into effect. The *Law Journal* probably expressed the general feeling in 1869 by saying, "Mr. Denman's proposition is recommended, not only upon the ground of uniformity in the law, but also on the higher ground of justice and fair dealing."[36]

Because of its vague wording, the results of the act were not perhaps as far-reaching as its authors had hoped. Both sides began taking the stand, but the material evidence rule was applied unevenly. *Bessela v. Stern* in 1877 was a good example. The plaintiff, a servant in the house of the defendant's father, claimed to have had sex with Stern on a promise of marriage, and she eventually gave birth to an illegitimate child. The corroboration for her claim came from her sister, Maria Bessela. Maria testified that the defendant had promised her that he would marry the plaintiff; in addition, after the child was born, she overheard the plaintiff tell him, "You always promised to marry me and you don't keep your word," which he did not deny. The lower court ruled that Maria's testimony did not constitute material evidence, but on appeal the Court of Common Pleas reversed the decision. The court considered the defendant's silence when confronted by the plaintiff as confirmation enough; material evidence, Justice Cockburn reasoned, was expected to corroborate the promise, but not prove it absolutely.[37] Despite the new law, then, a great deal of latitude was still afforded the plaintiff in proving a contract to marry.

But the act was not totally ineffectual, particularly if the plaintiff's honesty were questionable. In *Wiedemann v. Walpole* (1891), for instance, the material evidence offered by Valerie Wiedemann was simply that Robert Walpole had not replied to several insulting letters she had sent to him over a period of five years. Although she won over the jury, receiving £300 in damages, the appeals court reversed the decision. The court argued that there was a qualitative difference between failure to deny a face-to-face accusation and refusing to answer insulting letters.[38] Though used sparingly, the Evidence Amendment Act did affect rulings in breach-of-promise cases; 10 of the 875 cases under study were nonsuited for lack of material evidence.[39] The act may also have discouraged some dubious actions from being brought.

Nevertheless, the immediate result of the act was to increase the number of breach-of-promise cases brought each year. Opponents of the change insisted that a plague of dubious cases was sweeping the country. The *Law Times* complained bitterly in March 1870 about the stupidity of juries and concluded with a call for repeal.[40] The *Law Journal* was gentler but admitted that "both judges and juries have a disposition to be too generous to plaintiffs in actions for breach of promise." Even some judges and barristers took the opportunity during new actions to complain about the change.[41] Nevertheless, most legislators agreed with the *Journal of Jurisprudence* that to repeal the law would be to take a step backward, which they refused to do.[42] The Evidence Amendment Act survived as long as the action did.

The rights of minors was the next issue to affect breach-of-promise actions, due to the Infants Relief Act of 1874. This law required that all contracts made by persons under the age of twenty-one be remade once that person came of age. The law drew a distinction between mere ratification of the old promise and the creation of a new contract: only the latter sufficed. In all probability law reformers had not considered breach-of-promise cases when they passed this measure,[43] but solicitors soon saw the implications for their clients. After 1874 judges and juries had to determine if young lovers had made new promises or just ratified the old promise when they became twenty-one; in such a private matter, this was a fine line to draw.

The first major case decided on the issue was *Coxhead v. Mullis* (1878). Charlotte Coxhead and John Mullis first courted when they were both underage in 1874. John turned twenty-one in March 1877 and broke the relationship off in December 1877 to marry someone else. The Court of Common Pleas found for the defendant, since the judges did not believe that Charlotte had proved there was a new proposal after John's birthday in March (she had only his lover-like conduct to put into evidence).[44] If this interpretation had dominated legal thinking, the Infants Relief Act would have limited the number of possible cases in the later nineteenth century. However, two major subsequent cases modified this view. In *Northcote v. Doughty* (1879) the Court of Common Pleas ruled that the defendant's saying "Now I may and will marry you as soon as I can," three days after his coming of age constituted a new promise, not a mere ratification. In *Ditcham v. Worrall* (1880) the same court held that the defendant's asking the plaintiff to set a wedding date was enough to constitute a new promise. The court was not unanimous, however, since Lord Coleridge insisted that his decision in *Coxhead v. Mullis* should be followed, because otherwise the Infants Act was "practically a dead letter."[45] Obviously, there was no consensus on the issue, and suits continued to be decided on a case-by-case basis from that time forward.[46]

The final change in law in the nineteenth century was the County Courts Act of 1888, which allowed breach-of-promise suits to be brought in the

County Courts rather than the High Courts if both parties agreed. Until then, at least theoretically, the original jurisdiction of breach of promise was the assizes, although there were certainly breach-of-promise cases brought irregularly in the lower jurisdiction before then.[47] The County Courts Act made this practice legitimate; however, since both parties had to agree to change, the act had less impact than it might have done. Any defendant who wished to stop a destitute plaintiff from suing need only refuse to move. Nonetheless, such cases were not unknown.

Perhaps because of the limited impact of these legal changes, there were numerous attempts to abolish the action of breach of promise in the late nineteenth century. In 1879 Herschell introduced the resolution mentioned above, which argued that "the action for Breach of Promise of Marriage ought to be abolished except in cases where actual pecuniary loss has been incurred by reason of the promise, the damages being limited to such pecuniary loss." After a spirited debate, the abolitionists won the vote, 106 to 65.[48] However, repeated bills to abolish breach of promise, beginning in 1878 and continuing to 1890, failed. The resolution had passed in a lightly attended sitting and, since it had no binding power, it was able to attract the widest possible support. One contemporary observer suggested that the vote was a spontaneous display of frustration by men who often had to defend or prosecute these cases, but this does not explain why these same M.P.s did not vote for a bill.[49] For whatever reason, attempts at abolition failed. The ministries were unwilling to devote time and energy to what was, after all, a minor reform and one that went against the opinion of the majority of the population. So breach of promise remained a fact of life well into the twentieth century.

In the current century, in fact, the class of suit evolved and changed in remarkable ways, proving its adaptability. The main issue in the early twentieth century was promises made before or during divorce proceedings. As stated above, any promise made while one of the two people was married was void. But as divorce became easier, judges and juries had to determine at what point the first marriage formally ended and a new contract could begin. Between 1905 and 1935 most cases supported the old doctrine: a man or woman could not contract a new marriage until the old one had been completely rescinded.[50] Yet even in the 1920s this doctrine was challenged, and it was overturned in *Fender v. St. John-Mildmay* in 1938, an action appealed to the House of Lords. The decision was based on the Lords' belief that a marriage was truly over as soon as the decree *nisi* had been granted, even without the decree absolute.[51]

The second way breach of promise changed in the twentieth century was to expand into a vehicle to protect women from fraudulent marriages. The most important of these cases was *Shaw v. Shaw and Another* in 1954.[52] In *Shaw* a woman who had married a man bigamously (unbeknownst to her) was allowed to use breach of promise to regain her share of her so-called husband's estate. Although Olive Stone has called this use of the action bizarre, it apparently filled in a gap in the common law.[53] Finally, breach-of-promise actions in the late twentieth century often dealt with foreign and commonwealth marriage problems. First, several cases established that if a person promised to marry a foreign national, he or she could be sued in English courts, and the rejected lover could collect damages on the English scale.[54] Second, women from commonwealth countries could sue if their so-called husbands refused to go through the English wedding ceremony once they had emigrated.[55] Here again, breach of promise was used to protect those only nominally married in English law.

Breach of promise appeared to be expanding and growing stronger as the century went on. But appearance belied the reality. The number of cases declined after the Second World War, despite the use of the action in unusual circumstances. In addition, efforts at abolition continued in the twentieth century, although for many years there was the same lack of success as in the nineteenth century. Finally, in 1969 the Law Commission, after thoroughly studying the action, recommended that it be abolished, with adequate remedies for property disputes. These recommendations were accepted and passed as the Law Reform (Miscellaneous Provisions) Act of 1970.[56]

Breach of promise had taken almost one century to eliminate; it had flourished during the Victorian period and beyond. One reason for its longevity was the strong support of the lower middle class against the others. In this study, I have defined the classes in these groupings: upper class, including peers and gentry; middle class, including professionals, businesspeople, and large farmers; lower middle class, including small shopkeepers, master workers, and middling farmers; and working class, including anyone who worked for wages in industry, as a servant, or as a tenant farmer. I consider the upper working class those with regular employment and steady wages, even if the wages were low, while the lower working class as casual workers, paupers, and the criminal classes. It was the lower middle and upper working classes that staged the productions of breach of promise trials as melodramas, making the actual cases anything but dull.

II

The Court as Public Theatre

"I FEEL THAT personally I and my family have been grossly insulted and wronged by your disgraceful behaviour—and it is of course hardly necessary for me to state that legal proceedings will be forthwith taken against you with a view that your superior officer and others may know how you have so disgraced yourself and wrecked the life of one you have so many times professed to have such a tender regard for."[1] So wrote Thomas Parker, brother-in-law of Olive Bardens, to her ex-fiancé, J. H. Amey, in 1892. Amey, a boatswain, had refused to marry Bardens, accusing her of having had an affair with his brother. Parker wrote denying those allegations and warning Amey of the impending breach-of-promise suit. Within days, both parties had set the intricate process of bringing a suit into motion.[2]

Karen Dubinsky, in her recent study of criminal seduction and rape cases in Canada, has discussed the theatrical nature of the law courts. She argues that the use of the public court as an entertainment was ultimately conservative because of the moral lessons the audience learned.[3] The staging of breach-of-promise cases was similarly both theatrical and conservative, although in this case the conservatism was helpful to the women involved, making them the helpless, and ultimately redeemed, heroines in a melodrama. Indeed, those implicated in these actions recognized, at least implicitly, that the latter were dramas. Barristers for both sides frequently employed the language of theatre to make their points, quoting Shakespeare, *Pickwick,* and Gilbert and Sullivan.[4] Furthermore, there was little doubt that the trials were enormously popular as entertainment in the assize towns. Case after case recorded that the courtroom was filled, often with a "fair sprinkling of ladies." The audience responded to the action before them as they would to a play, laughing at jokes; "murmuring" at unexpected revelations; and applauding at the end. In one case the jurymen continually said "Hear, hear!" as the plaintiff gave her evidence.[5] Judges did not always like this aspect of the case, but there was little they could do. In *Lewis v. Jenkins* (1898) the plaintiff moaned throughout the defendant's evidence, and the judge, in disgust, told her "she had better do her acting outside the court." Nevertheless, the jury found for her. In *Kelly v. Bell* (1880) the audience laughed so loudly "that his Lordship threatened to have the Court cleared, remarking that it was not a theatre."[6] But no matter how much judges insisted the courtroom was for formal legal proceedings, breach-of-promise cases undermined them. And sometimes the judges played to the crowd as well; a judge in 1899 did not protest when the audience cheered his summation.[7]

Like putting on a large-scale theatrical production, suing for breach of promise in the nineteenth century was a long and complicated process. Much of the action in these cases followed a similar script, which got more familiar as use of the suit broadened in the late nineteenth century. That script closely resembled a domestic melodrama, with an innocent young woman as the victim of a scheming villain, high-flown discourse, and a triumphant final vindication in court.[8] Melodrama as a theatrical form had its heyday in the early nineteenth century, just at the time that breach of promise was evolving into a woman's suit for punitive damages. The convergence of these two processes was probably not coincidental. Dubinsky also finds a similarity to melodrama in her cases, but it did not have a beneficent result for women in the criminal courts, probably in part because of the differing punishments for the male villains.[9] In civil actions the awarding of damages to the "damsel in distress" was a sort of community healing that punished the villain without incarcerating him. However, the vindication of the heroine only worked while the verdict was being read. When the case ended, the melodramatic mode broke down and real life intruded.

The description that follows is a model or ideal type for breach-of-promise cases—not all of which was true at all times, but which can give a sense of the process for many couples. That many of the plaintiffs, defendants, barristers, judges, and juries played their parts in an almost formulaic way is not meant to argue that the participants were insincere. A woman could dress and talk as instructed by her counsel while at the same time feeling truly wronged; a barrister could use overwrought language yet still believe his client's case. Of course, both sides did what they felt would succeed, but that does not invariably mean that all their testimony was calculated or that love letters and rings had no meaning. This sage use of the courts argues for intelligence in lower middle- and upper working-class men and women rather than Machiavellian plotting. Indeed, the long process of bringing the suit demonstrates that only those who were greatly damaged or particularly tough would risk such publicity and expense.

The first step was for the plaintiff to believe that a defendant had committed a definite breach of his promise to marry; this could happen when he married someone else, admitted his changed mind, or stopped visiting and writing.[10] Plaintiffs saw such desertion as a betrayal, the central crime of melodramatic villains.[11] The plaintiff's family was usually equally outraged, and the parent or closest relative often wrote or visited the defendant, remonstrating—in words similar to those above—on the defendant's conduct, usually with emotional rhetoric and dramatic threats.

In the vast majority of broken engagements this was the end of the matter; only a minority of women were angry, knowledgeable, or independent enough to threaten a suit. Also, even if they did so, the defendants might change their minds or agree to pay compensation without a trial. Such cases never reached the courts.[12] But if the defendant still refused to admit any liability and the plaintiff was determined to force him to do so, she turned the matter over to a solicitor. At this point the formal script came into play, since professional litigators followed established lines in bringing cases to court. Her counsel's first action was to communicate to the defendant that he would soon be served with a writ and to advise him to find his own solicitor as soon as possible.

The plaintiff's position in the proceedings from this point was problematic. Although presumably a helpless victim, in actual fact she was taking initiative by bringing the jilter to court. The women involved, unlike heroines in plays, did not leave their defense to providence or male relatives. Even if the woman were encouraged by her family, the case was a personal one and had to be brought by the woman herself. And, indeed, some women openly admitted their motivations. When the defense barrister asked Margaret Jukes if she had first hired the lawyer, she replied, "Yes, I suggested it myself. I was paying him back in his own coin." Similarly, Anne Allmand insisted that "no one suggested to me to bring this action, and no one advised me to do it. I thought from the manner in which he had treated me that I should have some recompense." These women may have been victims, but they were also strong and assertive, at least in the courtroom. As Emily Blackham wrote to Clement Simpson after he had broken their engagement, she was not sure what she would do now, "but I shall not sit down and crie like some weake things do."[13] Anna Clark, in the context of the Queen Caroline affair, has pointed out the difficulty of combining melodramatic chivalry with the reality of plucky, active women. The contradiction of the active victim was never faced by those involved with breach-of-promise actions, and it seldom had much effect on the outcomes of the cases. It did, however, make for a subtle undermining of the cultural meaning of these dramas.[14]

It is unclear how women discovered their legal options or how they paid for them. Breach-of-promise suits had a popular reputation by the 1830s, since Buckstone and Dickens both wrote about them early in the decade. The action's long history as an ecclesiastical suit and slow evolution in the civil tribunals argues for familiarity in large sections of the English public. In fact, contemporary records occasionally reveal popular knowledge of the suit before midcentury. In 1841 Mary B., a servant, petitioned the Foundling Hospital to take her child, explaining that her lover, David R., a gardener, had refused to go through with their wedding plans. He was confident of his position, boasting, "She could not do anything to him, except bring an action for a 'Breach of promise of marriage.'"[15] In addition, as the century wore on, knowledge of the action grew, since hundreds of cases were printed in the daily newspapers. As for payment, solicitors and barristers may have taken cases on spec, agreeing to payment only if the case was won, although the legal community discouraged this practice.[16] There is also limited evidence that some barristers specialized in breach-of-promise cases.[17] I have no information at all, however, on how solicitors garnered their business. The important point is not so much how these women discovered their rights but that they took the trouble to do so and followed up on them with tenacity.

Like many theatre productions, a long preparation period ensued before the performance occurred; indeed, all involved knew that the play might never be produced at all. Both solicitors bluffed each other and the two principals in an effort to settle on the best possible terms for their respective sides. This process went on for months, often lasting into the trial itself. The correspondence in *Bardens v. Amey* was typical of the melodramatic, vilifying language of these communications. Albert Akaster, Amey's solicitor, wrote to Parker as follows: "I think from the tone of your letter that you must be entirely ignorant of the character of the person whose claims you are advancing." He also wrote to Bardens, warning her that she probably would not want to have the action come to trial and that his client "feels very thankful that the discoveries were made in due time and before it was too late."[18] Parker, undaunted, replied, "I think you will be conclusively satisfied of the utter worthlessness of your clients instructions. All his attempts to aggravate his base conduct by cowardice in bringing false charges against his intended wife will be comp[ensated]."[19]

In a substantial minority of cases the bluffing persuaded the parties to come to terms. Usually, however, no settlement was forthcoming, and the solicitors began communicating through formal legal papers. First, the plaintiff served the defendant with a writ, setting out her claims. These followed a standard form, stating that the couple had promised to marry one another, but that the defendant had "neglected and refused" to do so. If the defendant had married another woman, the plaintiff entered that fact, and added that she had always been "ready and willing" to marry him. She also claimed an exact amount of compensation, usually an enormous sum (£500–1,000).[20] The defendant's solicitors replied with a statement of defense. Usually, the defendant made a flat denial of the promise and then added several other pleas in case the denial failed (such as infancy, drunkenness, mutual exoneration, or fraud).[21] The plaintiff, after receiving the defense statement, joined issue with him on the points of disagreement, and the date for the trial was set.[22]

The plaintiff's solicitor had the responsibility of putting the action on the cause list for the next assize. Both sets of solicitors also retained barristers to argue the matter in court, and they tried to employ well-known stars of the circuit. Quite often actions were settled between registration and trial; between 1859 and 1922 over 22 percent of breach-of-promise cases on the lists were withdrawn.[23] In addition, a large number were settled during the trial itself, often after the plaintiff had proved the promise and the defendant decided his best course was to avoid a jury decision.[24] Particularly in cases that involved sexual improprieties, the plaintiff also wanted to settle to avoid revealing her "fall." Judges approved, too, since they disliked airing sexual scandals in open court.[25]

However, most of the suits did not end so amicably. In the majority of them negotiations failed, and the barristers began to build their cases, sifting through the evidence. The plaintiff's lawyer, in particular, often had to peruse stacks of letters, marking the places to read.[26] Both sides rounded up relatives and friends to be witnesses, and here the woman had a definite advantage, since she was usually still living at home and had numerous witnesses. The plaintiff's barrister also tried to get an idea of the amount of money the defendant made, for such evidence was admissible to help assess damages.

On the day of the trial the lawyers and participants arrived and the performance began. One of the characteristics of melodrama was its Manichaeanism, its insistence on strict polarity between good and bad with no gray areas in the middle.[27] Breach-of-promise cases fit into this mode, for both sides presented cardboard characters with no real psychological insight. Such characterizations are almost inevitable in court cases because of their adversarial nature. This superficiality was even reflected in the language used by newspaper court reporters. The people suing were seldom referred to by their personal names; they were always "the plaintiffs," while the people sued were "the defendants." In addition, the judge was "the judge" or "His Lordship," and the jurors were a collective character referred to as "the jury" or the "men in the jury-box." All were playing well-known parts: the women were pathetic maidens hurt by cruel seducers; and the men were hapless bachelors, caught in the snares of husband-hungry women. The judge and jury played the parts of avengers or conciliators, depending on the situation.[28]

Lawyers used a number of theatrical tactics to influence the jury. For instance, the plaintiff's barrister often instructed his client to wear a costume. If young, she dressed nicely, often in the clothes she had bought for the wedding. In addition, the plaintiff's barrister invariably found out what his client looked like and displayed her prominently if she were attractive. Barrister Jack Lee used this maneuver in a trial in the Norfolk Circuit early in the century, complaining pointedly of the "abominable cruelty" of the defendant to "the lovely and confiding female" the jury saw before them.[29] Lawyers firmly believed that a pretty face was an asset, although they had no proof, and newspapers seldom failed to record the appearance of the plaintiff as "interesting looking" or "fair."[30] Older women, too, had costumes, usually arranged to induce sympathy. An example was a seventy-year-old plaintiff in 1878; she wore widow's weeds and a wig in the witness box, the former in mourning for her husband, "and the latter, she said, was rendered necessary by her hair having all fallen off in consequence of the defendant's heartless conduct."[31]

The plaintiff's side always began the action; it was the first act in a two-act play.[32] The first scene belonged to the plaintiff's barrister, who made the opening speech, thus getting his client's side firmly in the jury's minds. Most of the barristers took great advantage of this opportunity, speaking for up to two hours. Generally, they took one of two tacks. One was to emphasize the bad behavior of the defendant in deserting his fiancée. As Mr. Addison in *Barrow v. Twist* (1886) declared, "This case was about as cruel and as wicked a one as was ever brought before a jury. The unhappy woman had not only been treated by the defendant with great cruelty, but he had put forward the sham plea that he broke off the match because she had been guilty of misconduct. This he would endeavour to show them was a wicked fabrication."[33] Epithets such as "false," "terrible," "wretched," and "cruel" were frequently used as a shorthand characterization for melodramatic villains, and barristers did not hesitate to follow this example.[34] When romance was absent, an alternative approach was to make a point of how prosaic the case would be; it would not afford the usual amusement. In 1886 Mr. Gully admitted that "there would be nothing comic or tragic in this case. . . . However, the circumstances, although very unromantic circumstances, were none the less worthy of consideration."[35] This was a way to blunt the defense that the plaintiff had lost little because she lacked a romantic attachment to the defendant.

Before 1869 the plaintiff then backed up her case with the evidence of friends and family and with any letters, gifts, or tokens she had kept. After 1869 the plaintiff herself took the stand and was usually followed by at least one relative. This evidence constituted the important second scene in the first act. Many plaintiffs also had props with which to support their stories. Letters, for instance, figured in 173 cases. In *Pettit v. Tough* (1898) Louisa Pettit had 117 letters from her traveling fiancé.[36] Other common pieces of evidence were gifts of jewelry (especially rings), the parents' acceptance of the man as their daughter's suitor, and the fact that they had walked out together for many months.

Occasionally, plaintiffs even had written promises.[37] These physical pieces of evidence are the best examples of the mixture of shrewdness and heartbreak the trials reveal. Most of the letters evinced real passion, but in the trials they became weapons against their faithless writers.

Plaintiffs tried to elicit sympathy from the all-male jury by emphasizing their timidity and sorrow, feelings that many probably did not have to manufacture. To counteract this effect, defense counsels severely questioned plaintiffs in the hope of breaking down their stories. They kept the women on the stand for long periods of time and even made fun of them, usually in an effort to ridicule the entire action.[38] Defense barristers realized they must complicate the presentation of the plaintiff as a victim or lose. Even younger women could be subject to harsh questioning, but defense lawyers had to be careful; bullying a young woman was not likable. Carried too far, it transferred the villain's part to the defense barrister, damaging his influence with the jury. For instance, in *Penny v. Rees* (1872), the plaintiff fainted after a long cross-examination, earning much sympathy in the process.[39]

After the plaintiff's case closed, the second act commenced, this one comprising the defense. Again the first scene belonged to the barrister. The defense lawyer also made an opening speech, but he labored under the disadvantage of having to negate the plaintiff's case rather than to assert one of his own. Most defense speeches were comparatively short, though good barristers managed to make a positive statement in spite of the difficulties. Much of their time was spent trying to make it clear that the plaintiff had no right to the position of melodramatic victim. For example, Mr. Lopes argued in *Penny v. Rees* that the suit was not brought for the young woman's benefit, since she was not really hurt, but for the benefit of her friends.[40] Others simply urged that the plaintiff had lost little (if she were still young), or that the plaintiff had trapped the defendant. Also, almost all denied the plaintiff's story and pleaded for mitigation of damages.[41]

Another common tactic of defense barristers was to center on the defendant's character. He, like the plaintiff, came into court wearing a costume and playing a role. If he seemed a noble and upright man, his counsel insisted that he could not have behaved in such a dishonorable way. If he appeared otherwise, the lawyer instead argued that the plaintiff had lost nothing in losing him. Sir Henry Hawkins, in fact, used both of these tactics in one trial.[42] Either way, the defendant did not fit the role of a melodramatic villain, a character who was usually outwardly attractive but also straightforwardly evil. Similarly, defense barristers argued that their clients could not pay high damages. As Mr. Coleridge put it in a trial in 1893, "He had never known a defendant in a breach of promise who was not a pauper at the trial."[43] As well as mitigating damages, such appeals underlined the unsuitability of the defendant as a villain, since most of the latter, at least by the 1840s, were rich landlords and factory owners.[44]

Costuming was particularly important at this point. A number of defendants dressed in shabby clothing, and some even acted like idiots or invalids. In *Shickell v. Warren* (1890), James Warren came into the court dressed in a disreputable coat. Mr. Blofeld, the plaintiff's barrister, asked him sarcastically "if he had got it off a scarecrow, and whether he had put dirt on the collar that morning." Warren replied unconvincingly that it was his "market coat." Even the judge was unimpressed. In his summing up he said that "a defendant in a breach-of-promise case ought not to take a coat off a scarecrow in his garden and come into Court with it on his back."[45] Attempts at acting insane or silly were also repulsed. The defendant in *Humphries v. Gain* (1884) would only answer "Hee-haw" when asked his name, and he presented himself as deaf and in ill health. The plaintiff's barrister demanded a doctor's report to prove these infirmities, which was not forthcoming. The jury in this case ignored such obvious shamming.[46] Although usually not this excessive, most defense barristers devoted at least part of their time to denying the wealth of their clients, if only to assure reasonable damages.

Like the defense speeches, the evidence called by the defendant varied much more than that of the plaintiff. First, defendants testified on their own behalf less often, for they assumed that they would not automatically get a sympathetic hearing the way an injured member of the weaker sex would. They were in the role of the purported villain, and they were also adult men who should be able to fend for themselves under cross-examination. Second, they called fewer witnesses and seldom submitted tokens or letters, except in unusual cases, such as the defense of mutual exoneration.[47] The few witnesses defendants did call primarily testified about the purported bad character of the plaintiff. In *Jones v. James* (1868), for example, three different men accused Ann Jones of loose conduct. In this instance the attempt failed, since the jury did not believe them, but many times calling such witnesses at least gave the jury a different side to consider.[48]

The second act was, then, much shorter than the first, although some defendants did decide to testify and give their own side of the story, thereby adding a second scene. However, the defendant did not control the script after his testimony was done, and plaintiffs' barristers relished the opportunity for cross-examination.[49] They vigorously attacked the stories of the defendants, and they felt free to do so, since men hesitated to appear weak by fainting or protesting that they were being bullied. Men were in something of a dilemma, since they needed to appeal for sympathy but could not do so through appearing pathetic and unmanly. Clever barristers made the defendants look extremely silly, particularly if they tried to deny everything in the face of irrefutable evidence (which a surprising number did). The plaintiff's counsel whittled away the defendant's story until there was little left, and this seldom failed to make the defendant look deceitful and foolish (sometimes deservedly so).[50] This danger explains why few defendants braved the witness box. Like the unusual activity of the plaintiffs, the silence of the villain contradicted the melodramatic mode; the victim usually was unable to speak, while the villain spoke continually.[51] Juries ignored this contradiction as well.

The final scene of the trial was the summing up by both counsels and the judge. Usually, the summations simply recapitulated the trial, although the plaintiff's barrister often tried to refute whatever defense had been raised. The judge's speech, however, was different. The judge, in his splendid costume and elevated seat, had an important role, even though his influence was largely left until the end. Often in melodramas the problems in the play were resolved by a trial, with the judges discovering the true villainy and releasing the innocent.[52] Judges in breach-of-promise cases seldom made decisions, but their summations usually influenced juries. Most of the time judges sided with the plaintiff, particularly in cases involving sexual intercourse. Baron Huddleston, for example, was outraged at the behavior of Evan Jones in an 1879 case, and "in the course of his observations expressed his strong disapprobation of the conduct of a man who came into court and tried to save his pocket by blasting the character of a decent woman whose favours he had enjoyed." The jury awarded Mary Roberts £150.[53] But the woman need not have fallen to get a chivalrous response from the judge; Justice Field was equally angry at the defendant in *Hancock v. Davies* (1889) who had courted a servant and induced her to give up her position, despite the fact that he was already married. Also, judges were furious at "light" behavior. In a case in 1892 Samuel Southern, the defendant, constantly made jokes and laughed his way through his testimony. The judge was not amused, calling Southern's laughter "stupid" and concluding that "the defendant's conduct in the witness box showed a disregard of decent feelings."[54] Judges were careful not to overdo it, though, because the jury might award too much for the defendant to pay. Justice Brett, for instance, cautioned a jury in 1880 that they should not give too heavy damages, or the plaintiff would get nothing.[55]

Although judges were on the whole more sympathetic to the women bringing the cases, some actions elicited the opposite response. As in the divorce court, the plaintiff had to pass a character test in order to collect. In particular, she had to fit the role of the deceived maiden. If she had been sexually or even socially aggressive, she was not the properly passive victim. In *Lamb v. Fryer* (1881) Justice Williams sided with the defendant, since he was sure that the plaintiff had courted the latter relentlessly: "It would be affectation to say that the lady did not make love to him, as it was as plain as daylight. . . . His Lordship afterwards suggested that the case was one for reasonable damages."[56] Furthermore, the plaintiff had to have been "blighted" by the broken engagement because of a strong emotional attachment. The plaintiff in *Adams v. Leach* (1895) laughed merrily during her trial. The judge summed up against her, insisting that she could not have been hurt much, and she received nothing. In addition, widows or elderly spinsters received less consideration because they could not play the role convincingly. Widows, after all, had already benefited from marriage, while elderly spinsters hardly fit the part of romantic heroines.[57]

After the judge had his say, the matter was left in the hands of the jury. The jury had a peculiar position in the proceedings as both audience and actors. They came from the local area and had probably sat in the audience at other trials; now they were expected to produce the climax of the drama.[58] Jurors were entirely independent; they could follow the advice of the judge or they could ignore it. Most of the time the judge influenced them, but they could disregard him if they chose. When the judge summed up for the plaintiff, the jury agreed with him 77 percent of the time. But when the judge summed up for the defendant, the jury found as he suggested only 51 percent of the time. They particularly gave verdicts to plaintiffs based on questionable evidence if the plaintiff had fallen, clearly desiring to help a ruined woman. They also sometimes disregarded the defendant's ability to pay. In *Lamb v. Fryer* the jury ignored Justice Williams's plea for moderate damages, awarding Kate Lamb £1,000.

The foreman's announcement of the verdict was a dramatic climax, often resulting in applause from the audience. The audience could feel that the wrongdoer had paid for his sins, while his victim's reputation was restored. The appeal to melodrama, in short, was effective, whether or not it was deliberate, and it was apparently widely used in the nineteenth-century courts. Ruth Harris finds that women who maimed or murdered their seducers in the heat of passion in nineteenth-century France were almost always "ritually acquitted," when they employed a similar dynamic.[59]

By the time the jury gave its verdict, the production could have been anywhere from half an hour to three or four days, although the typical length was between two and four hours.[60] Juries often took little time to come to decisions, not even leaving the box, or taking a short consultation. But in more complicated cases they took hours, and in some cases they never agreed.[61] This was an unsatisfactory ending for the audience, like a play that had no last scene. It was also the worst possible outcome for the plaintiff, since her expenses doubled. Such a prospect probably led some plaintiffs to drop the suit entirely; however, if the plaintiff persevered, the defendant's expenses also rose. Judges did their best to avoid this result, urging the jury to meet until they could come to some kind of agreement, and a hung jury was rare in breach-of-promise cases.[62]

The last word in the assize trial was that of the judge. He pronounced the jury's judgment and then certified which party paid costs. He acted as the voice of authority, either withholding or giving his blessing to the action of the jury. If the jury's decision seemed completely wrong or against the evidence, the judge could set it aside and make his own decision, but in no breach-of-promise case on record did a judge do this. However, costs were entirely up to him, and when he felt the verdict was incorrect, he could deny them to the victor. Judges could also stay execution of high awards to give the defendant a chance to appeal (Williams did so in *Lamb v. Fryer*).[63] By the same token, however, the judge at times ordered immediate execution of decisions to keep the defendant from avoiding payment.[64]

The end of the trial at the assizes was not always the end of the issue. A few cases were appealed to the central courts, either on a technical point of law or by arguing that the decision was against the evidence, the damages were too high, or the judge had misdirected the jury in his summation. If the defeated party succeeded in getting a hearing, both principals had the expense of a second trial, in which most of the facts of the case were reiterated. And if the appeal succeeded, there would be yet another trial, since most appeals resulted in new trials rather than reversals. The rehash of the facts by barristers before the appeals courts rarely had the dramatic punch of the original trial; it lacked the pathos and the main performers. Despite the lack of the melodramatic setting, defendants (or plaintiffs) had little luck in appealing on anything except the technical points of law. Central Court judges had great respect for the decisions of juries; their discretion on damages, especially, was seldom gainsaid.[65] The decisions on points of law, on the other hand, were decided on a case-by-case basis, since the jury's discretion was not at stake in these suits.

The announcement of the verdict should have been a satisfying conclusion to the play. The evil seducer was banished (or, less often, the victimized male was rescued from the clutches of a grasping husband hunter), and "justice" prevailed. But after the trial, the fact that these were real people with complex emotions rather than symbolic actors came back into play. Most of the principals disappeared from public view once their cases left the court, but the few that reappeared showed that the outcome was often in question. Though the jury might award £100 to the plaintiff or the defendant might be exonerated, neither party was assured satisfaction.

For example, probably a large number of defendants never paid damages. Time and again defendants hid assets the moment they were served with the writs. James Hamer changed the name on his pub to "James Greenhalgh" to give the impression he no longer owned it; James Wilkins transferred his shares in his fishing business to his father; James Haythornethwaite transferred his two houses to his son; and Henry Tucker "sold" his farm to his new father-in-law, acting as a tenant until the case he was involved with was over.[66] Other defendants disappeared. In 1889 Simeon Holden escaped to America to forestall being served, and the defendant in *Drake v. Blake* planned to leave England if the jury found against him. The plaintiff's barrister asked for immediate execution, but since the action went undefended, Blake had probably already gone.[67] In most cases there is simply no way to determine if the damages ever reached the plaintiff, but contemporary records—such as those of the Foundling Hospital—indicate that plaintiffs had little reason for optimism. For example, a young woman identified as Eleanor O. gave her baby to the Foundling Hospital in 1866 because she could not support it, despite the fact that she had won £100 in a breach-of-promise case. She had apparently received nothing by the time she decided to part with the child.[68]

Indeed, men would go to extraordinary lengths to avoid paying, as two examples from the 1890s demonstrate. Eliza Kennedy was a mantle-maker, who was barely eighteen when Thomas McCann, a boot and shoe maker, promised to marry her in December 1892. The couple decided to wed when Eliza turned twenty, but in December 1894 McCann refused to fulfill the promise. (He claimed mutual exoneration.) This was a rare trial without a jury, and the judge decided that there had been a definite promise. He remarked that there was no blemish on the character of the plaintiff and that McCann "appeared to have acted towards her in an unmanly and unfeeling way." He therefore gave a judgment for Kennedy for £75, with costs, on April 18, 1895.[69]

By February 1896, however, the plaintiff had yet to see a shilling of her award. Before the trial McCann had put his business in his father's name and all his stocks in that of his mother. When the court insisted he pay the damages anyway, he fled to America, where he stayed until December 1895. When he returned, Kennedy's solicitors pressed him for the money. McCann's response was to declare bankruptcy. At his bankruptcy hearing he claimed assets of £50 savings, £16 in a building society, and other assets of about £7, out of which he had to pay her award (£75), her costs (£46), and his own solicitor's fees (£25). He offered to settle with Kennedy for £20, but since this amount would not even pay for her costs, she refused. The Bankruptcy Court was unimpressed, particularly since he had admitted in the trial to £400 savings, but there was little they could do when they could not uncover these funds. Although the record is not complete, Kennedy probably had to settle for a much reduced award, all of which would go to her counsel.[70]

In *Knowles v. Duncan* the plaintiff was twenty-year-old Gladys Knowles, granddaughter of Sir Francis Knowles, third baronet, and she lived with her mother in Fulham.[71] One day in 1889 she received a free copy of *Matrimonial News,* a matchmaking publication. "For fun," she decided to put in an advertisement herself. While at the newspaper's offices, she met the elderly proprietor, Leslie Fraser Duncan, and became engaged to him within two weeks. Duncan spent the next several weeks promising to get a special license but in reality merely trying to get Knowles to spend the night with him. Gladys went to his home unchaperoned twice. She also stayed at a hotel with him, although she sat up all night in the bathroom rather than share a room with him. Although the engagement continued for a few weeks after this episode, Knowles eventually realized that Duncan had no intention of fulfilling his obligations. With her mother's support, she sued for breach of promise, asking for £25,000 damages.

Duncan did not come to the trial nor did his counsel offer much defense. William Willis, the plaintiff's barrister, was able to paint the editor as a dissipated old roué out to seduce an innocent young gentlewoman, and Duncan's case was further weakened by the fact that he had recently married another of his clients. The jury had no hesitation in finding for the plaintiff, with damages of £10,000. Duncan ignored the judgment, and when the court levied execution he escaped to France, taking his business ledgers and all the cash he could find. He eventually returned to stand public examination, and the official receivers uncovered most of his assets and committed him to stand trial for violations of the Bankruptcy Acts. Duncan spent the next six months in jail, but he used the time wisely, appealing the judgment on the grounds of excessive damages. Lords Esher, Bowen, and Fry agreed to reduce the award to £6,500, but only if the entire amount were paid in one month. Though they were disgusted by Duncan's character and actions, they also put some blame on Knowles. Before she had received anything, then, Gladys found her award reduced by £3,500. She did finally collect the remainder, but she had one more scrape with the law, since she sued an English publication, *Hawk,* for libel in its report of the suit. She lost that case completely.

Knowles obviously got more out of her breach-of-promise action than Kennedy. Nevertheless, both these cases demonstrate that the verdict at the end of a case could prove illusory, leaving the plaintiffs penniless or notorious. On a more serious note, the people involved in the suits did not always stop feuding when the case came to an end. In melodramas the villain is banished or killed, but the real defendants and plaintiffs had to continue living near each other, a situation fraught with difficulties. *Barnard v. Marks* is a case in point. Barnard was the daughter of an umbrella manufacturer, and Marks was a picture-frame maker. The couple became engaged after a short acquaintance. Marks came into some insurance money when his premises burned down, and he broke his promise soon after. He then tried to sue Barnard for some gifts he had given her. Though he failed in the attempt, her family was furious and retaliated with a breach-of-promise suit. Barnard won the case, but Marks refused to pay. Rather than try to force him through the courts, the plaintiff's brother, Frederick, instead told the police that the defendant had committed arson to get the insurance award. A few days later Marks shot Frederick three times, killing him instantly. Although he pleaded insanity at his trial, he was found guilty and hanged. Rather than receiving any of her award, Barnard had to mourn two deaths—that of her faithful brother as well as that of her faithless fiancé.[72]

So being declared the winner in a legal battle did not necessarily ensure happiness. Interestingly, this fact was true even when the damages were paid in full (or in the case of the defendant, when the jury decided for him). For example, in 1883, Ada Buhrer sued her lover, a man named Holloway, for breach of promise. She won only forty shillings and the judge did not give her costs, essentially a victory for the defendant. Yet Holloway, shortly after the proceedings, "took as much phosphorus as he thought would kill him . . . confessed that Ada had been the death of him, and expired." The publicity and worry of the trial had apparently been too much for him, and at his inquest, the jury gave a verdict of "suicide whilst temporarily insane." His victory in court clearly gave him no peace of mind.[73]

Nor were winning plaintiffs always pleased with their victories. Mary Hamilton brought a breach-of-promise case against her longtime lover in 1896. She had lived with Joseph Jacobs for ten years and had two children with him (both had died). He kept promising to marry her, but after ten years she realized that he was not going to do so, and she sued him, winning and receiving substantial damages. Yet, after the trial, Mary refused to accept the award, saying that "it was marriage she wanted, and not money." She only took the damages when she was starving. When the money ran out, she broke into Joseph's house, intending to kill herself. She was caught before she succeeded and committed for trial by the magistrates. Jacobs, obviously feeling responsible, offered to pay her one pound a week for the rest of her life, a suggestion the magistrates accepted gladly.[74] Yet for all Jacobs's "kindness," Hamilton remained unhappy because he would not give her the one thing that she really wanted—marriage. No trial could do that, and she remained discontented.

Certainly these examples are too few to afford many generalizations. Probably most of the defendants paid at least part of the awards, and most winners felt some pleasure and relief. But these instances offer cautionary lessons: an award from a jury was not the same as money in the hand, nor did winning a case give women (or men) everything that they wanted. Large damages were better than nothing, but they did not provide the comfort and prestige of marriage. After the extensive trouble and expense of a trial in the High Court, both plaintiffs and defendants may have found themselves feeling empty, poorer, or even publicly humiliated. Still, female plaintiffs usually at least had the satisfaction of a friendly verdict. The reasons for women's success went beyond their ability to frame the trials in melodramatic terms. They also were able to convince juries, who were often of the same class, of their peculiar difficulties in courtship and breaches, and of their hardship due to sexual misadventures. But most important, expectations for the masculine gender proved to be more onerous than those for the feminine one. Though seldom helpful to women in the criminal courts, the assumption of manly responsibility for providing, promise-keeping, and sexuality was a great asset to female plaintiffs in the civil tribunals.

III

Gender Roles

IN THE LAST SEVERAL YEARS historians have begun exploring gender and its impact on both men and women. Recent works have emphasized that gender is not something that only women have; masculinity should be as problematized and historicized as femininity, and both entities changed during the nineteenth century.[1] However, with a few exceptions, such as the work of Keith McClelland, historians have concentrated on the middle class, and have dealt with manliness primarily in the public sphere.[2] Domestic life, however, as John Tosh and Michael Roper have pointed out, was central to the construction of both genders; it was the foundation of masculine self-identity. Breach-of-promise cases, then, can offer two unusual perspectives on gender: first, they encompass the lower middle and upper working classes; and second, they deal with men in a domestic setting.[3] The remarks of plaintiffs, defendants, judges, and jurors about manliness and womanliness give a firm sense of the characteristics of "proper" men and women.

Indeed, what emerges most obviously from these cases is that one of the reasons that the lower middle class was so supportive of breach-of-promise cases was its firm belief in correct behavior for both genders. These ideas often matched those of the middle and upper classes, and they stressed the difficulties, rather than the advantages, of manliness. In fact, at least in the expressions used, the men in the courtroom and the women bringing the actions were more concerned about masculinity than femininity. Though certain behaviors disqualified a female plaintiff, breach-of-promise cases showed clearly that masculinity was not a total boon, despite men's obvious advantages in Victorian England. The heavy expectations for men made them unsuccessful in breach-of-promise cases, while women were able to use their gender to great effect. And though the actions often supported patriarchal assumptions about both sexes, they also subtly undercut them.

Correct masculine behavior consisted of several things; one of the most important was that a man should keep his word. If he made a promise, particularly to someone deemed inferior, he must fulfill it. Thus, breach-of-promise cases struck at the very heart of manliness; a proposal was a contract, whose terms must be enforced. Officers of the court and plaintiffs both placed a great degree of importance on promise-keeping. Maria Brookfield had kept her sexual liaisons with Joseph Wilcock quiet in the hope that he would marry her. When he refused, she wrote to him: "You promised me the morning you seduced me, that if I would promise you on my honour not to say one word to any one, particularly my mother, that you would marry me. Now I have kept it while ever I could from them, and now you are not man enough to keep your promise."[4] This insistence that men should keep their word related to a distinct distaste for men who vacillated. Juries, in particular, were repulsed by indecisiveness. In 1824 Maria Foote received an award of £3,000 from her lover, Joseph Haynes, primarily because he had set the wedding date four times and failed to show up each time. She wrote to him indignantly, "Your conduct is as inconsistent as it is cruel and unjust." Fifty years later Margaret Adams and Thomas Jeeves got engaged and broke up three times before he finally married someone else. Although the couple apparently were incompatible, Margaret and the jury believed that Thomas was at fault for being unable to make up his mind either to the marriage or to the breach. Adams called him a "villain," and her barrister defended her term as follows: "He made an engagement. . . . Then he broke it, then he renewed it again, then he broke it again, then he renewed it again, and then he broke it again. Could they wonder that after such conduct she should on the spur of the moment have called him a villain? Was there any name too bad for her to describe him?" The judge, too, sympathized with Adams, claiming that he had seldom "met with a case of such heartless and inhuman treatment," and she received £1,000.[5] Moreover, this disgust was limited to men. In several cases the female plaintiff had already jilted at least one man herself, but the jury did not hold this against her when it came to a verdict.[6] Women's inconstancy was assumed, but men should be firm and consistent.

This obsession with a man's promises was in part because of the importance of men's words in the business world. Broken contracts were a threat to all social relations. In *Brookes v. Cox* the plaintiff and the defendant began a sexual affair when she was in her teens; she then waited ten years for him to marry her. He ultimately refused, and Brookes even had to have him affiliated to get support for their child. Justice Hill summed up firmly against Cox on these grounds: "The plaintiff had given up ten good years of her life to the defendant. If men were to be allowed to act generally in that way, society would be worth nothing."[7] The emphasis on male promise-keeping alone was highly ironic, since most of the female plaintiffs in breach-of-promise actions were also businesswomen (if in a small way) and could have been held to the same standard. But judges and juries persisted in seeing women primarily as potential wives, not as people with careers who should be trustworthy in their businesses. Furthermore, the court was more insistent on men's promises because of the man's peculiar advantages in courtship. The male was assumed to be the initiator in the relationship. Having persuaded the woman into a closer intimacy, he must not then repudiate her. Since he had special advantages, he also had a special responsibility.

In addition to firmness, a man should be honest in his addresses to a woman, an attribute that Allen Warren has identified as crucial in late Victorian manly development. Plaintiffs' barristers stressed the dishonest conduct of the defendants in leading these women on and then deserting them. And the standard of honesty was just as high for male plaintiffs as male defendants. In *Morris v. Leigh* the plaintiff was a man who had persuaded the defendant to enter a secret engagement with him, despite her family's disapproval. The defendant's barrister insisted that no proper man would countenance a secret engagement, nor would he then drag his fiancée into court when she broke the pact: "Any right minded man who wished his courtship to be above board would have put his hand to the wheel and tried to improve his position, and would have had nothing to do with secret meetings." The jury found for the female defendant, apparently untroubled by her equally dishonest cooperation in the clandestine courtship.[8]

Furthermore, men were expected to be brave, facing the consequences of their actions without flinching. For one thing, men were cowardly to refuse to go through with the bargain. Jane Alderton had been engaged to Charles Hunt for two years and had received many affectionate letters from him. All the same, he fell in love with another woman, and instead of telling Jane at once, he tried to provoke a breach by flirting with his new love in front of his old. Alderton's barrister complained that Hunt had "behaved in a most cowardly and unmanly manner." It was also reprehensible not to acknowledge illegitimate children. Emily Kitteridge's mother begged her daughter's lover, Thomas Crowe, to marry Emily before the birth of their child; he replied indifferently that "she has got into trouble, and she must get out." Justice Cockburn was incensed with such a cavalier attitude, claiming that "in his long experience, he never recollected a more unmanly or cowardly expression."[9]

Additionally, judges or juries considered it cowardly for men to be afraid of disappointing their families. A man should put his future wife's needs first, not those of his parents or anyone else. This was particularly true in the case of older, mature men who should have been economically and emotionally independent. The plaintiff's barrister in *Bebbington v. Hitchen* ridiculed the defendant's claim that his parents forced the breach: "Poor little boy! Only 42, and could not get married without his father's consent!" Edith Williams also garnered much sympathy in her case against Edward Hughes. He was ten years older and had induced her to live with him, and she had his child. He then repudiated her, claiming that his father disapproved (Hughes was twenty-nine at the time of the trial, while Williams was eighteen). The judge summed up for Edith, and the jury gave her £150. Again, these expectations of independence were for men alone. A woman might obey her parents until she was in her forties, but a man should be making his way in the world. If he were man enough to make the promise, he should be man enough to keep it.[10]

In addition to being a coward, a wayward fiancé was also ungenerous. A man should face up to his debts; not to do so was mean. His behavior was bad enough when he refused to keep his promise, but in forcing his ex-lover to sue for compensation, he was especially cheap. And since so many defendants pleaded poverty, this criticism was effective. In *Orford v. Cole* the mere fact of a breach was enough to inspire the plaintiff's barrister to brand the defendant as "unmanly and ungenerous." Any kind of additional cheapness made the damages higher. For example, James Thompson blamed his fiancée, Kate Fleming, for their breakup because he claimed she spent too much on the linens for their future home, ending a letter, "I was not aware until lately that I was expected to provide clothing for the lady before marriage." He then broke off the match. The jury reacted to this evidence of miserliness by finding for Fleming with damages of £1,500. Also, the defendants who had seduced the plaintiffs looked bad if they had been affiliated before they agreed to support their illegitimate offspring. In all of these cases, but especially in the latter, the defendants were not living up to their duty to provide for those weaker than they.[11] As Keith McClelland has argued about artisans and Sonya Rose has argued for working-class men as a whole in the mid-Victorian period, part of their construction of masculinity was in becoming independent providers while insisting on female dependence. If they demanded such a role, however, they must be prepared to provide for all women and children connected to them.[12] Indeed, probably one reason breach-of-promise cases increased after midcentury was this assumption of male responsibility and female helplessness in all classes.

Defendants were also accused of bullying the plaintiffs. The simple act of jilting alone was enough to brand a man "base" or "cruel." "Brutality" also embraced actual violent behavior, drunkenness, and sexual overtures that the plaintiffs rebuffed. Albert Taylor talked Maria Harworth into living with him, frequently got drunk and beat her, and then tried to plead at the trial that she was unfaithful. Not surprisingly, such a collection of brutal behaviors earned Albert a verdict of £1,600 against him and the epithet of a "wicked knave" from the plaintiff's barrister. Ada Ibbetson called her fiancé, Walter Strickland, "unmanly" because he was drunk one night and also because he had "pushed her off a chair and knocked her down." Strickland apparently agreed with her assessment, because he apologized for his unmanly behavior in a letter, and the jury gave Ada £200. Ellen Ross and Pamela Walker have shown that working-class masculinity often involved violence and drinking in the late nineteenth century, but the judges and jurors did not think this was acceptable in the artisan and lower middle classes. Nor did the development of the more virile, hard-hitting manliness of the late Victorian period change their minds. Women were inferiors and thus required gentleness, not bullying.[13]

Brutality was particularly difficult for defendants to refute, since the very act of defending the action was (at base) accusing the plaintiff of lying. In addition, the only defense that was fairly successful was to accuse the plaintiff of unchastity, which was seen as very cruel. If the man did not present a defense, the jury only heard the plaintiff's side of the story, but if he did launch a vigorous defense, he was regarded as a bully. Furthermore, a woman could commit much more violence than a man and escape reproof. For example, Ellen Wood threatened John Irving on the public street, claiming she would "clip his wings" and have him "in a cage" for not fulfilling his promise. Sarah Nates was described as being "a girl of violent temper" and apparently struck her ex-fiancé with an umbrella in a rage. All the same, the juries in these two cases gave Wood £250 and Nates £150. In both instances they assumed that a man could look after himself. After all, it was natural for a woman to be hysterical and emotional, especially when she had been jilted.[14] A man, however, must control his temper.

Probably the most interesting insight into masculinity from breach-of-promise cases was the court's reaction to male sexuality. As Leonore Davidoff, Catherine Hall, and John Tosh have found, the middle classes in the mid-Victorian period believed in chastity for men, but they made few legal penalties to force men to behave.[15] Instead, women had the sole responsibility for illegitimate children, and the Divorce Act enshrined the double standard for married couples. However, in breach-of-promise cases the plaintiff, her family, the judge, and the jury all felt firmly that a man who had intercourse with a woman had a duty to support her and any children they had. Once a man had sex with a woman (unless she was unchaste with others as well), he was responsible for her. In this way the action undermined the harsh Victorian strictures on female chastity.

One reason for this attitude was the common assumption that men were the aggressive sex. Most of those involved in the suits assumed that only men pushed for sexual intercourse.[16] Indeed, the plaintiffs accepted these conventions. Charlotte Windeatt used typical language when she claimed that Frank Slocombe "wished me to 'give up' to him, but I refused. When we got home he repeatedly asked me to give up to him, and said if I would he would marry me directly. Then I gave up to him." The jury sympathized with Windeatt's passive rendering of the relationship, assuming that Slocombe had taken her virtue from her.[17] Since the men were the initiators, then, they should act honorably toward women they had ruined.

The most honorable conclusion to a seduction was marriage, but if a man could not do that, the least he could do was to support the child and mother. Even some defendants agreed. William Stowe contracted to pay Florence Carter five shillings a week for support of his child, but then he reneged on his word, and she affiliated him. He complained that she was "persecuting him," but the judge and jury saw it as his duty and fined him accordingly. William Hampson sold Mary Wilkinson's child to a couple for £40 to get rid of the responsibility. Justice Grantham and the jury were appalled at his actions, profiting from the mother's distress on the one hand and failing to provide on the other. Mary received £600 and the judge urged her to reclaim the child.[18] Indeed, as the century wore on, the sexual double standard wavered even more, despite the new, virile version of manliness that John Springhall and Michael Rosenthal found emerging in the middle classes in the late Victorian period. Judges and jurors held to a more domestic view of manliness and insisted that men be sexually responsible.[19]

Even some defendants agreed that they were at fault. In *Hairs v. Elliot* (1890), the defendant, Sir George Elliot, admitted to having had a long affair with the plaintiff, saying, "It is the sorrow of my life that I fell." He used the exact language mid-Victorians had reserved for seduced women, assuming that a man could fall into sin. In *Herron v. Mort* (1890), Justice Smith angrily rejected the defense barrister's assertion that the plaintiff was unchaste, since the defense had not produced adequate evidence to support those assertions. Smith instead called Mort "a bad and abandoned man." Again, a word usually meant to designate a sexually aggressive woman, "abandoned," was applied to a man. By 1893 Robert Harding could write to Caroline Fawkes that his failure to marry her after her pregnancy preyed on his mind: "I cannot blame you, for my conscience tells me I have done with you as though you were a dog."[20] The insistence that women were responsible for their own chastity was limited even at the height of the Victorian period, and it lessened steadily as the century wore on. Such ideals limited the dominance of the aggressive masculinity and "flight from domesticity" that some historians have seen in the 1880s and 1890s. This is not to say, of course, that purity in the female sex was not important; most of the attributes of womanliness were related to it. But manliness involved chastity, too, and men were expected to do their duty when they failed to remain pure.

The male defendants accepted many of these attributes of manliness, but they argued that they were exercising these traits precisely when they broke their engagements. In particular, they insisted that they were being honest and courageous when they admitted that they had changed their minds about marriage. William Ramwell, for example, argued to Eleanor Green that he wished "to be perfectly honourable," but he had to choose between the wishes of his fiancée and his mother, who opposed the marriage, and he felt he must side with his family. After a two-year engagement to one woman, Robert Franklin fell in love with another. When he wrote to break off the engagement, he insisted, "I consider that I am only doing my duty by so acting."[21] In addition, men firmly believed in the need for independence, a trait riddled with contradictions in these actions. The men wanted to be independent from their fiancées, disliking domestic ties as much as dominance by employers. But bids for this kind of independence did not impress juries. Juries, instead, expected men to put their fiancées first—even ahead of other dependent women. In other words, men had to be independent of their families, particularly after they came of age, but they could not claim that same independence from their fiancées. In contrast, because the awards were so high, these suits granted some women enough capital to begin a new life. The action, then, allowed women to pursue economic independence, despite its assumptions of female helplessness. In short, in breach-of-promise cases men were partially tied down and women were partially freed. Though not desired by most judges and juries, this outcome was a product of the contradictory nature of masculine gender roles, accepted in different ways by all concerned.

The only part of the idea of masculinity that the men did not seem to accept fairly readily was the need to support illegitimate children, for not all men voluntarily paid maintenance. Many of them may well have believed that women careless of their virtue should pay the consequences themselves. Nonetheless, a substantial minority did at least pay for the mother's confinement, and many had been affiliated before the action was brought. This act of providing, however, showed another conflict in interpreting male gender roles. Most men assumed that their maintenance payments were an end to the matter, but women (usually supported by their male relatives) sued when they realized that a more permanent bond was not forthcoming. And judges and juries usually agreed that unmarried support was a poor substitute for the permanent responsibility of marriage.

Womanliness was a less important topic in breach of promise. Still, there were obvious expectations of the female gender embedded in the entire process of breach-of-promise actions, many of which related, if only indirectly, to chastity. An honorable or honest man was one who provided, kept his word, and told the truth. An honorable or honest woman meant one thing—a sexually pure one.[22] Purity was so vital that almost all barristers described their clients as "respectable" or "coming from a respectable family," whether or not they were virgins. As long as the woman had intercourse only with the defendant, she could present herself as respectable.[23] Occasionally, defendants argued that the woman was the seducer, but this seldom worked, at least with young women. Andrew McMaster insisted that Esther Dales had followed him into a stables to seduce him, but the plaintiff's barrister ridiculed the idea of a seventeen-year-old girl stalking a grown man, and the jury ignored it, granting Dales £400.[24]

If the plaintiff had not fallen, her innocence was also a great asset—plaintiffs were invariably described as "modest," "timid," "accomplished," and "delicate."[25] In order to win, they had to conform to passive, good-natured behavior patterns, at least until they entered the courtroom. However, as previously stated, they could justify some aggressive behavior as hysteria, "caused" by the "cruel" treatment of the defendant. In particular, women excused angry letters and threats after the breach as "justifiable" emotions of the moment. Jane Turner wrote a blistering letter to Herbert Jackson after he broke off their engagement, calling his behavior "heartless, shameful and contemptible," and adding, "what a mean, despicable, cowardly creature you are." She even hired a private detective to prove that Herbert was seeing another woman. Yet the judge insisted that the jury ignore this epistle, since it was written immediately after the engagement was broken off. The jury awarded her £200.[26]

This assumption of female emotion was an asset in other ways, too. It excused a woman's yielding to her fiancé's wishes to anticipate the marriage date. It also aggravated damages, since a woman's feelings were assumed to be deeply hurt upon losing a lover. In fact, one thing that could hurt a woman's case was if she did not seem to have loved the man much. Sarah Chedzoy lost her action against Harry Woodbery in part because she became engaged to him almost immediately after her previous fiancé's funeral and in part because the connection lasted only a few weeks. Justice Lush insisted that Chedzoy "did not look as if her feelings were very much wounded or hurt, and it was impossible to suppose that the previous engagement had taken very deep root."[27] Women should also be forgiving and willing to take back their errant lovers after quarrels. George Kelsall wanted to make up with Annie Wilkinson before and during their trial, but she refused. The jury gave her only forty shillings.[28]

In addition to chastity and strong emotions, the woman had to have lived fairly quietly. For instance, she could not drink alcohol to any great extent. Several plaintiffs had some difficulties with this, since they worked in pubs. Just being that close to strong drink made them suspect. The defendant in *Harbert v. Edginton* charged Maria Harbert with drinking brandy and smoking a pipe and cigars. The judge warned the jury that if they believed him, they must not find for the plaintiff, since "a woman who could so far forget herself was not entitled to ask for heavy damages."[29] A related defense was the "bad temper" of the plaintiff; she could not be a "scold" or the defendant could plead that he had a right not to marry such a woman. However, few defendants were successful in this plea, since they were expected to determine the woman's personality before proposing.[30]

The most interesting aspect of the assumption of femininity in breach-of-promise cases were the descriptions by the plaintiffs' barristers of their clients as "hard-working." Despite the fact that the man was seen as the provider of the family, many of these women supported themselves or at least supplemented the family income. However, rather than a mere compliment (although it did speak well of them as potential wives), barristers used the hard work of the plaintiffs to insist on their need for marriage. They were laboring not because they wanted to but because they had no choice. This argument had pathos since many of these cases dealt with cross-class matings. Barristers stressed that the difference in station was not a good reason for a breach; indeed, promising to raise a young woman out of the ranks of the working and then dashing her hopes was doubly unkind. The plaintiff in *Hagger v. Bush,* for example, was a housemaid, while the defendant was a doctor. She had left her job for him, and her barrister pointed out that she had been interrupted in "earning a virtuous and honest livelihood." Similarly, Elizabeth Davies, also a servant, "was labouring hard" and after the breach had nothing to look forward to but continuing to "bear with the temper of the persons under whom she served."[31] Furthermore, when there had been an illegitimate child, the plaintiff's hard work contrasted with the irresponsible behavior of the child's father. Gwen Williams was an attendant in a ladies' room at a train station, while John Roberts was a sea captain. She was a widow with children, and her barrister insisted that "she was a hard-working woman." This not only blunted accusations that she might be loose, but it also played up her plight as a widow, deserted when pregnant by a heartless sailor. The appeal succeeded, and she received £100.[32] Ironically, then, the insistence on hard work shored up the idea that women should not provide for themselves, a constant theme in the construction of gender from midcentury. But the fact that a woman's job was at issue still undermined that point, one which was at the heart of breach-of-promise cases.[33]

As stated above, judges and juries did not hold sexually active women totally responsible for their difficulties; the man was an equal or even a dominant partner in her disgrace. This was partly a result of the assumption of female passivity, but it also reflected firm sympathy for any woman who was a mother. According to Davidoff and Hall, the sanctification of motherhood was part of the middle-class construction of gender roles early in the century. It only grew stronger as the century progressed, even becoming a justification for improving women's education and widening their influence in society.[34] Obviously, motherhood should occur within wedlock, but even unwed mothers were able to command tender feelings from the court. In *Wilkinson v. Hampson* the judge and jury assumed unthinkingly that Mary Wilkinson would never have parted with her child except under the influence of her fiancé, and they penalized him accordingly. Juries also punished men who suggested abortificants to their fiancées. Even a woman who was sexually aggressive could be redeemed through her child. Mary Williams was unable to put herself forward as a victim, since she had aggressively pursued her lover. Yet the judge approved of her case being settled for £100, and he lectured Captain Mathias, saying that he should not forget that Williams was the mother of his child.[35] Though it might not cover all sins, motherhood ennobled women and bonded them with the fathers of their children permanently. Fatherhood did not have the same impact, in part because men tried to escape its responsibilities.[36]

The interactions of gender expectations were extremely complex and were made even more so by the public nature of a lawsuit. They worked in very different ways, depending on the type of action. A good example was *Bull v. Robinson* in 1870.[37] Caroline Bull was a slight acquaintance of Henry Robinson until February 1864. At that point Henry wrote to her, asking if she would marry him. Caroline was understandably surprised, since they did not know each other well, but she asked him to visit her family within the week in order to make up her mind. The visit was a success, and, in consequence, the two became engaged after having spent about six hours together. Henry was ordained as a minister and spent the next six years struggling to make a living without a place, primarily through taking students. He wrote to Caroline faithfully, and they were able to see each other occasionally on religious holidays. His letters expressed great affection until late 1868, when Caroline began to notice that he was growing cooler. When she questioned him, Henry admitted that his feelings had changed and he did not wish to marry. Indeed, he insisted that he had never loved her in the way that led to matrimony. He acknowledged that he should have spoken sooner, but blamed social expectations: "When I first began to feel my mistake, I had two courses before me— one was socially and conventionally wrong. I avoided this, and chose the other—a false position, and therefore, in some measure, morally wrong, but which I hoped a change of feeling might some day justify."

Caroline was devastated by Henry's announcement and insisted that his feelings for her had been genuine until the beginning of the last year. She suspected that his feelings had changed because she did not have the means to help him in his quest for a position, and she considered such a motive unworthy; it "soiled what I regarded as a most noble character." Henry was apparently taken aback at her emotional response, because his reply was less harsh. He refuted her assessment of his motives, but he also denied repudiating her utterly. This letter bewildered Caroline, but she took heart and urged Henry to "come to his senses." She was convinced that his hard work and the long separation from her had made him unnecessarily gloomy: "Men are so occupied and busy with the world's affairs that they need contact with the object of their regard to keep alive that interest and love that natures such as yours, whose whole soul is given to the occupation of their hands and mind, feel to be waning without . . . as you ever hope for happiness yourself, do not trifle with mine."

Caroline's hopes were premature. Henry did not reply for almost a month, and, when he did, his tone had grown testy. He began to place himself in the role of the victim, forced to continue communication with a woman he did not love. He said he supposed he had to marry her and give up all thoughts of future happiness. Caroline's brother-in-law, a Mr. Pledger, then wrote to Robinson demanding to know if he intended marriage or not. Bull wrote as well, admitting, "I confess I do not understand your letters; what you say in one you unsay in another." Henry replied angrily that he did not recall refuting anything and insisted that they write less often, still without making a firm decision. Caroline patiently waited for two months, then wrote again, asking his intentions. She even went with her brother-in-law to Manchester to confront Henry, but the meeting resolved nothing.

Only in late March did Henry finally make it plain that he would not marry her. He had lost all patience, evidently having hoped that his reluctance to fulfill his contract would have convinced her to release him. His insistence that he was the truly aggrieved party was stronger than ever: "I have, in times gone by, complied too much with your wishes in this respect, [in continuing the connection] and with over consideration for you, have resisted the promptings of my own feelings." After all, he reasoned, she should not want to marry if he did not love her, and an engagement was a probationary period during which a couple learned whether or not they would suit. He acknowledged that she would not agree: "you will probably stigmatize me as you have already done, as infamous, a villain, wretch, &c., but I make allowance for your ebullition of feeling." All the same, he admitted that he did owe her compensation and promised to make restitution.

After this plain repudiation, Pledger took up the burden of the correspondence, disgusted that Henry, "professing to be a christian gentleman, could write such cruel and undeserving things to her who has ever shown to you the truest, noblest love." He vigorously defended Caroline against Henry's accusations of name calling and made clear that he supported her in her resort to legal means: "I should be something less than a man did I not determine to vindicate her to the utmost of my power." He also replied acidly to Robinson that an engagement of five years was a bit long for "a time of probation," as Robinson well knew. In the end Henry offered Caroline £250, but she decided that she would go to court to clear her name: "I seek to know and to let the whole world know what justifiable reason he can give for a change that leads him . . . to trample thus cruelly and ruthlessly on every hope I have of happiness in the world. I will accept no private money satisfaction, but will meet him in open court."

Henry's only defense at the trial was that Bull had behaved badly, calling him names and showing temper, and that he had only been trying to be "conscientious and honourable" when he broke off the engagement. His barrister insisted that he was "unfortunate" rather than a villain, which certainly fit with Robinson's view of himself. After all, the young man was hard-working and had tried to make a home for the plaintiff, though he supported his mother and sister, too. And she did not show the disposition of a "true woman" when she held him to an engagement even though he did not love her. Despite this appeal, the jury found for Bull, with £350 damages.

Bull won because in many ways she embodied the perfect behavior for a female plaintiff. She had remained devoted to the interests of her lover through five years, her letters were models of good manners and thoughts, and she had remained pure. She had no interest in money or preferment; at least until the trial she was self-sacrificing, supportive, and very much in love. Thus her misery at Henry's defection was not feigned; if anyone had suffered "wounded feelings," it was she. Although she may have shown some anger in her meeting with him in March 1869, this could be excused as female emotionalism, as Henry himself characterized it. Bull had insisted on going to open court, but she could blame this on her brother-in-law. Without Pledger, her apparent vindictiveness may have hurt her, although she might have pleaded "excited emotions." All the same, this difficulty highlights the contradiction for plaintiffs in acting as passive victims while at the same time taking lovers to court. Though juries seldom let it worry them, it demonstrates the ambiguity of the action's view of femininity.

Henry Robinson, on the other hand, showed the difficulties of men in these cases, particularly since they accepted the general ideas of correct masculine behavior. Clearly, he struggled against repudiating his engagement, knowing that society would frown on such a move. He apparently did want to be honest, and he bitterly regretted his long hesitation. To Henry, telling Caroline about his doubts was the truly brave thing to do, before the decision was irrevocable. Furthermore, his desire for independence was a large part of his irritability. In the first place he mourned his failure as a provider, and in the second he wanted to be independent of Caroline. The more she held on to him, the more victimized he sounded. However, juries were unimpressed with such claims for liberty, and his vacillation in late 1868 and early 1869 was inexcusable. Even his assurance that he was a hard-working provider for his mother and sister, along with his offer of £250, did not overcome the bad impression he made. After all, Bull may have received a lump sum, but she would not have the security of a hard-working husband. Robinson also fit into some common Victorian assumptions about men and romance. As Caroline insisted, his depressing work was part of his malaise; men had too much public activity to devote as much time to love and marriage as women. And his actions proved her supposition that men simply were not as faithful without some kind of inducement, such as the presence of the loved one. Women were the faithful lovers, in part because they had little else in their lives. Men had more liberty to change their minds, but that freedom in the public world was precisely the reason they should be strictly held to their domestic responsibilities.

Finally, this case demonstrates that breach-of-promise actions were more than simply clashes of inter-gender expectations. The role of Pledger highlights the conflicting interpretations about masculine roles between two men as well as between the couple. Henry wanted to be dutiful to his own feelings, if not to Caroline's, whereas Pledger felt that he must protect his sister-in-law's position—also a man's duty. Pledger's disgust with Robinson's behavior was obvious, and he was aggressive and paternalistic in his role as the male head of the extended family (Caroline's father was bedridden and so could not do so). Tosh and Roper have pointed out that several types of manliness could occur at any time in history concurrently, but these clashes were not so much about different types of masculinity as about differing interpretations of agreed-upon attributes.[38] Nevertheless, breach of promise undermined patriarchal manliness, since the actual person suing was Caroline. As her letter made clear, it was her decision to go to court and she was awarded the money. The contradictions for gender roles in this case were never faced, much less resolved, nor would they be until the action was abolished.

A second example, this time from the opposite point of view, was that of *Hole v. Harding*.[39] George Hole had been a friend of Winnifred (known as Minnie) Harding's family for many years, since both families had farms near each other. Minnie had first been engaged to George's brother for a short time, but her father disapproved and so the match was broken off. She became engaged to George in April 1881, when she was thirty-one and he was thirty-four. They kept the engagement secret, since she knew her parents would not like this match either. By June the countryside was buzzing with gossip, and her mother confronted her with the news, disgusted that her daughter could give up one brother just to begin seeing the other, "a thing never heard of." However, these difficulties were overcome, and Minnie's father did not object when he was told of the prospective marriage, also in June.

Things went on well until September. Then Minnie wrote two somewhat incoherent letters to George, claiming that her father had been making inquiries and had discovered that Hole's farm was losing money. On September 18 she broke the engagement, explaining: "Papa has this morning had a long and serious talk with me, and he still tells me it would be the very best thing for us both in every respect to break off our engagement. . . . I could not do anything very much against my dear father's wish, and would not." Deeply hurt, George urged her to continue with the engagement. After all, she should not sacrifice her happiness for her parent, and he was confident that the whole matter would be forgotten soon. Minnie, however, refused to oppose her father, and so George went at once to his solicitor.

Interestingly, the solicitor wrote to Minnie—threatening the suit—in the same language that he would have used had the plaintiff been female: "Mr. Hole feels that you have cruelly treated him, blighted the whole of his future life, and also seriously injured his social position. . . . [He] feels bound to take proceedings in his own vindication . . . to let other ladies know that they may not trifle with gentlemen's feelings." Having been served the writ, Minnie met with George and tried to reconcile on December 8. She told him she would marry him, but George was concerned with his legal bills and asked her what he could do about them. She offered to get a job and pay for them, and he said that he would have to speak to his solicitor. Somewhat annoyed, Harding returned home and eventually wrote to Hole, saying that she did not wish to see him again. Hole then proceeded with his case, which came to trial in January 1882.

A man bringing a breach-of-promise case did not have the advantages that a woman did, and this became obvious during the trial. Hole's barrister, a Mr. Norris, did his best to explain why his client was so doing in his opening speech, insisting that it was solely to clear Hole's character, since Harding had accused him of fraud (she claimed that he had hidden his financial difficulties). Nevertheless, such an action was difficult to justify. Norris read the solicitor's letter to Harding, and the audience in the courtroom laughed heartily, particularly at the insistence that ladies should not trifle with gentlemen. Still, Norris persevered, making Harding's flightiness an issue. After all, she was thirty-two years old and had already broken engagements to two men, behavior that was irresponsible and vacillating. Norris also held up Hole as an example of "an honest, upright English yeoman" against a snobbish, large property owner. Hole had made an offer in good faith and had been thrown over; furthermore, his character had been maligned. Norris appealed to class solidarity with the men in the box to give "reasonable damages."

The appeal to class was not a bad idea, but it did not have the power of gender assertions. Collins, the defense barrister, forced Hole to admit that when Harding offered to marry him and pay his legal bills, he said only that he would talk to his solicitor. In his final speech Collins attacked the very notion of a "British yeoman" coming into court to complain about his fiancée and to demand money. Collins obviously believed it was wrong for a man to request money from a woman—men provided for women, not the other way around. Collins also insisted that Hole did not really love Harding. If he had, Hole would have reconciled with her in December. Instead, he only said he would talk to his solicitor. This was "mean" behavior, publicizing the love affair and letting others read her letters simply because of a few legal costs.

Chief Justice Coleridge, too, was thoroughly unimpressed with Hole. Like Collins, he complained about Hole's reaction to Harding's attempts at reconciliation, arguing that it showed no real sentiment. "He never saw a case in which less feeling was imported. People had a right to marry from a feeling of respect and Platonic regard, but then they must not talk so much about their feelings." Moreover, even if he had been hurt, a man who came into court and complained about wounded feelings was weak and foolish. Coleridge quoted the duke of Wellington on this point, that "men did not die for love. (Laughter.) They generally got over it, and married somebody else." Men's disadvantages in this action came to the fore in such statements. The jury found for Hole with damages of one farthing (one-fourth of a penny).

Certainly, Minnie Harding was embarrassed by the court case, but she could at least be satisfied with the results, unlike most male defendants, a fact attributable almost entirely to her gender. For one thing, it was far more acceptable for a woman to be vacillating and indecisive than for a man. She had jilted both Hole brothers, but the jury did not expect her to keep her word strictly. Of course, she could plead the influence of her father, but such pleas rarely helped men. In this case, however, the jury apparently agreed that an unmarried woman in her thirties still should not go against the wishes of her "dear father." In fact, George probably made a bad impression when he admitted that he urged Minnie to marry without her father's blessing. Again, this is an example of clashing male expectations—Harding's father demanded obedience from his daughter, while Hole wanted her to honor her commitment. In addition, Harding was forgiving and willing to reconcile, even offering to get a job to pay for Hole's costs. A woman offering to pay a man's bills was an inversion of the proper gender order, so Hole's ungenerous response was a major factor in his loss.

While Minnie's gender was a great help in her defense, George's masculinity was his undoing as a plaintiff. The judge and jury found it ludicrous that he should claim that his affections were "blighted" and his social prospects dimmed by Harding's actions. Such emotionalism should not be a part of a British yeoman, no matter how bad the provocation. The action also damaged Hole's standing as a provider. Even from the very beginning of breach-of-promise cases, men who sued wealthier women found themselves regarded with great suspicion by judges and juries. A woman "naturally" bettered herself through marriage, but a man should make his own way.[40] George seemed like a fortune hunter—looking for a rich wife, acting mean over a few bills, and suing for damages. The generosity expected of male defendants, then, was also expected of male plaintiffs. Finally, Hole failed a test of chivalry. Though Harding had more resources, she was a woman and therefore an inferior; Hole should have treated her with kindness. Instead, when she offered to marry him and pay his costs, he talked about his solicitor. In a way Minnie, too, was a rejected suitor, because George turned down her offer to reconcile. The jury found it easy to excuse Minnie's fickleness because of George's stubbornness.

The advantages of manhood in Victorian England were legion: men had power, public access, economic resources well beyond most women, and were allowed sexual freedoms that women were denied. Despite these benefits, however, men also suffered from the constraints of gender ideology. Men could not express their emotions openly and were seldom compensated when their feelings were hurt. They were expected to earn for themselves and for inferiors and to tolerate unpleasant but weaker beings with patience. And if they took advantage of their sexual liberty, they paid for their pleasures, at least in breach-of-promise cases. Finally, they had to keep their promises with great strictness. Even if it meant alienating family or enduring an unhappy union, a man was expected to fulfill his contracts. Failing on any of these points might result in public humiliation and the loss of time and money. Clearly, as Tosh and Roper have emphasized, even the most overwhelming advantages of masculine power could be at least *experienced* as oppressive even if in the long run they were not. Men in breach-of-promise cases may well have felt oppressed, since their gender precluded them from suing while at the same time holding them responsible for their own breaches.[41]

On the other hand, the advantages of femininity were decided in this class of suit. A woman's "natural" propensity for inconstancy and emotionalism meant she could jilt with impunity, while demanding faithfulness from her own suitors. In addition, her damages for wounded feelings would be high, since her heart was tender. Women asking for support from men was natural, so the dynamics of the case seemed normal to judges and juries. In addition, women's assumed passivity in sexual matters made it easier for the court to brand the man as a seducer who should compensate the woman he had wronged. Women also did not have to be chivalrous, although they did have to behave in a seemly way, at least until they went to court.

Of course, breach-of-promise cases were troublesome in their tendency to reenforce patriarchal assumptions of gender. Men as superiors and providers automatically relegated women to inferior status and secondary breadwinners. And any woman who failed to pass the crucial character test could not sue successfully—she could not be sexually aggressive or even display the main force in the courtship. However, in other ways this was an ambivalent statement on gender. After all, many of these women provided for themselves; a large minority even owned their own property. At the very least, all of them found the resources with which to go to court. They spoke for themselves in the male public space of the court, and the award money went to them, not their fathers. In addition, these cases highlight the clash of expectations for manly behavior; conflict between various interpretations of male gender roles often escalated a couple's problems into a full-blown lawsuit. In some ways, then, breach of promise taught men the disadvantages of the gender notions of their age and gave women some benefit from a usually unsympathetic male establishment.[42] But in other ways the action undermined those ideological limits, exposing their contradictions and fragility.

In either case, breach-of-promise suits showed a firm and fairly unanimous perspective about the actions of both men and women by the judges and juries. The courts did not demand complete chastity from women and expected responsibility from sexually active men. They ignored the hard work of the women as well as the economic independence that the actions brought them. Furthermore, they allowed women to be aggressive and even violent. All of the classes and genders involved in the cases agreed on basic principles, although their interpretations of those attributes differed. Their outlook revises historians' assumptions about male and female gender roles in the late Victorian period in two ways. First, class differences on masculine and feminine gender roles were not great by the end of the Victorian period. A second point relates to the purported change in masculinity that some historians have seen in the late nineteenth century. By focusing on the new imperialism, public school games, and boy scouts, historians have argued that masculinity became more violent and aggressive by the 1880s. But breach-of-promise cases demonstrate that the domesticated man of the midcentury still had strong resonance, at least in the courts. James Hammerton has recently asserted that both the domestic and aggressive modes of male behavior existed throughout the nineteenth century, interacting and conflicting with each other.[43] These suits support his argument. Those involved with breach-of-promise actions favored domestic manliness into the twentieth century, and a desire for domesticity also emerged in lower middle- and upper working-class courtship patterns. These couples developed their own system, one which made breach of promise a more justifiable alternative.

IV

Courtships
and Weddings

COURTSHIP AMONG the lower middle and upper working classes had changed by the late nineteenth century due to the revolutions in agriculture and industry. Children often left home to go to work by their teens, escaping the watchful eyes of their parents. Their newfound economic independence gave them more leverage against parental objections, even when they stayed at home. In addition, they did not have many communal functions to attend, as in the past, and, unlike the upper classes, they had no "season" to replace village customs.[1] Catherine Hall has recently argued for a "cultural identity" between the lower middle and middle classes, "which drew together in some ways the disparate elements of the class."[2] However, the evidence of breach-of-promise cases indicates that any such identity was fragile, at least with regard to courtship practices. Though they had few formalities, the lower middle and upper working classes had a distinct set of unwritten courtship rituals, including patterns of walking out, gift-giving, and organizing weddings. These courtships were a mixture of middle- and working-class mores, since the couples aspired to middle-class domesticity without the economic resources to secure it.

According to Davidoff and Hall, lower middle-class couples in Birmingham early in the century found their spouses through "kinship, friendship, and religious communities" as well as businesses. Francoise Barret-Ducrocq's study of working-class courtship also revealed a wide variety of ways for couples to meet in the Victorian period, including kin ties and work.[3] Couples in breach-of-promise suits in the last half of the century continued to find each other through a mix of business and family influences. Relatively few met at social events such as balls, picnics, or church-related activities (14 percent). Far more knew each other through relatives, mutual friends, or from being neighbors (42 percent). A further 6 percent met because of a landlord-tenant relationship. The second largest group (27 percent) knew each other through work, as when the defendant employed the plaintiff or was her or his customer. Finally, a large number of couples (11 percent) fit into none of these categories. Strangers to each other, these people met in the street, on travels, or through matchmakers.

Proximity was clearly the most important factor in determining whom one met. Many of those who met through friends and relatives were acquainted for many years; they had grown up together and their parents were longtime friends. In addition, over 13 percent of the couples were neighbors, often living on adjoining land in villages. Others were landlord (or landlady) and tenant. Putting two eligible people within close quarters often resulted in amazingly quick intimacies, sometimes unfortunately so. Catherine Lewis, a widow, took John Jenkins, an ironmonger, as a lodger in March 1897; they had sex by the end of May. She had a child the following March, by which time he had moved on. As Davidoff has pointed out, lodging romances were full of difficulties, since the two parties were usually not of the same class and the defendant often intended to leave. The landlady's peculiar position as surrogate wife (cooking meals, cleaning, and so on) always made the relationship problematic; sexual relations complicated things even more.[4]

Yet another example of easy proximity were servants, and they experienced similar difficulties. These plaintiffs were either domestic servants, helpers in businesses (such as barmaids), or poor professionals like governesses. As John Gillis has noted, female servants were in a peculiarly difficult position regarding courtship, and his conclusions are confirmed in Barret-Ducrocq's more in-depth study of the Foundling Hospital. Many of the servants' close relationships were with men who were either above or below them in class, which was frequently a recipe for broken engagements. Despite this, Gillis and Barret-Ducrocq found that most disrupted relationships were between well-matched couples, but my sample is primarily of cross-class matings (probably because women tended to sue wealthier men).[5] These women fell into intimate relationships with their employers and found themselves unable to demand fulfill-ment of marriage promises.

In over half of the servants' cases (eighteen of thirty), the plaintiff had sex with the defendant, a far higher proportion than in the cases as a whole. These couples usually consisted of a young woman involved with a much older em-ployer and suitor. Sarah Pearce, for example, was only twenty when she went to work as a housekeeper for a master plumber, Thomas Boardman (thirty-nine), and his invalid wife in 1866. Mrs. Boardman died in March of that year, and by May Boardman and Pearce were lovers. He assured her parents he would marry her, but he and Sarah quarreled, and he married his cook instead. In *Haynes v. Haynes* the two parties were second cousins, the plaintiff being twenty-two and the defendant forty (she was the daughter of a "cab proprietor" and he was a farmer). She, too, went to work as his housekeeper and soon became pregnant.[6] These women became intimate with men of slightly higher station, risking abandonment and social disapproval, apparently in hopes of bet-tering themselves.

Often the class difference was frankly stated to be the problem when the couple failed to marry. For example, in *Crosswell v. Hearn* the plaintiff taught music to the defendant's children. He broke off his engagement to her specifically because his family opposed the marriage, since Crosswell was socially inferior and twenty-three years younger. Elizabeth Morris went to work for Thomas Bonville's father as a servant at the age of fourteen. She endured a secret engagement for over ten years and had two illegitimate children because Thomas told her he would marry her when his father died. Once the elder Bonville died, however, Thomas married someone else.[7] Many of these relationships involve housekeepers, and the ambivalence of their roles as surrogate wives (like landladies) contributed to the strain in their relations with their employers and their families. Unless the employer drew a firm line between them, the relationship could slowly modify into cohabitation. And it is not surprising that other family members found it difficult to accept a former inferior as mistress of the home.

Unlike servants, other couples who met through work did so as customers of each other's businesses. Although proximity helped in these situations, it was not essential. A great many of the women involved in breach-of-promise cases earned their living as milliners, dressmakers, small shopkeepers, and innkeepers. They thus met a number of men simply through serving the public. Men and women also met by working for the same people (for instance, two couples met because both worked at the mill), or because they shared train carriages or omnibuses on their commutes.[8]

Finally, at the other extreme, a number of people began courting as strangers (30 of 371). Seven times the couple simply met in the street or road, eight times the man wrote to the woman introducing himself and asking to court her, and six times the couple went through some kind of matchmaking service (the other nine are miscellaneous ways). Such methods were outside community control and a result of urbanization and industrialization. Almost always the matchmaking cases were widowers searching for wives to be step-mothers of their children or to assist in businesses. In 1890 Joseph Daintith, a merchant, went looking for a fourth wife at the age of seventy-six, employing a man named Hampson to find suitable candidates. Hampson presented him to Emma Clark, a fifty-year-old widow who owned her own muffin shop. Daintith proposed at the first meeting. John Owen Roberts, a builder and farmer, asked the local innkeeper (a woman) to find a wife for him in 1884, and proposed to her choice just as quickly. Women, on the other hand, used advertisements, as Mary Crookshank did in 1889 or Gladys Knowles attempted in 1890.[9] There were no sexual intimacies in these cases; relationships failed because of lack of familiarity, not from too much.

The situation was quite different for those couples who claimed to have met "in the street." Most of the plaintiffs were young working women who met the defendants casually as they went home from work or were out for a walk. Lower-class parents did not have the resources to control their children on the way to and from situations or when out for well-earned pleasure. The defendants were usually considerably older, of a higher class, and had sex with the women in short order. A typical example was the case of Susannah Brown, aged nineteen. She was accosted by William Friend (thirty-five), a sea captain, as she walked home from her job as a servant in November 1872. She ignored him, but the next day he called and proposed marriage. She eventually accepted him and, before he left on his next voyage, he had sex with her, assuring her that they would soon be husband and wife. Unfortunately, Friend was already married.[10] Again, a cross-class romance proved dangerous for the working-class woman, particularly when she risked pregnancy.

Most interesting of those who began to court as total strangers were those couples who met when the defendant wrote to introduce himself. All of the people involved in these cases, with the exception of one plaintiff, were lower middle or middle class. In each case the defendant was an almost complete stranger to the plaintiff before writing and asking to call. John Harrison, an insurance collector, admitted in his 1889 letter to Emma Abbot, a milliner, that they were strangers, but he insisted she was the perfect wife for him, and he presented his attractions to her: "I am a total abstainer and a dissenter; age, a little over 40 years, with good expectations." Harrison's letter was similar to that of William Williams, a tailor, who wrote to Sarah Roberts, a cook, in May 1884: "Truly, I desired you the moment I saw your becoming manner. . . . Well, to break through the ice, I pray you to name an evening to meet one another, and the place." Naturally, the primary emotion of the women receiving such epistles was surprise; women were more wary of making sudden commitments than men. Roberts, for instance, declined to meet Williams after his first try, while Abbot consulted her mother before agreeing to court Harrison.[11] These men were attracted to the appearance and manner of women and set out to win their hearts. While only one of these cases involved a sexual relationship, women in these situations found it extremely difficult to release men who had so insistently courted them.[12]

Whether the couple met through proximity or chance, the period of time between the meeting and the engagement was usually short. The average length of courtship before a proposal was only nine months; the median was less, at three months.[13] These figures are probably too low, since women listed the date of their engagements as early as possible, and often only their side of the story survives. Still, many men admitted to proposing after only a few weeks. Nor was this short time made up in frequent visits. Couples saw each other an average of sixteen times per month, or four times a week; the median was ten times per month. Though frequent, many couples still only had thirty visits before making a serious commitment.[14] In addition, many couples were separated for long periods and got to know each other primarily through letters. They felt fortunate to see each other four to six times a year.

Though courtships were usually short, engagements were long. The average engagement was almost 3 years (34 months), while the median was 1 year and 3 months (however, cases that went to court were probably biased toward length). Though most people were engaged for under 3 years (340 cases), a substantial number (167) stayed engaged longer. Of the latter, 67 were engaged 3–5 years; 48 from 5–8 years; and in 52 cases—a surprisingly large number—the couple was engaged 8 years or more. Michael Anderson has pointed out that "the process of courtship and entry into marriage was a much more protracted one" for everyone after 1851.[15] However, in my sample, class made a great difference in length of engagements. Middle-class couples were engaged over 3 years in only 6 cases; indeed, middle-class advice writers frequently warned of the dangers of long engagements and discouraged them, though some certainly suffered through them anyway. Lower middle- and working-class couples, on the other hand, were spread fairly evenly across all the time periods, including 35 lower middle- and 17 working-class couples engaged for over 8 years. Except for some unfortunate people, long engagements were probably mainly a problem for those below the middle classes. A lower middle- or working-class woman might wait 5–10 years for marriage; consequently, she lost a great deal when the relationship failed.

There were two main reasons for long engagements in these classes. First, these couples had to save carefully before setting up a household. Particularly lower middle-class men strived to earn enough so that their wives did not have to work outside the home. They were, then, the victims of their combined economic weakness and social aspirations. More specifically, sons had to wait to inherit land or money with which to start a farm or small business or to finish schooling. Women used the time to save as much as possible and to purchase necessary items for the home. Geoffrey Crossick's work on the lower middle-class family demonstrates the difficulties of these families in providing for children, and things could be even harder for the working class. Though the goal of economic independence was common to all classes, the means of achieving it were easier to find in the upper ranks, as Pat Jalland has shown, and at least a jilted middle-class woman had a comfortable home if the match failed.[16] Second, illnesses or deaths forced postponements. Naturally, if either of the parties were ill, the wedding was delayed; in addition, women often nursed sick relatives and could not marry at such times. For example, Elizabeth Jones and James Southworth met in 1868, became engaged in 1872, and broke up in 1878. During that time they had set the date twice in 1874, only to have it postponed because of business setbacks and Jones's illness. They again planned to marry in 1877, only to have it put back due to Southworth's bad health. Southworth finally broke it off in 1878 when Jones was thirty years old, having waited ten years for a wedding that never occurred.[17]

Courting men and women of the lower middle class and below, then, expected a long wait before they fulfilled their commitments to each other. In the meantime they took part in a number of almost ritualized activities. Though without balls and entertainments, these couples shared with the middle class the ideals of sentimentality and domesticity. This feeling of companionship was not necessarily new to the lower classes; they, indeed, had married for love far longer than the upper reaches of society, although not necessarily due to sexual passion. Probably middle-class feelings merged with older ideas to form a strong desire for a true affection in a spouse, without dimming the need for practical skills in both partners. As Hall has pointed out, those beneath the middle class may have believed in domesticity, but they also needed more prosaic abilities in their partners, such as "household management, cooking, cleaning and bringing up children."[18] A combination of romance and reality, then, was their goal for companionship.

Despite their limited amount of time together, couples found any number of ways to solidify these ties of affinity. Sometimes they literally walked out— taking long strolls. They also went together to infrequent social occasions, such as church meetings or picnics. However, by far the most common activity was for the man to call and take tea or supper with the woman or her family, then to sit with her for the rest of the evening. Even when the woman did not live by herself, the couple had privacy, since parents were lenient about time alone together. Such evenings were almost universal, and the privacy sometimes led to complications. Kate Curtis, the daughter of a farmer, got engaged to Ernest Olden, a master miller, in August 1884; her father went on an errand a few days later and left them alone. Ernest and Kate had intercourse during the absence. Some parents even allowed their daughters to travel with their fiancés. The mother of the plaintiff in *Kerfoot v. Marsden* permitted her daughter to go on a trip overnight to Liverpool, only to find herself with an illegitimate grandchild nine months later. When questioned about their judgment in allowing such freedom, parents invariably protested that they assumed they could trust the honorable intentions of their daughters' suitors.[19] Though this trust was probably genuine, lower-class parents also had to acknowledge that they did not control their children's social lives, even their daughters.

Informal socializing between the families of the couple was also a major part of courtship. As stated, the bride's family was most often the host, but it was considered obligatory for the woman to be introduced formally to the man's relatives, especially his parents. In breach-of-promise actions this introduction was often used as proof that there had indeed been an engagement, while the lack of it was a telling point for the defense. The woman often corresponded with the female members of the man's family as well. It appeared to be less important to the couples that their families socialize together before the wedding. Often the two families already knew each other, but if they did not, they seldom had more than one meeting.

Engaged women also expected gifts, the number and variety depending on the wealth of their choices. More affluent lovers gave jewelry, handkerchiefs, or even paintings. However, men more often gave food (for example, a Christmas ham). Only three gifts were practically universal. First, men gave engagement rings, often accompanied by a "keeper" ring (and sometimes he had even bought the wedding rings before the breakup). Possession of this ring or rings was one of the key pieces of evidence in breach-of-promise actions, and women resisted returning rings under even the most trying circumstances. Second, couples exchanged locks of hair; this was a gift that involved no expense and was a sure sign of intimacy. Finally, many couples exchanged photographs of each other, or had their picture taken together. This, too, was a sign of a serious relationship. If a man had presented a woman with a ring, a lock of hair, and his picture, she was perfectly justified in assuming that he intended marriage. Women, too, occasionally gave presents, such as watches, neckties, and books, although this was less common. Women's gifts usually consisted of service, such as cooking meals or nursing members of her lover's family. For example, the plaintiff in *Green v. Patey* in 1887 cooked dinner for her fiancé every evening for the ten years of their engagement.[20]

These exchanges mirrored the expectations of sex roles in Victorian marriage: the male was the provider, while the female oversaw domestic duties and functioned as the primary caregiver. To some extent women were trying out for the role of wife and mother by demonstrating their competence for their future tasks, which was particularly important for homes that would not include paid servants. Occasionally, men admitted that they broke engagements because they felt their fiancées could not fulfill their domestic needs. Thomas Dommet, a supervisor of an insurance company, claimed that he rejected Alice Hawkridge, a waitress, when he found that "she was unable to cook, and that she was a very poor needlewoman." One man who settled his case out of court told the arbitrator that he had begun to doubt his decision when his intended had made "a bungling mess" out of some sausages she was cooking for him.[21] This divide between the providing male and the domestic female shows that middle-class notions of gender had penetrated into the lower classes by the late nine-teenth century. Such conclusions support much recent work on gender forma-tion in the mid-Victorian period, especially that of Sonya Rose, who argues that working-class masculinity had adopted the role of sole provider by the 1850s. However, lower middle- and working-class women had wider duties than the notion of separate spheres allowed, such as helping in small businesses. The lower middle class apparently adapted parts of the middle-class ethos while rejecting those that were useless. This mixture of ideas supports F. M. L. Thompson's argument that each Victorian class created its own version of re-spectability; it also supports Hall's assertion that the acceptance of parts of do-mesticity by the working class was part of a complex negotiation with, not a wholesale consent to, upper-class norms.[22]

Couples exchanged one other thing far more often than gifts: the written word. In an age with no telephones and relatively slow transportation, letters were the primary source of communication between separated lovers. This was particularly true when both couples were working and changing situations. Many of the female servants changed jobs two or three times during a single relationship, while many of the men traveled on business or to school. Couples in these situations wrote to each other regularly. In fact, in some cases one can trace the warmth of the regard growing and then cooling through the saluta-tions and lengths of these epistles.[23]

Ellen Rothman and Karen Lystra have both used letters to explore the American middle-class experience of courtship in the nineteenth century. They found a distinct courtship pattern. Men hesitated to become engaged, but ea-gerly pressed for the wedding once they had made the commitment. Women, by contrast, were anxious for the engagement but were reluctant to go through with the marriage. Indeed, according to Lystra, women put men through a series of tests before the wedding.[24] English lower middle- and working-class lovers went through a different pattern, either because of differences in class or because these courtships were unsuccessful. Indeed, the complexities of their relationships demonstrate the importance of studying failed courtships as well as successful ones to understand fully Victorian courtship.

The courses of these relationships were long, convoluted, and showed shifting balances of power. Because these women had dowries and hard work to offer, they were not invariably in the position of supplicant. Indeed, in the early stages of courtship, the most ardent and pleading words came from men. They expressed total love and devotion and begged for letters and other signs of affection. Charles Hunt, a farmer, wrote to his lover, Jane Alderton (the daughter of a farmer), "I never loved a girl so much as I do you, I shall never deceive you, dear, and I hope you wont me." Susanna Jones had a similar profession from her lover in the early 1890s: "Don't think that I mean to alter one bit from what I have told you." Such protests must have seemed highly ironic to those hearing them for the first time in breach-of-promise actions, but especially so to those who originally received them. As Alderton wrote to Hunt in 1879, "I am at a loss to understand your cool treatment after all those ardent professions and promises to me."[25]

At least at first, the letters show the sincerity of the men's protestations. Most men expressed frustration at not seeing their loved ones often enough and their loneliness without them. John Irving complained to Ellen Wood in 1881, after making a trip to see her and finding her gone: "I write this note on the bank beside your house, and am nearly broken-hearted at your absence from home. Do come home again as soon as you can." Henry Davies, a builder, was even more blunt in his letter to Annie Hancock, a cook, saying, "I am craving to see your dear face and sparkling eyes and to strengthen you in love." In addition, rows of "Xs," representing kisses, often accompanied the body of the letters, sometimes as many as five rows. Barristers invariably counted them, to the great amusement of the court.[26]

Although most of the letters that survive are from the men (since the women used them as evidence), the few surviving letters from women were similar in tone and fervency. Harriet Roper wrote to her lover Sam Hills in 1867 that he might think she had forgotten him, but she had not: "Although absent you are ever present in my thoughts, and [I] only feel my utter inability of words sufficiently impressive to express my love for you." Polly Wynn, the daughter of an innkeeper, tried to reassure Thomas Hurst, an engine fitter, that she would not mind living with him, and promised to promote domestic harmony: "Dear Tom I know I shall find it very diffent then being at home Dear Tom I do not care for the diffence so as we are happy with each other . . . I am willing to do the best I can to please you."[27]

Yet the tone of the men's letters began to change once the longed-for woman was assuredly won and had accepted the man as her future husband. The balance of power shifted, and the men's letters became shorter and more perfunctory, while the women's remained long and ardent. Toward the end of the relationship the women, rather than the men, pleaded and searched for signs of affection. Usually, the women noticed a coolness in letters or behavior and wrote to discover the reason. Susanna Jones's fiancé, Joshua Williams, stopped writing to her after she asked him about a rumor that he was seeing another woman, and she wrote to him, greatly worried: "I have always placed the fullest trust in your honourable intentions to me, and I am, my dearest Josh, very loath to believe that you are now going to throw me over after all the years we have been waiting for one another." Women who had allowed sexual intercourse were even more agonized at the prospect of desertion. Elizabeth Jones, the daughter of a widow, was engaged to her cousin, Pryce Griffiths, a preacher. He urged her to come to Liverpool and stay with him, and when she complied, they had intercourse. When she became pregnant, he denied that he had promised marriage. Elizabeth wrote to him, her desperation clear: "I whent to the Post this morning and found no answer to my letter you know how i am and a dont know what to do for I am in such trubble and do right and let me no what I am to do for you no that I am in the family way to you." Most of the women, even if not desperate, were bewildered by the changes in the attitudes of their lovers.[28]

The current wisdom behind breach-of-promise actions was that the man could not break off an engagement honorably, since he had pursued and won the heart of the woman. Having made her love him, he could not change his mind. To some extent, the correspondence in breach-of-promise cases bears this interpretation out. In the beginning women were ardently wooed and their affections engaged. For a brief period women had more power, since they decided whether or not to accept the men's addresses. In some ways men temporarily gave up the normal gender power relationship in order eventually to restore it to the norm. The closer the courtship came to an actual marriage, however, the more the power shifted to the future husband's benefit. Once a woman had decided to accept a man, she became dependent on him, while at the same time unable to attract other men. Working women often gave up their situations or sold their businesses, losing their financial security, and women who had become pregnant lost their reputations as well as their ability to earn. Although in theory men were similarly circumscribed, in practice they courted other women without suffering a loss of reputation; they did not give up their jobs; and they could not become pregnant. In addition, in the late nineteenth century men had a wider choice of a spouse and were considered marriageable until an older age. Thomas Powell, a veterinarian, admitted the man's advantage to Minnie Reeves, the daughter of a small farmer, when he wrote to break off their match: "I have for years, after having obtained your love and confidence, kept you chained, as it were, to myself, in the hopes of long ere this marrying you. . . . All these thoughts crowd upon me from time to time, and what an amount of reproach they bring you cannot imagine."[29]

The women's puzzlement was doubly understandable considering the (mostly original) poetry men frequently wrote to them. Even poorly educated men wrote romantic verses as an expression of their affection. This again seems to be a grafting of middle-class sentimentality to a long-standing ideal of lower-class courtship. Sometimes, men wrote specifically for the woman they loved, naming the poem after her, for example, or referring to incidents known to both of them. These were usually silly or very bad poems, full of idiosyncratic spelling and meter. John Jackson, a miller, wrote poems in the place of letters to his "Miss Bell," including the following:

> I wish you wood com back and stay
> for I hav been quite sad ever since you went away
> The loss of you I do deplore
> for I never fell in with eaqual before.

However, some were more serious and better written, and expressed a strong need for companionship that many men were not afraid to admit. William Williams, a machine clerk, declared his affection for his "Nellie," a servant, by creating a poem about their last meeting:

> My Nellie, I am thinking
> Of Monday night all week,
> When you and me were happy,
> With face and cheek to cheek.
> It was you that made me happy
> By giving me your company;
> And so you are both far and near,
> Feel that you are my dear.[30]

Many of the poems communicated common themes, illuminating some of the features of courtship in the lower middle and upper working classes. Significantly, the most frequently used theme in original poetry was "forget me not." Poem after poem pleaded that the recipient not forget her lover, since he would never forget her. Such verses were understandably popular, considering the long waits and frequent separations most couples endured before they could wed. Joseph Taylor, the son of a tenant farmer, sent one of the more distinguished versions to Ellen Hall in the early 1870s:

> Forget thee! Sooner shall the waves
>   Forget and leave the sea,
> Sooner the stars forget to shine
>   Than thou forgot shall be.

> No love, my best and fondest prayer
>   Ascend to Heaven for thee,
> And till my lips are closed in death
>   I will remember thee.[31]

These rhymes show the anxiety of men during painful separations and their fear that their fiancées would lose patience. But they do belong to the early period of the relationships, when the men were still ardent.

A similar theme was to express loneliness and a longing to be with the lover. One of the best poems, "Come to Me, Darling," was on this subject:

> When the red sun in the clear west is glowing,
> And the soft wind from the sweet south is blowing;
> When the day's trials no longer are near me,
> Come to me, darling, to soothe and to cheer me.
>
> Thou art the sun that dispels my sad hours,
> Sweeter thy breath than the odour of flowers,
> Only thy smile can my sombre life brighten,
> Come to me, darling, my sad heart to lighten.

Written by a farmer in 1877, this poem was one of many passages of poetry he sent to his lover. Similar sentiments were voiced by those forced to rely on letters for long periods of time.[32] The frustrations with long engagements that the men had expressed in their prose, they also represented in verse, and both sexes found the extended wait for independence distressing.[33]

Clearly, with all the visiting and writing, the relationship of the couple developed from friendship to courtship to engagement. Nevertheless, to some extent the previous discussion of courtship and engagement has put too definite a line between the two periods. The prolonged waiting and informality of courtship often meant that there was no definite point when walking out or courting turned into a legal commitment. Most of these relationships shaded slowly into serious intentions without a public announcement or setting of the date. Exactly when a couple became engaged was therefore often difficult to determine—even for the couple. For example, Harriet Micklewright and John Bryning courted for eight years, waiting for John to take over the family farm from his father. John "spoke" to Harriet in 1870, saying he was not in a position to marry, but promising to "talk about marriage" when he was. She agreed to wait, and in the meantime ran a lodging house. They exchanged sixty-seven letters for the next nine years until John's father died in 1879. Yet John married someone else in 1881, and he claimed at the trial that they were not engaged, despite exchanging locks of hair and writing love letters and poetry. Although John's denials were not convincing, he did have a point, for at no time were he and Harriet formally engaged. It simply did not work that way in the lower middle and working classes.[34]

Indeed, in several cases the defense barristers used this ambiguity to argue that the courtship period was a time to determine if the couple were compatible. Mr. Metcalfe argued in 1895 that "people in the position of life of the parties in that case [a housemaid and the second whip of a hunt] often walked out together as a sort of trial to see if they liked each other well enough to get married eventually." Mr. Coleridge said much the same thing in a case in 1880 between a housemaid and a dairyman: "They were merely on the same terms as so many people were who kept company with each other, without meaning anything serious." To these defendants, at least, courtship did not necessarily lead to marriage.[35]

Women did not take this view. They assumed there was an engagement after the man "spoke" to them for the first time. In fact, women and their parents considered any serious courtship (and this occurred as soon as the man asked permission to "keep company") as tantamount to an engagement. They had justification for their views, since women were barred from seeing other men as soon as they seriously courted one. Furthermore, such walking out could go on for several years, so a woman should receive some kind of commitment after that investment of time. Even so, in most cases there was no way to draw the line between courtship and engagement, and this was the basis of many of the misunderstandings that ended in court. Some men admitted to "making love" to plaintiffs or being on "friendly terms" with them, but insisted that they had not proposed. Robert Scotter confessed to courting Maria Appleton, but explained that "having considered the matter he had arrived at the conclusion never to propose to her." William Orchard, too, claimed that although he had spent time with Elizabeth Spender, he had never asked to marry her. To the women, however, any courtship was serious, and usually judges and juries sympathized with the women's point of view.[36]

These ambiguities were even more pronounced in the courtship of mature couples, whose courtships had a different pattern from those of younger people.[37] Typically, at least one of the two people (and sometimes both) had been married before, producing numerous children. They knew what to expect from marriage and had a clear idea of what they wanted in a spouse. Kate Taylor, for instance, had nine children when she became engaged to Mr. Hardman, who was the father of eight. Catherine Smith had been married four times and had seven children; her fiancé, James Strickland, had been married three times. With such histories, many of these couples felt no need to fulfill courtship rituals. The men, particularly, preferred second courtships to be short and simple. James Horrocks angered Jane McCleod when "he told her that three months was long enough for a man at his time of life to court." The defendant in *Wheeler v. Jones* tried to hurry his fiancée as well, saying, "There was no necessity for a long courtship as with young people—a very short time would do for us."[38]

Mature couples found each other in one of two ways. Several had known each other for many years, either as friends or neighbors, and decided to marry after having survived their first spouses. The plaintiff and defendant in *Lacy v. Frankeiss,* for example, had known each other for fifty years. They met again at the ages of sixty-nine and seventy-one and agreed to spend their old age together.[39] Second, some met as almost total strangers and decided to marry on outward attributes. Older courters frequently met through marriage brokers or well-meaning friends and relatives. Margaret Halliwell and Phillip Rigby met because Margaret's daughter overheard Phillip saying that he wanted a wife. The daughter introduced them, and they might have made the match had Phillip's brother not interfered.[40] These were clearly marriages of convenience, yet the desire for companionship was not absent. Indeed, the men often backed out of the marriages precisely because they had not developed the affection they thought essential.

Despite the desire for sentiment, both parties—perhaps because of their life experiences—knew not to neglect practical needs. The men frankly expected the women to be able to cope with domestic arrangements. James Horrocks, in breaking off with Jane McLeod, complained that, among other things, she had refused to mend his trousers, which were "always out at the knees." Even if this were only an excuse to escape the match, it is significant that Horrocks thought such a reason acceptable. Men were also attracted to women who displayed sound business sense. James Strickland proposed to Catherine Smith after watching the efficient way she ran the Bridge Inn. Smith's previous four husbands had been publicans, obviously having valued the same characteristic in her, but on her fifth try, she agreed only on the proviso that she be able to give up the pub. Strickland consented at first, but soon changed his mind and married a younger woman—not surprisingly, since it was Smith's business that had attracted him in the first place.[41]

Men were not alone in their pragmatism. Women made a point of determining what their future husbands intended to settle on them before they committed to a second or late marriage. The plaintiff in *Wheeler v. Jones* questioned the defendant closely before they set the wedding date. As she put it, "I told him that leaving my house would be a serious thing for me, and said that if anything should happen, where should I be then? He promised in reply to make me comfortable for life." The couple in *Thomas v. Edwards* discussed money matters thoroughly during their courtship. Thomas agreed to give up her business upon marriage, while Edwards said "he would make a will in her favour which she could have in her own custody."[42] Though the women may have been overstating their future husbands' intentions (to get higher damages), they apparently did not think that their frank interest in money would prejudice the jury against them. The women needed some assurance of security when marrying relatively old men while at the same time giving up lucrative businesses. And the men had every reason to want an efficient housekeeper or why marry again at all? Settling such issues before the wedding presumably avoided incompatibilities after the ceremony.

For older couples courtship rituals seemed out of place, since such customs assumed youth on the part of the bride and groom. A formal wedding was redundant, since the bride had already been given away once before, or her parents had long been dead and she supported herself. Indeed, as Gillis has argued, most second marriages remained quiet and private into the twentieth century.[43] However short on ceremony, these cases also showed the popularity of marriage with most adults. Both men and women willingly took three or even four spouses in a lifetime, preferring conjugality to independence. Women wanted the increased security, and men wanted someone to look after them and any children they had. Even with all of these pragmatic considerations, both also wanted companionship. James Horrocks insisted on his next wife being "agreeable," and one reason he broke up with Jane was her unenthusiastic reception of him. And though Thomas recognized that she would have to act as nursemaid to her elderly suitor, she argued that "he was all right. He was for me, because he would have been a companion to me."[44]

Mature couples may not have considered weddings as an important rite of passage, but younger couples certainly did. In fact, the last major activity of younger courting couples was planning the wedding. Most of the arranging fell to the women and their families, but some men also took an active interest. Like the process of getting engaged, weddings of the lower middle and upper working classes were not formal, but they still had definite rituals and expectations. Wedding dates were set and then changed; dresses were several different colors; people were invited haphazardly; and, in fact, the whole affair was casual. Yet many of their activities appeared in case after case, showing that most men and women knew what a proper wedding should be.

Most couples made extensive preparations, including finding couples to attend them, assuring the cooperation of both families, renting carriages, and planning the wedding breakfast, the wedding clothes, and the honeymoon.[45] With such a number of concerns, women often spent a considerable amount of money—a particularly large expense for lower middle- and working-class women, whose wages were low. The biggest expense was the trousseau, or the wedding clothes. In addition to the bride's dress, the woman needed two or three other dresses as well as underclothes. Florence Carter had "several" dresses made, and Susannah Brown had "three dark dresses" in addition to her wedding dress.[46] The wedding dress was seldom white, but it was almost always an expensive fabric, usually silk. Sarah Owens and Elizabeth Higgs had black silk dresses made; Martha Bebbington and Susannah Brown both settled for blue; and Elizabeth Adams had grey.[47]

Besides the trousseau, the bride also provided household goods. For example, Emma Pryke bought "some spoons, glasses, and ornaments" in London before her wedding. Some women went to even more expense by improving their property or homes. Sarah Owen claimed that she spent £50 in draining and otherwise upgrading her farm in preparation for marriage.[48] The women were spared the expense of paying for their bridesmaids' dresses, since these were purchased by the bridesmaids themselves. The groom, too, provided his own clothing, though he did not necessarily buy a new suit. Attention usually centered on the waistcoat and ties that lent the proper formality to the groom's appearance.[49]

The bride and groom between them decided who would stand up with them, and almost always at least a few of the wedding party were relatives. The number of bridesmaids and groomsmen was usually small, seldom more than three. Mary Hill had only one bridesmaid, the defendant's sister; Susan Williams picked two of her friends; and Annie Wilkinson invited her fiancé's daughter to stand up with her.[50] The woman's family gave out the invitations to the wedding; if the groom had friends he wanted to be invited, he had to give a list to the bride's family. Many times the invitations were simply handwritten letters, although more formal cards were available.[51]

Though the couple seldom had newspaper announcements, they did have two communal rites as part of the engagement. The first, and less common, was "standing the wedding glass." Usually this coincided with the announcement of the engagement at a public gathering. The groom-to-be proclaimed the engagement, and the wedding glass passed from person to person as those present wished the couple good luck. If the wedding were hastily done, the "standing" could occur afterward.[52] The second rite, the wedding breakfast, was almost universal, from the working to the upper middle classes. It was a simple meal that took place after the wedding ceremony. There was always a wedding cake (or "bride's cake") as well as various other refreshments. Occasionally, these affairs were elaborate: Mary Hill's breakfast had "pheasants, partridges, bride's cake, jellies, &tc." Most of the time, though, these were humble affairs, consisting of light refreshment. The wedding breakfast served the same purpose as the modern reception, giving those close to the couple a chance to celebrate their union with them.[53]

Of course, the woman did not endure the entire financial drain. The groom's primary expense was in finding a place to live and furnishing it, though women often devoted time to these matters as well. For instance, the couple often picked out furniture together. Mary Jane Pattinson and Edward Heslop (a servant and a farmer) quickly settled on a farm to take, which possessions would remain with his mother and sister, and the furniture for the new home. Susan Williams and her fiancé, the Reverend John Thomas, divided up the furnishing chores by sex: "He selected the male portion of the furniture, that was for the dining room, and she selected the drawing room suite and the fancy articles." The groom was also expected to pay for the license and the cost of the preacher (or other official).[54] In general, men were more likely to want to use a license; women preferred the publicity of the banns, unless there was some urgency (for instance, if she were pregnant).[55] However, the man's expense was largely in the future; few couples had reached the point of purchasing homes or licenses by the time they split up.

The couples usually planned modest honeymoons (and sometimes none at all). Occasionally, the grooms hired carriages to bring the bride to the wedding and then take the couple away, but this expense was not usually undertaken. Nor did couples go far on their visits; often they went to the largest town nearby. Julia Burton and her fiancé, Frederick Howlett, planned to stay in Llandudno, while Susan Williams and John Thomas were to go to London. Annie Allmand intended to spend even less, for she and Elijah Forrester planned to stay with her cousin.[56]

One final preparation was made by the women: time after time they gave up businesses, jobs, training, or school before marrying. Any number of examples could be given of women who happily left the world of employment in anticipation of becoming full-time wives. Many times this action was at the defendant's request, although the women did not express any reluctance. Sarah Graves "gave up the house in which she was earning her living as a lodging-house keeper" after her lover, a draper, requested it. Other times, as in the case of servants, marriage automatically meant losing their situations. Even women working in factories were not always exceptions. Mary Ann Langley's fiancé, John Trickett, a woollen printer, gave her mother £1 a week to support her so that she could leave the mill. Moreover, women preparing for careers, either as governesses, schoolteachers, or musicians, halted their training. Edith Williams was a sixteen-year-old pupil teacher, preparing for her last examination, when she met Edward Hughes, an accountant, in 1879. She walked out with Edward, gave up her schooling, and eventually got pregnant before the age of eighteen. With an illegitimate baby, she undoubtedly lost her career in education.[57]

It may have been difficult for some middle-class leaders of the women's movement to understand the lower-class desire to leave the workforce. All of these examples took place in the late nineteenth century, the same time that upper middle-class women were pushing into the public sphere. Most women in classes below the middle were behind their sisters of higher status in their expectations. They had yet to feel stifled in the confines of the home; having faced uncertain futures of making their own way, they preferred to have a husband provide for them. Indeed, as Ellen Ross (among others) has pointed out, a providing husband was a sign of respectability for working-class women in late Victorian London. Women expressed great indignation at having lost their careers, but only because they gave up their businesses for no reason. And, as Joan Perkin has argued, a woman had many other reasons to prefer marriage, including "a home of her own, a spouse to love and share her life, legitimate sex, [and] children." All these had been lost by the breach, so it was no wonder that women protested.[58]

A final consideration about lower middle- and upper working-class courtship was the role of parents. Relatives had a complicated role in courtship and weddings, a mixture of leniency and interference. For instance, most parents allowed a great deal of freedom early in the relationship, seldom trying to veto courtships. Although women expected men to ask for consent to court them from the nearest relative, they assumed that the consent was automatic. The plaintiff's father in *White v. Aird* in 1872 replied to the defendant's letter asking his consent to an engagement that "as he had every confidence in his daughter, he could have no objection to him as her future husband." In *Ibbetson v. Strickland* (1889) Strickland asked for the mother's consent, "and her mother said her daughter could do as she liked."[59] Most parents were not this blasé, but only a few voiced objections, and those parents who did had limited influence. Anne Blakeman's father, a farmer, disliked Eli Bowers, also a farmer, thinking him irresponsible. He refused to allow Anne to see Eli at first, but he relented after only a few months. Sophia Dainty's mother pointed out to T. M. Brown the differences in their ages and religious opinions, but he overrode her objections (both families were in farming).[60] Parents were simply unable to prevent engagements, try though they might.

All the same, the families of the man and woman exerted enormous authority over the course of the courtship, and, especially, on the breaking up. Though seldom successful at stopping engagements, they were most effective at stopping weddings. Time after time the men pleaded that they did not carry out their promises because of the disapproval of family or friends. Of course, they may have been lying to excuse their breaches, but they apparently believed that juries would accept such reasons. Parental interference in courtship is one of the great continuities of modern family history: Bridget Hill documents it in the eighteenth century, Barret-Ducrocq in the nineteenth, and Diane Leonard into the late twentieth.[61] And although most historians have focused on the woman's kin, parents (and other relatives) sought to control the choices of their sons as well as their daughters.

Indeed, there were two ways that family members went about stopping a male child from contracting an unwise marriage. The first was to use the power of the purse. In several cases the defendant broke off the impending union because of threats from a family member from whom he had "expectations." William Barnes's rich father, for example, raised objections after Theresa Bingley's stepfather, a steelworks director, went bankrupt, leaving her without a dowry. But it was not just the parents who exerted control. The defendant in *Scrine v. M'Kay* claimed he could not marry because if he did, his sister would do nothing for him; other men were dependent on relatives outside the immediate family, such as an aunt or uncle.[62] Most of the time, however, relatives took a subtler approach. Instead of a threat, they used persuasion and unpleasantness to encourage a breach. In *Shickell v. Warren* the plaintiff, the daughter of a farmer, alienated her future mother-in-law by remarking that "some grapes which were offered to her were mouldy, and upon that the old lady took offence. . . . From this time on she was very disagreeable to the plaintiff." John Humphreys, a grocer, courted Fanny Wood secretly because he knew his mother would disapprove since Fanny was very poor (an assistant in a milliner's shop). When Mrs. Humphreys discovered their engagement, she objected so strongly that Fanny went to a different town for two years and lost touch with John.[63]

As these examples indicate, this subtle opposition worked well and could be used by all members of the family; in fact, several older couples were broken up by their children's objections. In *Bath v. Williams,* a case involving a dressmaker and a blacksmith, the defendant's grown children told him "that if he married the plaintiff they would leave him." Williams was twenty-three years older than his fiancée, and his children evidently feared that she would threaten their inheritance. They also may have disliked her class, since she was acting as his housekeeper. Evan Jones, a farmer, delayed marriage because his twenty-year-old son William "naturally objected to having a step-mother." Evan eventually married another, leaving his first fiancée with an illegitimate child.[64]

Although the defendant's family was the catalyst the majority of the time, the problem did not always exclusively stem from their jealousy or snobbery. On occasion, the woman's family caused the trouble. In the few cases in which the man was the plaintiff, the woman's family or friends were almost always strong influences. *Hole v. Harding* was such a case, with Harding breaking off her engagement with two men because of her father's disapproval. Interference also came from friends. Jane Ormand, who had an annual income of £750, got engaged to a land surveyor named John Eden. Her landlady, a Mrs. Todd, talked her into breaking it off, apparently convinced that Eden was only after Ormand's money.[65] Far more often, though, the woman's family and friends drove her suitor away unintentionally. The bone of contention could be anything, but money was a primary factor. Amelia Sutton's mother wrecked her engagement to William Aronsberg by demanding a large settlement for her daughter. Aronsberg became so angry that he changed the wedding date, insisted on a wedding by registrar, and refused to settle a penny on Sutton. Needless to say, Sutton refused to accept these terms. An almost identical case was that of Sarah Owen and Humphrey Williams, although this time it was Owen's daughter who asked for a settlement. Williams refused, and that difference was the beginning of the trouble between them.[66]

There were also a few occasions when the families of the principals feuded through the couple. In *Smith v. Woodfine* the defendant's mother and sister felt that Margaret Smith's family were looking down on them and "slighting" them. For his part, Margaret's father thought Woodfine's conduct was vacillating and had words with his future son-in-law about it. Finally, the couple had a heated interview in which Woodfine told Smith he would marry her only if none of her family were allowed to visit them. Naturally, Smith refused, and the families moved their bitter fight to the courts. In *Hart v. Clinker* the defense counsel insisted that the action was the result of the defendant's mother and the plaintiff's father feuding with each other. In fact, the defendant's entire family disliked the plaintiff, and her father reciprocated.[67] This bitterness shows the explosiveness of class and wealth distinctions, no matter how minor. Such bickering was apparently not limited to any one class or stratum in Victorian society, although the lower middle and working classes may have been more subject to it, since they married out of their class more often. According to Thompson, lower middle-class men found "between a third and two-fifths" of their brides in the working class from 1850 to 1900, usually the daughters of skilled artisans. Yet even such small degrees of status made a difference in whether the two families could tolerate a closer union.[68]

Clearly, the influence of family and friends was strong. This conclusion is hardly unexpected, since parents in all classes had informal controls of their children's courtship, even in the working class, as Lawrence Stone, Jalland, and Thompson have shown.[69] There are two noteworthy aspects of lower middle- and upper working-class relatives' roles, however. First, these families showed the influence of extensive kin networks. Cousins, aunts, uncles, and even guardians and in-laws took an interest in the courtships of their relatives. Although parents and siblings had the most say, others were not excluded; in fact, the expression of opinions of other relatives was expected. Industrialization and urbanization do not seem to have overridden kin roles in most families, at least in times of stress; whatever triumph the nuclear family experienced in the modern period, it was limited. Second, it is important to note the frequency with which male members of the family were involved. Most historians have assumed that women were primarily concerned in courtship. Thompson, for example, insists that "the effective determination of marrying standards, and their enforcement, were substantially women's business." And though Davidoff and Hall note the social influence of kin, they do not apply this conclusion to courtship.[70] Female dominance, however, was true only for successful courtships. Whenever relationships were troubled, fathers, brothers, and even uncles and male cousins concerned themselves vitally in romantic affairs.

There were even a few cases in which fathers seemed to do everything. For instance, the plaintiff's father in *Nixon v. Moss* played a large role in her complicated courtship. Nixon, a mantle-maker, and Moss, a stone mason, first knew each other in 1847, as neighbors in a small community. Nixon became pregnant and had a child in 1848. Her father, John Nixon, then spoke to Moss, who assured him that he would marry her as soon as he could afford it. After a few weeks, the father insisted that the child be affiliated to the defendant, who agreed. After a few more weeks, John demanded that the two stop seeing one another unless Moss could marry his daughter at once. Consequently, the two lost touch; Nixon even formed an engagement with another man. Despite all Mr. Nixon's efforts, his daughter still favored Moss and rejected her second fiancé for the first. John Nixon's judgment proved correct, since Moss eventually jilted Nixon for another woman. Although the plaintiff's mother testified with her husband at the trial, she appeared to have little role in the courtship. In contrast, her husband's actions defined its course from an early stage.[71]

This is not to say that women did not have a strong role in courtship, only that they had little to do with certain parts of the process. In other words, male and female members of the family had gendered roles. Women evaluated prospective mates, while encouraging suitable matches and discouraging unsuitable ones. They also did most of the planning for social occasions and weddings. Men gave their consent or withheld it at the beginning, discouraged perceived mismatches, and, in particular, stepped in during times of trouble. For example, most fathers assumed a protective role when their daughters got pregnant or when they were jilted. The closest male relative had the duty of writing to the jilter to demand explanations, even if he were only a distant relation or guardian.

In three ways, then, lower middle- and upper working-class courtship in the late nineteenth century was an odd mix. First, although the most important relationship was between the man and the woman, both of the families were intimately involved. An engagement was a private affair, but it invariably affected more people than just the bride and groom. In this way the lower middle class was similar to all classes in Victorian society. However, in examples where the courtship went wrong, the roles of wider kin and male relatives in courtship were emphasized. <u>Second</u>, despite their aspirations to the domesticity of the upper middle classes, many of the informalities of the lower classes intruded, especially in courting activities and weddings. For instance, lower middle-class men and women had both a great deal of freedom to meet members of the opposite sex and privacy with them once they were on intimate terms. Their relationships were also ambiguous, because of the difficulty of determining the difference between courtship and formal engagements. This made the lower orders vulnerable to breaches, while at the same time less able to prove engagements. <u>Finally</u>, the lower middle class aspired to the middle-class standard of respectability and domesticity without the financial resources to make the process easy. The results were long engagements, frequent separations, and unfortunate pregnancies. Furthermore, a woman spent a great deal of money on preparations and gave up her business or job to marry; this left her in a difficult situation if the wedding did not take place. These three circumstances help explain the intense frustration and worry that dogged the courtships of these couples. What is impressive is the faithfulness of the lower middle class to their own rites of courtship, despite the difficulties. Both partners knew the rules and tried to follow them. Indeed, these distinct rituals appeared among the complicated reasons for broken courtships.

V

Broken Engagements
in Victorian England

ALTHOUGH MOST PEOPLE in Victorian times assumed that success—a wedding—resulted from courtship almost automatically, possibly thousands of courtships per year failed, far more than made it to court in a breach-of-promise suit. The reasons for failure were complex, and those that eventually appeared in the legal records show difficulties closely related to the courtship rituals peculiar to the lower orders. These reasons fall into three areas. First, there was the vexed issue of class. Cross-class matings faced numerous problems; in addition, intra-class courtships ran into obstacles because of the delays and separations inherent in the lower middle and working classes (and a few middle-class couples as well). Second, the romance of courtship often conflicted with practical needs, while at the same time suffering from internal contradictions. Third, these structural obstacles were complicated by interpersonal factors, such as age, religion, and incompatibility. Whatever the reason, many couples found the engagement to be a difficult and sometimes tragic time in their lives.

As already discussed, the most common negative factor in the breakup of a couple was their relatives. Family opposition was effective in stopping "unsuitable" weddings, usually through indirect means. However, the motives behind familial interference deserve closer scrutiny, because in most of these cases the reason was differences in class, wealth, and status. And even when no parents or other relatives intervened, differences in class could derail a relationship very quickly. Recent works by Patrick Joyce, Judith Walkowitz, and others have de-emphasized class as a defining factor in many people's lives in Victorian England, revising the primarily Marxist interpretation of social relations that previously dominated.[1] These historians have instead privileged considerations such as populism and gender. However, the evidence of breach-of-promise cases indicates that class, wealth, and status were crucially important in the choice of a spouse for numerous couples. Such a conclusion does not necessarily contradict the revisionist position, but it does indicate that class was more important in private than public life in the Victorian period. In addition, though gender was central to these actions, class interacted with it in complex ways.

This conclusion is supported by other studies of courtships in Victorian

times, including those of Joan Perkin, F. M. L. Thompson, and Geoffrey Crossick. Although women were expected to try to marry into a slightly higher
social class, they were not to leap too many social barriers.[2] Middle-class pre-
scriptive literature emphasized the dangers of interclass love. One writer in the
1890s insisted that all cross-class matings ended in "trouble and humiliation and
shame." Annie Swan of *Woman at Home* did not feel that cross-class matings
were hopeless but advised great caution.[3] Most middle-class advice writers believed that though marriage without love was wrong, unions based only on
sexual attraction were also a mistake. Love appropriate for marriage was a deep
companionship or affinity, not sexual attraction or fancy. Affinity grew from
similar outlooks, beliefs, and ways of life, a difficult process for those from
different classes. Since marriage also had a religious meaning, only the most
foolish would go before God with someone they did not believe was a twin
soul in every way.[4]

All the same, saying simply that class or wealth differences broke up an
engagement oversimplifies the matter. As Thompson has pointed out, the middle class was the most exclusive and rigid about cross-class matings, while the
working and lower middle classes, the ones most likely to appear in breach-of-
promise cases, were the least. Lower middle-class men often married women in
the working class, even the daughters of manual laborers. Indeed, Hall's research
has shown the crucial importance of women's capital in starting small businesses
in the lower middle class. Although her research mainly concerns those with
dowries, such capital could come from a variety of sources, including the wages
of servants, making some working-class women attractive marital prospects.[5]

Not surprisingly, then, in many cases the objection to the lower-class party
was not simply that he or she was not of the same class but that his or her
occupation was not respectable. Most of the few cases involving peers and gentry, for example, had models, actresses, or chorus girls as the plaintiffs. In *Fitzpatrick v. Curling* the defendant was a gentleman of independent means, while
the plaintiff was an "artist's model." Curling accused Fitzpatrick of lying to him
about her occupation (he claimed she told him she only modeled her head) and
insinuated that she posed nude (which she denied). Although Fitzpatrick refuted the charges, many assumed that a woman who modeled her body for a
living displayed dubious moral tenets.[6] Actresses, both in the early and later
parts of the century, had similar difficulties, although their reputations improved
as the century went on. Maria Foote, a celebrated actress in the early nineteenth
century, lost Joseph Hayne because he was unable to face the disapproval of his
friends. Her profession was troubling, and she had also lived for five years as
the mistress of another man and had two illegitimate children.[7]

Though most cross-class cases involved smaller social distances, the emphasis on respectability remained. Any woman working in a bar or hotel, particularly as a barmaid, was suspected of being a prostitute, or at best a woman of easy virtue. Such confusion was easy, since until the Contagious Diseases Act of 1866 (and even afterward in districts where the acts were not enforced), prostitution was temporary and often run from women's lodging houses or inns. In addition, barmaids were important sexual symbols in Victorian England, as Peter Bailey has argued (though his term is parasexual). His conclusions focus on the higher class of the occupation and assume that part of the appeal of barmaids was their unattainability. My data indicate that his analysis has applications for the poorer parts of the business's population. Barmaids often dated their customers, with poor results, perhaps because of their seemingly sexualized occupation.[8] Although formerly a dressmaker, Julia Ford was a barmaid when she met George Strongitharm, a young man from a well-to-do family. They ran off together, but his family found them and stopped their wedding. The plaintiff in *Haun v. Bradford* worked in her father's hotel where she met her fiancé, a bank clerk. Bradford left her after a short courtship; his mother wrote to Haun with the explanation that such a relationship was foolish because of their class differences.[9]

Though class was important, then, these cases support part of the revisionists' arguments, because they refute simplistic readings of "class" in the Victorian period. Class was not merely an economic affiliation but also a scale of behaviors and norms that varied by status and gender. Both parties, but especially women, had to pass character tests to be considered marriageable. The main requirement for a man was that he be a good provider; the primary requirement for a woman was chastity, and an occupation with an unsavory reputation was enough to sully the most blameless woman. Moreover, any fall in her past life or even one with the defendant, indicated to some men that such a woman was not due the title of "wife." A good example is *Gardner v. Thomas*. Ellen Gardner was a machinist who met Alfred Thomas, a gentleman of private means, in 1872.[10] The two began to live together shortly thereafter, Ellen claiming that Alfred had promised marriage. To support her story, she produced a written contract, dated April 23, 1873: "I, Alfred Thomas, do promise to marry Miss E. Gardner, if she does not run from her promise that she will have nothing to do with any other man before June next.—A. THOMAS." Alfred jilted her just seven months later. Although she had written evidence, Ellen's past was not pure; when much younger she had intercourse with "a young man with whom she was keeping company." In addition, Alfred's barrister painted the boarding house where she lived as a brothel with the landlady as the madam. Though the attempt failed, it illustrated the precarious position of a woman with sexual experience.[11]

Even women who had lived chastely before meeting the defendants were not always treated as suitable material for marriage. Servants were particularly vulnerable to sexual overtures, with little hope of matrimony. For example, Sarah Jane Watkins worked as a housekeeper for Edward Davies, a wealthy farmer almost twenty years her senior. After only three weeks in his service, Sarah received romantic overtures from him. Because of the disapproval of his two grown daughters, Sarah left his employ, and two years later he married a wealthy widow. Wanda Hadad was even more unfortunate. She worked as a maid for Hamilton Bruce, a retired naval officer. His daughters objected to their relationship, but Bruce insisted that Hadad stay, and the couple had a sexual affair. When she became pregnant, he sent her to London and never saw her again.[12] Though in some of these cases the men's protests that they had never promised matrimony were self-serving, in others there was an obvious (and perhaps intentional) misunderstanding between the two parties. The men never expected to go beyond a sexual relationship, while the women hoped for a legal union. Barret-Ducrocq's work on the Foundling Hospital also revealed the difficult position of servants vis-à-vis their masters. They hesitated to reject overtures for fear of losing their positions, but the likelihood of marriage was small, even if their employers were shopkeepers or small farmers. Many had to appeal to the Foundling Hospital or to the civil courts for help.[13]

All the same, though respectability was crucial, wealth and status were also important. Couples that at first seemed eminently suited to one another became less so after changes in business or reverses in fortune. Eleanor Allen, a school-teacher, became engaged to John Hutchings in 1867. Her family loaned John £140 so that he could begin his medical training, and the couple corresponded for ten years as John progressed through the various stages of medical school. Finally, John became an assistant to a Dr. Colebrook, and Eleanor gave up her job and prepared for the wedding. At the last minute John jilted her for the daughter of Colebrook, thereby ensuring his professional future. Having helped prepare him to support a wife, this defection must have been especially galling to Eleanor. Annie McGrath lost her fiancé, Henry De Valve, after he won £800 in a chancery suit. De Valve felt after this windfall that he could do better than McGrath.[14]

If the plaintiff's family suffered business reversals, this could also alter the balance. Early in the century Amelia Wharton lost her fiancé, William Lewis, after her father and brother went bankrupt. The bankruptcy disgusted Lewis's father, who persuaded William to break off the match. Arthur Pemberton, a clerk of shipping merchants, became engaged to Violet Brice in 1892, even though she was a barmaid. However, two things changed Arthur's mind. First, Violet's mother wrote to him asking for a large loan. Arthur, taken aback, offered Mrs. Brice £10, which she refused as not enough. Second, Arthur came into £2,000. With so much cash, he worried that her family would never stop asking for money. Thus, when the engagement was only three months old, he broke it off for good.[15]

For the most part, then, class differences were insurmountable in four instances: when the family strongly disapproved and had power over the defendant; when the plaintiff's job was not respectable as well as being less remunerative; when the plaintiff was viewed (for whatever reason) as simply a sexual partner; and when the difference in status between the couple became noticeably wider during the courtship. Class differences were also fatal when combined with one or more other factors. If, for example, a couple faced both class differences and some other incompatibility such as religious beliefs or wide age differences, then their chances of staying together declined markedly. Class, then, was complicated by expectations about respectability and gender, although wealth and status were also crucial. For the most part, the upper middle classes could avoid these problems since their children seldom met people well below them in class, although it was not unknown (indeed, some of the examples above were from the upper class). But a middle-class woman jilted by an upper-class suitor would not be left destitute or pregnant when he left, as was often the case in the lower orders. Class may not have been all-powerful, but for lower-class women it could be a firm bar to happiness and security.

In fact, as divisive as these interclass struggles were, there were also structural problems within the classes, particularly in those that did not enjoy financial security. The protracted nature of their courtship forced some couples to remain half-committed for periods longer than many marriages. Long engagements for poorer couples in the Victorian period were a common phenomenon. David Vincent found that working-class men recorded courtships of up to five years in their autobiographies, and Gillis called servants' courtships "extended" and "ritually protracted" because of their economic vulnerability.[16] These obstacles were doubly powerful when combined with the romantic ideal, a value system that encouraged men and women to search for true love. This quest for a perfect mate sometimes led couples away from each other rather than toward a closer union.

Indeed, in a large number of cases the breach was the result of a slow process of growing apart due to the frequent delays and separations. Out of the 875 cases under review, 248 involved either a delay, a separation, or both. These cases were heavily weighted to lower middle- and working-class couples; they outnumbered the upper classes over 3 to 1 in separations, and 10 to 1 in delays.[17] The most common reason for delaying the wedding was financial weakness.

Both men and women used long engagements to save money, receive legacies, and tie up loose ends in their former lives. Unfortunately, these waits opened the door to changes in personality and expectations that often led to the end of originally promising relationships.

For this very reason, most middle-class writers on the subject felt that long engagements were to be avoided. Jalland has found that the ideal length of engagements for the upper classes was two years or less. Contemporary upper-class women also enumerated objections in their published writings. First, in such a situation "a young man and a young woman [were] neither bound nor free." Therefore, they risked lapses of fidelity, changes in affection, and the loss of all the freshness of their love. Nor did the couple really get to know each other during long engagements, since they were under a constant strain for too many years.[18] Finally, and most tellingly, "an engagement of undue length is apt to become a fixed and chronic condition which ends in nothing but itself." Indeed, in many breach-of-promise cases the engagement lasted so long that it seemed to be enough, a position the couple appeared unable to go beyond.[19]

The advice of these middle-class women was undoubtedly correct, but, unfortunately, many couples had no choice but to wait if they wished to avoid poverty, and all of these objections were borne out in their experiences. Margaret Nelson met Thomas Taylforth in 1882 when he became a worker on an adjoining farm to her father's. They courted for several months, and Margaret had his child in 1884. Thomas kept putting off the marriage because he could never find a farm that he wanted. In 1885 the couple found two excellent prospects, but Thomas never made up his mind to take either of them. This state of affairs dragged on until 1898, when Thomas married someone else, without ever having settled on a farm at all. Taylforth may well have been purposely delaying marriage to Nelson, but their economic situation gave him the excuse he needed, and the jury did not find such a long engagement difficult to understand. A similar case was that of Alice Kennerley, a dressmaker, and T. W. Boulton, an engineer. They were engaged for ten years and he saved £70, but they had a quarrel in 1896 and never made up.[20]

In addition, financial constraints often combined with family objections to derail engagements. Usually, the couple was waiting for legacies or for the man's parents to pass on a business or farm. In *Roper v. Bagley* the defendant's father was against the match, and he was able to break it up simply by waiting four years before retiring from his grocery and drapery business. By the time he had turned it over to his son, the young man had become engaged to a more acceptable young woman. William Cox's family was unenthusiastic about his romance with Mary Anne Brookes. Thus, they were forced into a secret engagement until William could become "independent of his father and uncle." Ten years later he finally broke it off rather than be alienated from them. After giving the best years of her life to Cox, Brookes understandably felt bereft.[21]

The obvious main danger from the plaintiffs' point of view was that delays gave the defendants a chance to change their minds, either because they did not want to marry at all, grew apart from their betrothed, or met new women (or men). In short, the desire for a perfect love made long-term courtships dysfunctional. Couples expected to find and retain true affinity for each other, while struggling with innumerable impediments to intimacy. These problems struck the lower middle and upper working classes (as well as some middle-class couples) hard, since they had romantic goals yet lacked the financial means to overcome their difficulties. Any kind of delay involved risk, including those due to illness and traveling for jobs and recreation. Illness was particularly perilous, since it involved cessation of almost all contact. Louisa Burgoyne was twice on the point of marrying James Oldrieve, only to be thwarted by his bad health, first through his "bad neck" and then "an attack of the gout." After the second affliction, a "coldness sprung up" and James stopped answering her letters. James may well have pretended at least the second of these problems in order to avoid marriage; since his coldness did not begin until the second attack, though, he probably was sincerely ill with the first. Illness and death of relatives could also derail courtships. In *Ditcham v. Worrall* the plaintiff's mother fell ill shortly before her daughter's wedding in June 1879. Ditcham dutifully nursed her mother through the illness and in the process saw very little of Worrall. Perhaps because of this perceived neglect, the couple quarreled in May 1879, and Worrall refused to fulfill his promise.[22]

Even those couples who did not expect to have long engagements suffered from numerous separations, and the results were equally disruptive. Quite often absence led to forgetfulness. Defendants met new and closer people or simply lost touch with their faraway lovers. Frequently, one or both of the couple was pulled away due to his or her work. For example, in *Pierce v. Smith* the defendant came to live with the plaintiff's family in 1863 to learn the carpentry trade. She had two children with him, and when his training was over, he went to a neighboring town to set up business. She did not go with him, since he wanted to get the business going before marriage. They thereafter only saw each other a few times a year until 1871, when Pierce became suspicious and sought Smith out. She discovered that he had a flourishing business and had married another woman some time before. Similarly, Alice Dods lost William Woollett when his regiment went to Hong Kong. He soon married another young woman and forgot about Dods.[23]

Nevertheless, the most common problem of separation was simply that the couple did not live near each other and did not have enough money or leisure to visit with any frequency. Many times, the lack of proximity was crucial; the defendant invariably met and married another woman, an event that precipitated the breach. Katherine Martin lost Bertrand Secker after an engagement of eight months because he met another woman whom he preferred in London where he worked. Martin, who lived in Dawlish, was jilted without ever having seen her rival. Constance Lewis and Eva Hancock had similar experiences. Their fiancés also lived far away and married women who resided closer by. Constance and Robert Franklin had been engaged for two years when he met someone new, while Eva and her lover had courted eighteen months.[24]

Although not always true, delays and separations were sometimes symptoms of trouble rather than the causes. On occasion, the defendant was clearly making excuses to keep from having to set a date for the wedding. Robert Owen, a ship broker, got engaged to Sarah Jane Walker, a lodging-house keeper, in October 1888 after lodging with her for seven months. Sarah bought a trousseau and made preparations, including giving up her lodging house, but Robert made excuses throughout all of 1889. Finally, in June 1890 the couple set a date, but on the day of the wedding Robert sent word that he was too busy to come. Similarly, James Wilkins put off his marriage to Adeline Parker for two years, even though she had a child by him in 1884. He showed up drunk at her door one night and they quarreled. Wilkins then used this as an excuse to never visit again.[25] In these and similar cases the couple (or at least the defendants) had already grown apart, so the delays and separations were purposeful. These cases were the exceptions rather than the rule, however.

Somewhat similarly, it was not unknown for couples to break up once or even more times before reaching the decision to marry or break up forever. In twenty-five cases the couple got engaged and broke up at least twice, sometimes with quite lengthy periods in between. Most of the time the couple had a genuine affection for each other but were incompatible, so their relationships were punctuated with quarrels and reconciliations. For example, Thomas Jeeves and Margaret Adams were related by marriage and had known one another since childhood. They first became engaged in 1868, but they argued in June 1869 and split up for five weeks. Thomas then returned and renewed the engagement until December, when he again decided to break it off. Two months later, however, he asked her to take him back yet again, and this time the engagement lasted until early 1871. Tom left for good that time, saying, "I cannot bear your temper . . . I shall not come again." He married another woman two years later. Numerous other cases show the same pattern of breakup and makeup. Robert Lloyd, for instance, married another woman after having a fight with Mary Jones; after his wife's death, he wrote to Jones and proposed a second time, only to split up with her again later.[26]

Most of the time the men admitted initiating the breaks, while the women accepted the men back, apparently willingly. Dora Otte, for example, renewed her engagement to Charles Grant after a lapse of almost three years. The couple had first been engaged in 1863, but Grant left for India in 1864 and never replied to Otte's letters. He came back to England in 1867 and they reunited, but he returned to India later in the year and forgot her again. Only after having been jilted twice did she sue. A similar case was that of Sarah Ann Mitchell and Francis Hazeldine. The two became engaged in 1862, but Francis stopped visiting her after a few months, and she did not hear from him for four years. In 1867 he wrote to her asking if he could renew the acquaintance, and she agreed. They were to be married in 1869, but before the ceremony could take place he broke it off. Mitchell refused to release Hazeldine, even though he threatened her with cruel treatment, so he had to repudiate her plainly. Mitchell was apparently willing to risk an unhappy marriage rather than be jilted for a second time without compensation.[27]

Obviously, long engagements, frequent delays, and numerous separations took their toll on relationships. And, despite the fact that most people in these classes assumed that they would have to wait, they did not seem to be prepared for the hardships they experienced. Defendants, in particular, did not demonstrate much faithfulness. In 259 of the cases under study, the defendant had married someone else (or become engaged to someone else) before the trial had begun. This total is artificially inflated because some plaintiffs mistakenly believed that they had to wait until the defendant married to sue. Furthermore, others waited because such a marriage was irrefutable evidence of a breach, or because until the defendant married they had not lost hope for reconciliation. But a substantial number lost their lovers to another woman or man who had more to offer, even though flirting with another when engaged was forbidden to both sexes. The desire to marry for love often overcame scruples about correct behavior, while protracted and long-distance engagements made straying undeniably easy.

Middle-class writings on courtship were unanimous in condemning those who flirted with others when engaged, although most of them were preoccupied with women's behavior, warning them of the dangers of being thought of as flirts or coquettes.[28] Such behavior justified a breach, since any woman who indulged in random flirting diminished her chances of finding a husband. However, a more lenient criterion was applied to men. The sexual double standard operated even before marriage, and this fact enabled men to find alternatives to

their first fiancées without incurring social ostracism. Despite societal disapproval, unfaithful men had little difficulty in finding new partners—a freedom
that highlights men's advantages on the marriage market. Lower middle- and
working-class women, the most likely victims of these inequalities, also sued
most frequently.

Unfaithfulness in a few cases resulted from money problems; that is, poorer
women and men lost out to wealthier rivals. The defendant in *Redhead v. Huddleston,* a man of small independent means, jilted his milliner fiancée for a Miss
Dodgron, a woman who had an income of £100 a year. Joseph Tonge lived for
fifteen years with Sarah Langford, and they had five children. He never married
Langford, though; instead, he married the landlady of a successful inn.[29] Other
times defendants decided to marry men or women who were in closer proximity. Although housekeepers and landladies were often the victims of breaches,
they could also be the causes. Robert Routledge, an ironworks builder, jilted
Elizabeth Kelly, the daughter of a foreman builder, for his landlady, after a relationship with Kelly of five years. The plaintiff in *Chapman v. Rushman* lost her
lover to his cousin, despite a courtship of over ten years and an illegitimate
child.[30]

There were also numerous cases in which the woman was thrown over
after having had sex with the man; he married someone he considered more
suitable as a wife (that is, more chaste), even when there were no clear class
divisions. For instance, Elizabeth Williams, the daughter of a farmer, courted
Evan Jones, a farmer, for ten years. He promised to marry her after his father
died, but in the end married someone else. Williams may have seemed unrespectable to Jones, since she had had an illegitimate child two years before
courting him as well as having a child with him. Augusta Davis, the daughter
of a baker, and her lover, a Mr. Goddard, a farmer, grew up together, and they
became engaged in 1875. In August of that year Goddard invited her to his
brother's farm where they had intercourse. When she became pregnant, he refused to see her. His family accused her of trying to trap him, but Davis replied
that "it was quite clear that he had entrapped her, to her very great sorrow."[31]
These women had either already had illegitimate children or had so compromised themselves with the defendants that they were left in disgrace.

All the same, in the majority of cases the defendant simply decided to
marry someone else, without finding anything wrong with the plaintiff. For
instance, Letitia Lewis and John Davies were engaged after he had returned
from Australia. Letitia suggested that before they marry, he should go back to
Australia to finish school. John did so, but the results were of no benefit to
Letitia, since he eventually decided to marry the schoolmaster's sister. Abraham
Wright courted Ellen Lee for six years before leaving her for a Miss Primrose,

despite the fact that Lee had a fortune of £500 a year and Primrose had none. Wright married Primrose three years later in what was clearly a love match.[32]

The defendants felt some shame for their behavior because they knew that they were not following the rules. They almost always denied heatedly that they were seeing other women until they had actually married. They often tried to force the plaintiffs to break the engagement rather than admit their unfaithfulness. Samuel Stone, for example, began to find fault with everything Caroline Brett did in an effort to alienate her so he could be free to marry a Miss Gale. Eventually, Brett's brother was driven to complain to Stone about his coolness. And even when taking responsibility for the breach, the defendants did not admit their true reasons. William Weston wrote to Sarah Chamberlain that he had simply changed his mind about marrying; in the same way, W. Hooper told Mary Tittle that he had decided not to marry at all. Both men married other women shortly after breaking their promises.[33] Most men seemed to regard their first fiancées as embarrassments to be put off as quickly as possible, for they wanted to devote themselves to their new loves. In addition, they probably wanted to avoid reminders of their bad behavior. This led to callous disregard of those jilted at best and gross cruelty at the worst.

In these cases the defendants did not set out to two-time anyone; they met someone new, decided to marry them, and almost at once tried to end the relationship with their original fiancées. However, some men (no women did this in any case under study) courted two or three women at the same time purposely. Thomas Morse courted Jane Appleton, Miss Wells, and a widow, Mrs. Sandell, dividing his attentions between them. According to one of his employees, Morse entertained Appleton early in the day. When it was time for Sandell to call, he found an excuse to hurry Appleton to the omnibus. Morse eventually wed Sandell, the owner of a pub. In most cases the men went beyond courtship and convinced at least two women that they were engaged. Agnes Richards courted Robert Palmer in 1884 and had intercourse with him. In November 1886 he married someone else to whom he had been engaged for eighteen months. Agnes heard rumors that he was married, but he strenuously denied them, not admitting the truth to her until he had been married for six months. Such duplicity could go on for surprisingly long periods of time. Andrew Cox was engaged to both Amy Hayes and a Miss Gardiner for six years before he finally married the latter.[34]

These kinds of cases illustrate several points. First, men had far more ease in flirtation than women, for a woman who had courted more than one man would have lost both. Middle-class obsession with coquettes was misplaced, since men were equally—if not more—likely to indulge in flirtatious behavior. Second, the idea that men were victims of female wiles was naive. Although there were certainly occasions on which the women were to blame, the men in breach-of-promise cases were rarely hapless dupes; indeed, they could be deceitful, heartless, and duplicitous. Finally, the view of marriage one forms from such cases is a mix of pragmatism and romance. All these men appeared to view courtship as a kind of wife-shopping. They did not necessarily want a particular woman, but the best one to fulfill the position of a wife. Yet, most of the time these needs did not obscure the search for someone who was also attractive and compatible. On occasion, practical needs overcame everything else, especially in the lower middle and upper working classes. More often, however, the practical and romantic needs resided in an uncomfortable union, a mixture that facilitated breakups.[35] What was particularly unpleasant for women was the volatile mix of the romantic ideal and the sexual double standard; men could commit to more than one woman and excuse their behavior by appealing both to romantic love and to the view of men as the aggressive, sexually active gender. They also could court one woman for her sexual favors while courting another for marriage without incurring any loss for their behavior, at least until they were sued.

Indeed, such dishonorable actions did not make the women angry enough to break off relationships; they merely seemed disappointed at not having been chosen. The only one to reply with spirit was Susannah Berry, who informed her fiancé, Frederick Dunn, that "she would have nothing more to do with him" if he visited with his first fiancée, a Miss Blundell. Despite her harsh words, however, she forgave him when he assured her that he loved her best. Ruth Brown was even more forebearing. She had courted John Barnfather five years, waiting for him to get a farm. Before they could marry, John told her that he was responsible for his housekeeper's pregnancy and he would have to deal with that problem before he could marry Ruth. Instead of a furious rebuke, she only said "she hoped he was not going to let anything come between them after their long engagement."[36] These mild responses certainly emphasize men's advantages in courtship. Ruth still wanted to marry John, even though he had betrayed her. If Ruth had had intercourse with another man, however, John probably would have had nothing to do with her (and she could not have sued successfully).

The romantic ideal produced a final, more complicated reason for failed courtships in the Victorian era. Popular notions of romance and courtship encouraged couples to become engaged quickly, so many couples did not know each other well when they became engaged. Indeed, in ninety-eight cases the couple knew each other only a month or less before they promised marriage. Of course, these figures are exaggerated because plaintiffs dated engagements as soon as possible. But in the majority of cases either the defendant admitted to the engagement or the plaintiff provided letters or other convincing evidence to prove it. For instance, Alice Owens was introduced to Arthur Horton on August 4, 1889. They went for a drive together on August 5, and Arthur wrote her several letters from his army camp. Several days later they went for a walk, and Arthur hinted that he "was in a position to get married." The next Sunday he went to see her father. Without revealing what they discussed, he urged Alice as he left to "be true." On August 19 she visited his mother. Arthur then gave her an engagement ring and spoke to her father a second time. At that point the two became formally engaged, fifteen days after having met.[37]

Such brief courtships were not unusual. For example, Bertha Smith and Arthur Mitchell met on September 14, 1891, and were engaged on October 13, after having seen each other almost daily during that month. Annie Copeland insisted that her employer, William Hopkins, proposed to her only four days after she had gone to be his housekeeper. He denied the engagement, but they certainly did have sexual relations shortly after she arrived, since she quickly became pregnant (and he admitted paternity). Jessie Elder received a proposal from a man she had never seen. She had come to the attention of Michael Brearly by sending him a letter requesting a position for her brother. A few months later Brearly wrote to her to propose, since he was not happy as a widower: "I cannot do without a wife very well." She agreed, though they did not make it official until he had visited her home.[38]

In some cases the reason for the brevity was the nature of the union. Mature couples quite often arranged marriages without knowing each other well, due to a desire for a comfortable home and companionship. Ann Edwards, Margaret Halliwell, and Catherine Smith all made marriage arrangements with older men after a few days' acquaintanceship, only to be jilted when the wedding day neared.[39] At other times swift engagements were due to the couple's (or the man's) desire to have sexual relations. According to Sarah Bath, she worked for Thomas Williams as a housekeeper only one month before he spoke to her about marriage. Ten months later she had his illegitimate child. Apparently, Thomas and Sarah began acting out all the roles of husband and wife as soon as possible.[40] In this and similar cases the promise of marriage was partly a ruse to legitimize, at least in the woman's mind, premarital relations. This need for reassurance explains these hasty engagements.

Nevertheless, in most cases a brief courtship was dictated at least partially by the rules of society. If a man saw a woman three or four times, he was expected to state his intentions; even if the couple did not become formally engaged, the man had to indicate that the courtship was serious. This rule was meant to protect women from triflers; if a man did not intend marriage, he would be asked to desist in his attentions. However, such rules could backfire.

Men who had become quickly attached might just as swiftly change their minds, particularly over long engagements. Brice Wilkinson, a lieutenant in the army, spent one week in the beginning of June 1857 courting Laura Killick. His regiment left for Ireland and did not return until the end of the month, when he again called on her. At this point, after barely three weeks' acquaintance, Killick's father asked Brice his intentions, and Brice was obliged either to propose marriage or cease his visits. Brice assured Killick that he had marriage in mind, but he left with his regiment and stopped answering Laura's letters by October 1857.[41]

Part of the problem was that men often were attracted by superficial qualities, such as the looks or manner of a woman. For instance, David Harman was "at once struck" with the "appearance" of Mary Williams, and the two were engaged in a few weeks. Within ten months, however, Harman had been even more powerfully attracted by another woman and had married her instead. Brief courtships and long engagements also gave men a chance to have second thoughts. The defendant in *Woodward v. Clarke* was an officer in the Indian Army. He met the plaintiff on one of his leaves, and they quickly became engaged. Once back in India, Clarke reconsidered, and he wrote to her, explaining his change of heart: "When I came home I was so excited by my long absence and so pleased with the reception I met with that I hardly knew what I was doing. I feel that I have acted most foolishly and wrongly, and am very much to blame for allowing matters to go on so long without explaining."[42] Short courtships did not give a couple long enough to get to know one another; the engagement period (or courtship with a view to marriage) was the only time that they could discover whether or not they suited each other. In other words, for many couples the engagement was the beginning of formal courtship. Even in the lower middle and upper working classes, where there was no clear line between courtship and engagement, women expected much more from serious courtship than men. Unfortunately, many couples found that they were not compatible after the first flush of physical attraction wore off.

In fact, middle-class writers in the nineteenth century observed that these social conventions maneuvered men into a false position. "The Perils of Paying Attention," an article originally written for the *Saturday Review,* charged that courtship was "reduced to a matter of numerical calculation—that a certain number of dances, or calls, or polite speeches will justify a stern father or big brother in asking his 'intentions.'" Another writer told a story of a young man who had taken a lady to "a few theatres and dances" and had been forced to propose by social pressure. Although these writers were dealing with the middle and upper classes, the lower middle and working classes had the same problem. Flora Thompson, a servant, claimed that most of her friends conducted their courtships "by letter, for they seldom met except during the girls' summer holiday." Thus, the two people most involved saw each other infrequently before they made a life commitment to one another. The possibilities for misunderstandings and changed minds were great.[43]

In short, the conventions meant to protect women from being jilted—obliging men to state their intentions soon—at times led to broken engagements. Some couples discovered incompatibilities or differences that made marriage impossible. Additionally, the murky concept of romantic love caused problems. Men fell in love with the manner or looks of a woman, a type of love based on sexual attraction. Yet they also recognized that they needed a deeper love, or affinity, for a woman they married (companionate love). These different forms of love were well known; Gay found both types of love in middle-class courtship, which he labeled "sexual" and "affectionate" (or "tender") and which also mixed together during courting and marrying. Sexual love was not illegitimate, but it did clash with the more prosaic and pragmatic considerations of daily life, and advice writers considered the latter more important for a successful union. These varied types of attraction did not always go together, and when there was a divergence, a broken engagement was often the result.[44]

Contradictions within the romantic ideal, then, were as disruptive as those between and within classes. The complex interplay of economic and ideological needs, particularly when the two conflicted, led to the end of many relationships. Yet structural influences did not always set the course of engagements; personal factors, such as differences of age, religious beliefs, and temperaments, also played a part. In fact, differences in age and religion, though almost never strong enough to split a couple on their own, often functioned as contributing factors.

Age differences were common among late-Victorian couples. According to Jalland in her study of the upper classes, "The husband was expected to be older than the wife, ideally by three to seven years, since women were supposed to age faster than men." Small age ranges supposedly promoted marital harmony, an assumption that had some basis in reality. M. Jeanne Peterson found, in her study of Victorian gentlewomen, that in successful marriages the couples were approximately the same age. In my sample defendants were older than plaintiffs 84 percent of the time, but the ranges were quite often higher than the ideal, since half of the older defendants were more than ten years senior to the plaintiffs.[45] However, few people involved in the trials disapproved of these age ranges. In several cases a woman in her twenties was considered well suited to a man in his forties or fifties.[46]

Age led to failed courtships in only two instances. First, very large differ-

ences were problematic. James Hall was a fifty-six-year-old widower and a retired auctioneer when he proposed to his servant, Elizabeth Rice, who was
twenty-one. Despite her parents' strong objections, Elizabeth and James got
engaged. However, a few weeks later as the two of them were strolling together,
"some boys called out to the defendant 'What are you doing walking about
with a good-looking girl like that?' and there was also some vulgar chaff." James
was furious and embarrassed and broke off the match. More frequently, the
defendants combined age with other reasons. Thomas Radford wrote to his
fiancée, Fanny Wade, that he felt breaking it off was only right "when I came
to think of the wide difference of our ages and my income so small" (he was
forty-six and she was twenty-four).[47]

The second way that age was a factor was when the woman was older than
the man. This situation occurred in 40 of the 324 cases in which both ages were
known, although the age disparity was seldom more than 5 years. Most of the
time this small difference did not greatly influence the courtship (or the jury).
Only if the defendant could make it seem that the plaintiff was a scheming,
older woman out to push him into an unhappy marriage did it matter. For
example, in the cases of both Julia Ford and Catherine Fitzpatrick the defendants portrayed themselves as inexperienced boys menaced by older women.
Such defenses implied that Julia (who was 30 to George Strongitharm's 22) and
Catherine (who was 7 years older than Jesse Curling) were sexually active and
thus threatening and predatory. Deborah Gorham has pointed out that one of
the persistent stereotypes of young women was the "husband-hunter," an image
often linked to the unchaste. Such a combination of images was apparently easy
to transfer to older women courting younger men. However, juries tended to
side with the older woman unless she was over 10 years the senior, at which
point the awards lessened. Nevertheless, the factor of age clearly favored men
in Victorian courtship, and these attitudes were not limited to the lower classes.
Jalland concluded that upper middle-class women could be as much as 25 years
younger than their fiancés, but it was highly unusual for a woman to be the
older party.[48]

Differences in religious beliefs worked much the same way. By the late
nineteenth century the intensity of religious controversy had decreased. In fact,
Elizabeth Roberts found surprisingly little religious bigotry about marriage
partners in her oral history of working-class women in the late Victorian period,
although the majority still married within their own denominations. Thompson
also found a great deal of in-marrying in middle-class dissenters and Catholics,
and Jalland argues that although a difference in religion between engaged couples was frowned upon, it seldom stopped weddings.[49] Breach-of-promise cases
support these general conclusions, although religion occasionally provoked

family opposition or led to critical delays. For instance, Susannah Jones had problems with Joshua Williams's family because her family was Anglican and his was Nonconformist. For this reason his family worked to frustrate the match. Even late in the century, however, a rare couple broke up due to religious incompatibility. Edmund Cave broke off his engagement to Blanche Chamberlaine because she was a Roman Catholic. He was a Protestant, and he refused to sign an agreement to rear their children in the Catholic church.[50]

Differences in religion and age were easily identifiable stumbling blocks; nevertheless, simple interpersonal disputes were also common. In particular, couples split up because they had a bitter quarrel (or series of quarrels) without any obvious structural causes. In a few cases the man became angry or disillusioned when the woman did not successfully fulfill her duties as wife-in-training. Arthur Horton was furious with Alice Owens because she did not join in the Christmas festivities with his family when she was invited. Owens was ill and had not even wanted to go, but she went to please Horton. However, Horton took her reticent behavior as a slight to his family and called it "almost unpardonable." A more humorous example was *Vibert v. Hampton.* Richard Hampton and Ann Vibert had arranged to marry in order to have a comfortable home in their later years. He postponed the wedding once because he was ill; the second time he could not get out of bed because, he claimed, the beef steak pie she made him was far too salty. This culinary dispute kept the couple from ever making it to the altar.[51]

In the majority of these cases, though, the ultimate argument showed a true incompatibility. Many times the defendants complained that the plaintiffs were cool to them and displayed no interest in the relationship. Sarah Blinkinsop became angry enough with Herbert Chapman (he had missed an appointment) that she broke off the engagement. She then wrote him an ugly and vituperative letter threatening him when he refused to see her again. Agnes Walker frequently showed great coolness to Edmund Boocock. In fact, she jilted him twice, only to beg him to take her back each time. Not surprisingly, he became exasperated and gave her up.[52] These couples would not have been happy together if married; despite the hardship being jilted entailed for these women, their situation may very well have been better with not marrying. Still, it was easier for the economically stable man to come to that conclusion than his less secure fiancée. What was surprising was how many women still wanted to marry men whom they apparently did not even like, much less love.

When "a coldness sprung up" between an engaged couple in Victorian England, any number of factors could be involved. However, the primary influences remained class and ideology. Sometimes class alone was sufficient. For instance, cross-class courtships faced daunting obstacles, particularly when the families were not supportive. At other times the companionate ideal's own internal contradictions were enough, for the need to protect women from jilting by requiring early engagements often backfired when the couple came to know each other intimately. Still, most frequent were interplays between the two in the lower middle and upper working classes (and a few poor professional couples). Their simultaneous desire for romantic love combined with their economic inability to sustain it made for unstable courtships and broken hearts. It was easy for the middle-class advice writers to warn against long engagements and to scold those who married for anything but love, but it was much harder for a working-class woman to arrange for a quick wedding or to lose a chance at a secure life with equanimity. When engagements failed, women had the most to lose because of their economic and social disabilities. Men could range widely and freely and remained marriageable longer. Most especially, men were less damaged by sexual relationships, and cases involving seductions comprised almost 25 percent of the total. For women, the cost of sexuality often proved higher even than long-term engagements or cross-class courtships.

VI

Premarital Sex in
Victorian England

THE NOTION that Victorians were straitlaced prudes, both obsessed and repulsed by sex at the same time, has largely been exploded in the past several
years. Sexuality was openly discussed in Parliament, newspapers, and journals;
furthermore, only a fraction of the population could stay ignorant of the facts
of life.[1] The evidence from breach-of-promise cases also indicates a wider par-
ticipation in sexual activity than the stereotypical view allowed. About 25 percent of the 875 breach-of-promise cases under study involved sexual activity
between the couple, and the true figure is probably somewhat larger since there
is little information on many cases.[2] Barret-Ducrocq has recently shown that
the working classes in London had a distinct set of sexual mores that defied
those of the elite. The evidence of breach-of-promise cases, particularly the
evidence of the high number of women engaged in sexual relationships, reveals
a separate set of standards for the lower middle and upper working classes as
well. These women used their sexuality in courtship, gambling that the intimacy would lead to a long-standing commitment or would push a reluctant
fiancé to the altar.[3] Most of these women must have realized the risks of pregnancy and desertion, but they entered sexual relations because of affection and
hopes of marriage. Often this behavior resulted in a satisfactory conclusion—a
wedding. But when the courtship failed, lower middle- and upper working-
class women had a great deal to lose.

Women reacted to sexual opportunities in a variety of ways. These suits
indicate a complicated interweaving of male-female desire for intimacy and
commitment. In the courtroom, however, the careful balance of the courtship
was ignored. Barristers, with the cooperation of most plaintiffs, instead framed
the relationship in a way to minimize female agency, insisting that the woman
was seduced by an active male. Though this device worked to the advantage of
many women, it excluded any woman who could not fit herself into the proper
passive mold. It also reemphasized the danger of sexuality for women, ignoring
the pleasure that some women surely experienced.[4] Ironically, this emphasis on
victimization occurred in one of the few cases that penalized men for their
sexual adventures.

Premarital intercourse was an accepted part of courtship in the lower middle and "respectable" working classes, but only in long-term relationships and infrequently even then. In most of the cases the woman had sex only with her fiancé or after an extended period of courtship. Although not acknowledged by most people outside of the working class, there was a long-held belief that sex with a fiancé was acceptable, since the couple were to be married anyway. The primary disgrace came if the woman became pregnant and the couple did not marry.[5] Certainly, a fall under a promise of marriage was considered much less reprehensible than one without such assurances.

Though sexual intercourse was not uncommon, most couples waited some time before consummating the relationship, often several months or even years. Women may have felt safer risking pregnancy with a man who had been faithful for an extended period, and the couple's many hours of companionship must have strengthened the affection between them. Mary Capron, daughter of a farmer, and Richard Denning, a farmer, began courting in 1859, but Capron did not have an illegitimate child until 1862. Joseph Rolph courted Harriet Bailey for a year before proposing marriage, and they were engaged another year before starting a sexual liaison. Harriet eventually had two children, in 1873 and 1875, but Joseph married someone else before the birth of the second child.[6] These long periods before the birth of children indicate abstinence more than birth control, since, as Angus McLaren has shown, birth control methods were either too expensive for the lower middle and working classes or were not widely reported until the early twentieth century. Most people below the middle class relied on traditional methods—rhythm and withdrawal—that required male cooperation and were often ineffective even then (the other two major methods, abstinence and lactation, do not apply in most of these cases). Furthermore, the majority of the couples had limited opportunities for privacy, so they most probably waited some time before starting a sexual relationship.[7] It may well be that these women decided to permit sexual advances in the hopes of pushing their lovers into matrimony, only to miscalculate the economic or emotional situations of the men. Instead of marriage, they achieved unwed motherhood and desertion.

Women and men in these cases were cautious, so the sexual contact was usually limited. Most women (and some of the men) reported having sex only once or twice before pregnancy or other problems split up the couple. Martha Bebbington only had sex with John Hitchen once, when they were visiting her grandfather's home after having been engaged four months. Charlotte Windeatt insisted that Frank Slocombe had "succeeded in twice seducing her" during their two-year romance. After those two times, Windeatt became pregnant, and so they did not risk a second mischance. William Smith testified that he had sex with Elizabeth Duxbury only twice after knowing her for over two years. These limited contacts were not unusual; John Gillis found the same basic pattern in his study of London servants between 1801 and 1900, a group who averaged only four sexual encounters.[8] Of course, the women may have been lying, trying to convince the jury of their innocence, but the men seldom contradicted them, even though it was in their interest to do so. Clearly, intercourse was an important step and a big risk, not to be taken lightly, though not taboo.

In addition, premarital intercourse was infrequent because the couple were rarely able to use their own rooms. Because so much of the courtship happened in the homes of the couple's parents, privacy was at a premium. Of course, in those cases in which the couple lodged together (for example, when the plaintiff was the defendant's housekeeper, landlady, or servant), opportunities for intimacy were easier to find. In other cases the couple did not become intimate until they took a trip alone together, either for entertainment or to make arrangements for the marriage. For instance, Annie Hooper claimed that William Stokes seduced her when she met him to look at an empty house they planned to buy. Similarly, Pryce Griffiths was unable to have sex with his young cousin until she visited his home in Liverpool.[9]

Although some of the cases indicated male pressure and female acquiescence, others demonstrate a mutual desire for intimacy. In particular, some couples worked together to find times and places to be alone. Since bedrooms were unavailable, they used other rooms in the house. Elizabeth Morris and Thomas Bonville had intercourse in the parlor of Bonville's home after his father had gone to bed. Ann Rees and David Powell also used the private parlor of her parents' house, which Ann carefully locked each time they sat alone together. At other times couples did not try to use their parents' homes. Mary Wilkinson claimed that William Hampson had sex with her in a railway carriage between Manchester and Leigh; even more inventively, Esther Dales and Andrew McMaster used the harness room of the stables that Andrew rented from Esther's employer. Walks offered another opportunity, since most couples took strolls together at some time in their courtship, and several of them took advantage of the relative privacy.[10]

The couple actually enjoyed the use of a bed in two circumstances. Most frequently, the man invited the woman to his house and then urged her to anticipate the wedding date. For example, Frances Owen visited Herbert Lawley's mother shortly after the two became formally engaged (they had known each other five years). They had intercourse while under his mother's roof; however, Lawley then almost immediately deserted Owen, to her dismay. Less frequently, the couple had sex at the woman's home when her family was absent. Ernest Olden and Kate Curtis did so at her father's house one afternoon when the latter was out. Agnes Barrow and William Twist resisted having inter-course until one day when both her sister and mother were gone. There were also a few cases in which the couple met at hotels or pubs, although these were rare.[11] Generally, most courting couples waited many months, had sex infrequently, and did so in hastily improvised conditions. Though sometimes men initiated the sexual contact, many women cooperated fully, enjoying sexual agency denied to most middle-class spinsters and widows.

If premarital sex was not uncommon, why did these couples end up apart? Much like the women forced to go to the Foundling Hospital, lower middle- and upper working-class women were victims of economic difficulties or class differences that interrupted the normal path of their courtships.[12] In better situa-tions the men might have married their pregnant fiancées before their children received the stigma of illegitimacy. However, a variety of problems led many men to postpone weddings, and this wait was often fatal. William Hurst, for instance, put off marrying Ann Hopley for two years because of economic rea-sons. Only a month after she had his daughter, William wrote that his "pros-pects" were too "gloomy" to consider marriage. Ann, urged by her brother, sued him. Most often, though, differences arose from family objections because of class conflict. Ellen Wood, the daughter of an innkeeper, and John Irving, a "statesman with property," endured long separations because of the opposition of his father. After several years, John married someone else, even though he had a child with Ellen.[13]

Despite occasional desertions, most men also saw sexual intercourse as a sign of commitment and a semi-normal part of courtship. Though they did not marry their lovers, the men almost always tried to help them through their confinements. Richard Denning wrote out two formal memoranda to Mary Capron "promising to pay the expenses of the confinement, to maintain the child, and to marry the mother." He also promised to leave £200 to her at his death and £10 a year for the child. The defendant in *Sherratt v. Webster* even agreed to pay an annuity for his child. If the defendant did not volunteer, the plaintiff's family often sued him for weekly support payments through the local magistrates, a process called affiliation. Despite the New Poor Law of 1834, there were still limited opportunities for getting support, and this act did not bar the woman from also suing for breach of promise. Agnes Nixon's father and Elizabeth Swift's brother both insisted that the women's children be affiliated. Neither defendant denied paternity, and both paid.[14] In short, though some men had to be prompted, many at least admitted that they should do something for the mothers of their children, even if they did not always follow through.[15]

Although many men stood by their fiancées, others deserted them as soon as they heard of the pregnancy and in spite of many years of companionship.

The ending of these relationships could be surprisingly cruel, and it requires some explication. Ann Sheppard had been engaged to Henry Forder for two years before they had intercourse in March 1877. Their sexual intimacy continued until March 1878, when Ann told him she was going to have a child. Henry was annoyed but decided he would have to marry her. Nevertheless, he changed his mind at the last minute, refusing to see her again. Eliza Heal and William Nicholls saw each other off and on for ten years before they became intimate in October 1896. Yet he grew cool and would not return her letters when she told him she was pregnant, and he married another woman by mid-1897. These women felt grossly betrayed by men who had professed great love for them. Frances Owen, who had known Herbert Lawley for six years and had been engaged to him for a year before she had intercourse with him, was devastated when he deserted her almost at once. When she became pregnant, she wrote several letters to him, and her bewilderment and despair are evident: "Let our child be born in wedlock I will never ask any more from you but your name if you wish after the child is born I will go away . . . Oh God have mercy on me for I do not think I am in my right mind."[16]

What would cause a man to desert his longtime lover when she needed him the most? At times, the sexual double standard came into play. Once the plaintiff agreed to sex with the defendant, she failed a crucial character test by proving unchaste. In other words, some men were ambiguous about female sexuality. Although assuming that premarital sex was fairly usual, they still lost respect for women who indulged in such behavior. John Jennings told Catherine Hamer that he did not want to marry her because of their religious differences, but also because she had fallen with him. Lizzie Eldridge claimed that William Rees "tried to insult her twice," but she stopped him. Rather than being angry, she claimed that "he said he was glad to find she was 'a brick.'" It never occurred to William that his actions made him in any way ineligible for marriage, but had Lizzie agreed, she would not have been "a brick." And she still wanted to marry him enough to sue him when he jilted her.[17] In addition, the man's relatives saw the woman's fall as a reason not to marry, particularly if they had disapproved for some time.

However, in the majority of cases the actual sexual intercourse was not the breaking point: only when the plaintiffs became pregnant did the men leave. This was the pattern that Barret-Ducrocq also found in her study of the Foundling Hospital records.[18] The imminent arrival of a child brought the relationship to a crisis, since the couple could no longer make do with vague promises of marriage sometime in the future. Understandably, the woman wanted to marry before the child was branded a bastard and she was disgraced. The man then had to decide if he were going to fulfill his promise. For a number of reasons, many men temporized. Sometimes the pregnancy came before the couple had completed their preparations for marriage—for example, before the man felt he could support a family. Alternatively, if the man had promised insincerely or thoughtlessly, he found himself tied to more responsibility than he had expected. Moreover, the woman's relatives got involved at this stage, demanding protection for their kin. All these pressures came to bear on the relationship, and the men often repudiated their fiancées rather than marry too soon or without enough affection.

Women's risk of unwed motherhood rose sharply with men they did not know well or with whom they enjoyed sex too soon. As Christine Stansell points out, women were always at a disadvantage in sexual bargaining, because the bargain was not between equals. These disadvantages grew greater with a virtual stranger, since his feelings of responsibility and affection were lessened.[19] Many couples met and became engaged quickly, just as quickly had intercourse, and then split as soon as the woman became pregnant. Most of the men left even before the child was born. In these cases the marriage proposal was presumably a ploy to persuade the woman to allow sexual intimacy. Women agreed, either because they desired the contact or because they hoped for a permanent bond. Despite the lack of a clear courtship in some of these relationships, juries tended to lump these women in with the other victims of male perfidy, seduced in spite of themselves, thereby ignoring the female sexual agency that such short relationships clearly indicated.

Indeed, although some of these women were certainly victims of fraud, they were not passive sexual partners. Carlotta Hutley, an actress, met Sidney Master, a club owner, in August 1893. Sidney proposed marriage a month later, and they had sex soon enough that Carlotta was pregnant in January 1894 (an independent witness at the trial verified the engagement). She, apparently, had few doubts about their relationship. Unfortunately, Master was already married and had four children, so he deserted her before her baby was born. Joseph Bell, a hatter and clothier, courted Ann Kelly, owner of a confectioner's shop, for a few weeks in late 1879. Ann claimed that he made "improper proposals" almost from the moment they met, but she resisted until he promised marriage. After that, she consented and was pregnant by February 1880. Only three months later Joseph broke off the engagement.[20] Both Sidney and Joseph apparently promised marriage (or at least pledged love) in order to persuade Carlotta and Ann to have intercourse. Both women in a sense were victims, but not passive ones. Kelly, in particular, held out against Bell's entreaties until he promised matrimony. She bargained for the proposal, hoping for a permanent relationship. In this case, because she knew him so slightly, she traded unwisely and had to settle for a monetary award.

One suspects, in cases such as these, that the men had no intention of marriage from the first; they promised simply to persuade their lovers to consent to sexual relations. Henry Sutton admitted his motive to Susannah Mallett's brother after he had intimacies with her for three years and then decamped as soon as she had a child. Mallett angrily pointed out to Sutton that he had promised to marry Susannah, and Henry replied that of course he had promised, but "all men do," and he had never meant it. Maurice Royston had sex with his servant, Jessie Mather, but insisted later that any talk of marriage had been in jest.[21] These actions indicate that the men knew the rules in courtship and were abusing them: they assumed that women would indeed fall if promised marriage. They also indicate that the women involved were apparently willing (if partly deluded) participants.

Naturally, not all women displayed the same degree of sexual agency. Some defendants used great psychological pressure to persuade the women to yield to their wishes, particularly as the date of the wedding neared. Dubinsky has found in nineteenth-century Canadian seduction cases that men coaxed women into sexual relations through a variety of mechanisms, and some breach-of-promise cases show similar machinations.[22] Maria Brookfield was a dressmaker who met Joseph Wilcock, a confectioner, because they lived and worked in the same town. They had known each other some time and became engaged in September 1869. In December Joseph invited Maria to his home. Early one morning he slipped into her room and persuaded her, by harping on the coming wedding date, to have sex. By using surprise and psychological pressure, Wilcock achieved his goal and quickly lost interest, especially after Brookfield became pregnant. Some men used both persuasion and willful deception. John Miller invited his fiancée to his home for a party, but when she arrived, she discovered that only he and his two children were there. They had intercourse that night, and he almost immediately left her.[23] These cases reveal duplicity and emotional pressure on the part of men, although still with some degree of female agency. The women presumably could have refused, but decided (unwisely in these cases) to participate.

In fact, the reluctance many women claimed to have indicates that they were aware of the dangers of desertion. The men succeeded in coaxing them only after several tries and especially only after a promise of marriage. Interestingly, the couples seem to have discussed the consequences of sex frankly, partly on the insistence of the women. Catherine Lewis stated that her lodger, John Jenkins, tried to seduce her three times before he finally succeeded. The only reason she eventually gave in, she said, was that the fourth time he promised to marry her. Robert Mitchell and Annie Grave actually split up once because of his "behaviour," but she gave in after they reconciled, since he assured her that "if anything took place he would make it all right and marry me."[24] Although some women might not have been as reluctant as they claimed, few would have taken such a serious risk without some guarantee in case of an unwanted pregnancy. For them, intercourse was a sign of long-term intimacy. They hoped for marriage, although, of course, such motives do not preclude enjoyment. But since women took all the risks and suffered the consequences, they had to be realistic when negotiating sexuality. As Stansell reminds us, women risked pregnancy first—before men had to follow through on marriage promises.[25] Women had to balance sexual agency and sexual danger; as a result, their responses to sexual overtures ranged from enthusiasm to reluctant acquiescence.

Whatever their responses to sexual choices, women seem to have believed that the men would honor the unwritten code: that if he promised, he would keep his word. As a consequence, most were desperate and bewildered at being left pregnant and unwed. Alice Spink begged John Lloyd to marry her; otherwise she did not see how she could face her father. Lloyd claimed he would not marry her without a more substantial dowry, but he ignored all of Spink's subsequent offers of income from her father. Although Alice miscarried, she was still disgraced. Ada Bennett's parents threw her out of the house when she became pregnant, and they took her back only when she became seriously ill. Furthermore, a woman's business was vulnerable to sexual scandal. Annie Grave, a milliner, wrote to Robert Mitchell that "the disgrace would fall very heavily upon her, especially in her business, where the better class of people came about." And Sarah Heywood lost her job as a servant after her intimacies with Albert Yeomans.[26] In short, an illegitimate child was such a disaster that few women would have agreed to risking one without some assurances of marriage, even if only vague ones. This conclusion is supported by the research of various historians of illegitimacy. Ann Higginbotham found that most unmarried mothers in London also insisted that men had promised them marriage before they allowed intimacies, and women forced to go to the Foundling Hospital told similar stories.[27] Indeed, the large numbers of breach-of-promise cases themselves show how seriously women took these betrayals.

Breach-of-promise cases, then, offer tentative suggestions of female agency in sexual relations. In general the testimony in the cases supports Gillis's insistence that "there is very little evidence of obsessive prudery or intense anxiety" about sexual intercourse among women, at least those of the lower middle and upper working classes. Indeed, their readiness to engage in sexual intimacy supports the revisionist view of Victorian sexuality in most recent historical work. Usually, women engaged in sexual intercourse only after a long period of courtship, but they do not appear to have been uninterested or difficult to persuade. However, they do seem to have had a firm idea of the dangers, which may have dimmed their pleasure, and most insisted on a commitment before taking such a risk. Thus, although I would not agree that the women's reluctance showed prudery or guilt on their part—as Barret-Ducrocq has argued—I would also not agree that women had sex with men purely through the rise of romantic love in courtship, as argued by Edward Shorter.[28] Instead, women walked a fine line between their desires and their prudence, making their sexual feelings necessarily ambiguous.

Most of the cases under study show no extremes of sexual behavior. Both women and men made decisions based on affection, future commitments, and degrees of trust, wisely or unwisely. However, a minority of cases show the limits of women's sexual freedom. First, a small number of cases involved sexual violence. Because of the difficulties of getting rape convictions in the nineteenth century, breach-of-promise actions may have seemed an attractive alternative to criminal charges. According to Carolyn Conley, respectable men were almost never convicted of rape; in particular, working women found it difficult to prove an assault against their employers.[29] Susan Edwards has suggested that middle-class women used breach-of-promise actions to repair their reputations after sexual assaults, particularly if the men were friends or relatives.[30] The evidence, however, supports a slightly different interpretation. For one thing, few rape victims in breach-of-promise actions were middle class (almost all were lower middle class), and none of their attackers were relatives or mere friends. The few cases that alleged force more closely resemble the modern crime of date rape. For the most part, these women were pressured or forced into sexual relations with men they courted. Since it was especially difficult to get a rape conviction if the woman were acquainted with her assailant, the circumstances encouraged them to explore other avenues than the criminal courts.

Only a minority of women accused their lovers of actual violence, but their feelings of betrayal were obvious. Elizabeth Beazor, a lady's outfitter, got engaged to David Gooch, son of a jeweler and pawnbroker, in 1867. One Sunday evening in July 1870 the couple were alone together in her parents' sitting room. David, as her counsel put it, "by violence committed a serious offence, for which . . . he might have been severely punished." Elizabeth was bedridden for eleven weeks. David expressed great remorse and promised marriage. Elizabeth became pregnant, but David then refused to marry her because of his father's opposition. Elizabeth's brother went to the Goochs' pawn shop and almost came to blows with the elder Gooch, but to no avail. Similarly, Caroline Williams insisted that the Reverend Frank Thomas "had obtained possession of her person by violence," an action verified by an independent witness. Despite entreaties from mutual friends, Thomas refused to marry her. Mary Nicholson claimed that on her second visit with David Maclachlan he "forcibly seduced" her. After the attack, she felt she had to marry him since her reputation was ruined (she was the stepdaughter of a clothier, and Maclachlan was a captain in the army). She had his child, and they communicated for three years until he married someone else.[31]

It is an interesting commentary on the position of women in Victorian Britain that these women wanted to marry men who had raped them. Many thought they had no choice. At least in their own minds, their attackers were the only men they could marry once they had been assaulted. Since the criminal courts were hostile to rape victims, many chose to regularize their relationships with the rapists. Indeed, the work of Gillis and Barret-Ducrocq shows that this reaction was not unusual.[32] The women felt violated, but they considered a wedding sufficient payment for the crime. They apparently adopted the traditional judicial view of women's chastity as property whose value was damaged by seduction. This loss was too serious to ignore, and women preferred to marry their attackers rather than have the burden of trying to overcome that stigma. Only when the rapist proved obdurate about matrimony did the woman turn to the civil courts.

Nevertheless, the use of breach-of-promise actions for rapes or other assaults was limited because the victim had to prove a promise of marriage. A rape by a stranger or even a friend, no matter how cruel, did not qualify a woman to sue. There had to be some kind of courtship and plans to marry. Moreover, the woman had to have material evidence to support her contentions. Justice Day nonsuited Mary Nicholson because he decided that she had no corroboration, despite several letters; he insisted, "I see nothing in those letters which suggests a promise to marry," only a promise to support the child.[33] Judges and juries were lenient about evidence for these cases, but they would not accept just anyone as a believable future husband for any plaintiff. Thus, again, the position of a rape victim in Victorian England was weak; the courts supported only special cases, even on the civil side. Indeed, juries may have feared opening up the defendant to a criminal charge and so strictly interpreted the evidence of a prior relationship.

Certainly, however, Edwards is right in that many breach-of-promise actions covered "cases of rather more serious seduction, where the women concerned had been cajoled or emotionally blackmailed into physical subjection." For example, Susannah Brown, who was eighteen years old when she brought her suit, was engaged to William Friend, thirty-three. One afternoon he "succeeded, notwithstanding her entreaties, in seducing her, quieting her fears by saying that he would be a good husband." Her mother was distressed, but William insisted that the action was his doing alone, admitting that "she begged me not to do so." Within days, he had deserted Brown, and she brought suit against him and won. In Victorian England the only other alternatives to rape charges were suits for seduction or prosecutions of married men who seduced young women under the Criminal Law Amendment Act of 1885.[34] Both of these alternatives were limited, the first because only a parent could sue for seduction and he or she had to prove "loss of service." The second was limited to married men and young women. Thus, for women like Brown, breach of promise could remedy an otherwise bleak situation.

Rape was the ultimate limit to women's sexual freedom, for male aggression highlighted the dangers for women in sexuality. At the other extreme, female sexual aggression was equally problematic for breach-of-promise plaintiffs. Women who enjoyed sex and pursued it found juries largely unsympathetic to their claims for compensation. Indeed, the sources are mostly silent on this matter, since female plaintiffs tried to hide any sexual agency, fearing— correctly—that their cases would fail if they appeared assertive. Nevertheless, many women obviously took some initiative in sexuality, even if only locking the parlor door, like Ann Rees. And a few cases had enthusiastically active plaintiffs. Mary Williams, the daughter of a farmer, claimed that her fiancé, Captain Mathias, had seduced her at her father's house a year after they became engaged. All the same, Williams admitted under cross-examination that she sat on Mathias's knee the first time she met him and that she wrote him letters that invited him over to her house as late as midnight. This behavior does not indicate bashfulness, and her counsel hurriedly agreed to settle the case. Ellen Roberts, daughter of a farmer, met Hugh Hughes, also a farmer, late at night when he came and tapped on her bedroom window. They sometimes sat up all night: "he had been seen coming out of the house at five o'clock in the morning."[35] In neither of these situations did the woman seem coy about late-night spooning. Some women also admitted to "frequent intercourse," rather than to the infrequent encounters of the majority. Charlotte Ball and W. H. Spickett had continual sexual relations over their nine-month engagement; Maria Levens, too, was intimate with Edward Hutton throughout their three years together.[36]

Any woman who had been openly sexually aggressive or who had some sexual experience did not receive the usual kindly response from the court. Although all women used their sexuality to bargain for a better future, some were more obvious about it, and they seldom garnered rewards. A good example of this is *Wiedemann v. Walpole* in 1891. Valerie Wiedemann met Robert Walpole at a hotel in Constantinople in 1882 where she was a governess and he was on holiday. She claimed they got engaged after eight days of courtship. After the proposal, the two had sexual intercourse, which resulted in Wiedemann losing her job. She had to leave her hotel room, so she stayed with Robert for four days. He then gave her £100 and left for England. The two did not see each other again, although Wiedemann made it a point to meet Walpole's mother and to resist all of his efforts to get back his signet ring. She later had a child and supported herself, periodically writing threatening letters to him. When Robert married someone else in 1887, she sued.

The first jury found for the defendant. Wiedemann managed to get an order for a new trial, apparently on the grounds that several of her witnesses had not been questioned. The second jury could not agree, however, so the principals went through yet another trial. This time Wiedemann won £300, despite the fact that her story had changed in each trial (she was unsure, for example, of her child's sex or if it were alive or dead). Walpole appealed, and the Court of Queen's Bench overturned the decision on the grounds that there was no material evidence of the promise. Whatever Walpole's behavior, Wiedemann was no mere victim. She knew how to use the courts, holding on to the signet ring for nine years and through four trials.[37] If in the end she did not win, she at least put Walpole through as much trouble as she could.

Wiedemann's case was not unique, nor was the outcome of her trial. A number of sexually assertive women sued for breach of promise, usually after a brief sexual liaison, and with poor results. Madge Hirst, a widow, got £50 from Humphrey Waddington for a child that did not exist and then sued him for breach of promise. She had to withdraw the action because of a lack of evidence. Emmeline Hairs was an "adventuress" who had to leave Paris because of her part in a scandal involving the sale of war decorations. In 1887 she began a sexual affair with Sir George Elliot, an M.P. She persuaded him to invest £3,000 in her coal business, and when he cooled toward her, she took him to court. Elliot admitted at the trial that he had seen her only twice before having sex with her at Brown's Hotel, and he appeared more broken up by the illicit connection than Hairs. This suit ended in a hung jury.[38]

In other instances the women may have expected marriage, but their sexual overtures ruined their chances as well as injuring their court cases. Sarah Anne Harrison and Henry Sherlock apparently wrote sexually explicit letters to one another during their four-year association. In addition, Henry claimed that Sarah went with him to a hotel in Manchester the day after they met; she then invited herself into his room. After he came back from a business trip, they had sexual relations regularly. Sarah got the derisory award of one farthing from the jury. Both Anne Palmer and Esther Dales had illegitimate children with men other than the defendants between their breakups with the latter and the trials. In the case of Palmer, Baron Bramwell stopped the trial, calling it "about the most impudent scheme he had ever heard of." However, Justice Day pitied

Dales and blamed Andrew McMaster, her seducer, for her subsequent conduct. Esther actually got £400, despite her second fall, but this was an unusually generous judge and jury.[39]

Occasionally, too, the woman was the mistress of her lover, either because he was married or because class differences made this arrangement sensible. Eileen Blum, the daughter of a dressmaker, met George Reeve, a soldier, in the street. After three weeks, she went into new lodgings so that he could spend the night with her. She was already the mistress of another man but decided to live with Reeve instead. Reeve eventually left the army, and she lost touch with him. He admitted promising marriage but claimed that she was a prostitute, which she denied. She won £30 but would probably have received more had she not been sexually experienced, particularly since Reeve admitted his promise. May Gore was for some years the mistress of Lord Sudley, as well as being the mistress of another man in between her liaisons with Sudley. When she tried to sue for breach of promise, her experienced past weakened her case and the suit failed.[40]

In many of these cases the relationship teetered between the fairly steady position of mistress and the insecurity of a prostitute. Prostitutes were notoriously poorly treated by the Victorian courts, for, as Walkowitz and Constance Backhouse have shown, they were considered public women who could not be assaulted.[41] Any plaintiff associated with prostitution, then, had a poor chance of success. Despite her outward respectability as the widow of an officer, Mrs. Thatcher's lover, Colonel D'Aguilar, admitted, "I looked upon Mrs. Thatcher, I won't say as a common prostitute, but I certainly did look upon her as a prostitute." Indeed, her own daughter "spoke of several gentlemen coming to see her mother, and of a Mr. Granville on one occasion stopping all night," thus effectively ending her case. The roommate of the plaintiff in *Irvine v. Vickers* admitted that several men, including the defendant, called on the plaintiff and used to give her money. Justice Piggott, in disgust, said "he had no sympathy either with the plaintiff or defendant" in such a case. Women with respectable characters often had to fight off suggestions that their lodgings were brothels. Ellen Gardner's landlady was strictly cross-examined about the nature of her house, and the defense counsel's insinuations were clear, although in this case they failed.[42] Though sometimes the defense counsel made unfounded accusations, then, these cases reemphasized the dangers of too blatantly disproving expectations of female "passionlessness."

In fact, any woman with a sexual past, even one who was completely respectable, was open to accusations of sexual aggression. Widows, ironically, had less sexual freedom than spinsters. Judges and juries were much more stringent with them for several reasons. First, most judges and jurors believed that widows, having been awakened to sexual feeling, would want intercourse again. At least for lower middle- and upper working-class women, this idea persisted, belying the allegedly common Victorian assumption of disinterest in sex on the part of "good" women. Second, widows were seen as predatory, always looking for the next husband. Third, and most important, people expected widows to know what they were doing and to protect themselves. One can plainly divine these assumptions in the language describing sex in these cases, because it was not passive. Instead of the man seducing an innocent girl, the barristers said instead that the couple "became very intimate," or a "connection took place between them," or even the fairly active phrasing, "she admitted him to closer intimacy."[43] Widows seldom won large awards, then, since they should have known better.

The one exception to this rule of experience were couples who had co-habited for many years. Most couples had sexual relations for brief periods of time, but a minority had intimate relationships for extended periods. These people lived as though married for several years but never actually went through the ceremony. Eventually, however, the man deserted the woman, who was often left with children to care for. She sued for breach of promise to recover support for herself and the children. As Stephen Parker and Chris Barton have pointed out, cohabitants' legal rights were whittled away in the nineteenth century, including claims on maintenance, insurance, and charitable bequests.[44] But that does not mean, as both have implied, that they were invisible in the law courts. Instead, deserted cohabitants found a sympathetic hearing as breach-of-promise plaintiffs. They were able to claim seduction because, at least before the cohabitation, they were virtuous.

Cohabitation, or "living tally," was not uncommon among the working classes, even in the late nineteenth century. Both men and women had reasons to prefer it to marriage, although the penalties of illegitimacy had risen so high that it was less common as the century progressed.[45] Even some lower middle- and middle-class women participated in cohabiting relationships. Maria Harworth was the daughter of a butcher and was studying to be a schoolteacher when she met Albert Taylor, a cotton spinner who owned part of a mill, in 1880. Just before she was to leave town to take her first job, Albert persuaded her to go away with him. They lived as husband and wife for several years "at various watering places" and had two children, both registered as legitimate. Albert was a good husband when sober, but he beat Maria when he was drunk. He left her twice, the final time in May 1885, and she sued to get support for the children. The resulting trial was much like a divorce hearing, since Albert's defense was that she had been unfaithful. The jury believed Maria, awarding her £1,600. Jane Tamikin, who lived with Lowther Wilson for several years and had his son, owned a grocery shop (Wilson was an "engine man" with property).[46] Neither of these women were working class, and both claimed to have been ruined when too young to know better.

Another reason these women engendered sympathy was that they were often induced into pseudo-marriages by deception. Hannah Maddocks, twice widowed (her last husband had been a cook and she had a small business), met Benjamin Bennett, a butcher and cattle dealer, on a carriage ride to the markets in 1888. They began seeing each other, and she soon moved to Flint with him as one of his tenants. Maddocks was content until a neighbor warned her that Bennett already had a wife and children. When confronted, he admitted the deception, and Maddocks got £275 in the subsequent trial. Frances Jennie Day, daughter of a postal inspector, went through two phony marriage ceremonies with Morris Roberts, a hotel proprietor, before he ejected her from their home. She did not discover his first wife was still living until she was denied maintenance after their separation.[47]

Though there were a few middle-class cases, most cohabitants were working-class women, usually involved with men who were wealthier. These cases divide into two groups. First are couples who chose to live together rather than marry (for whatever reason), and when they broke up, the women sued to get support for their children. These relationships lasted many years. Jane Elliot met James Stranger when she went to work on his farm as a dairy woman. They courted for a few months, and she had his child; afterward they lived together until 1875. Stranger, meanwhile, gave Elliot £100 in support of the child. In 1875 he met another woman, and he turned Jane and her child out of the house. The couple in *Dixon v. Brearley* knew each other for thirty years and had several children together before Brearley jilted Dixon (she was his servant, and he was a farmer).[48]

These women had no legal claim on their pseudo-husbands, despite several years of cohabitation. They could have sued in the magistrates court, but affiliation proceedings were highly restricted, and the amounts received from successful suits were small.[49] Breach of promise gave women another option, a way to get substantial amounts of cash fairly soon. In this way the suit acted as a kind of rough divorce court (or, in a twentieth-century alternative, a palimony suit). Sympathetic juries accepted the woman's word that she had lived with a man for many years only because he had promised marriage and awarded damages to help keep her off the poor rates. Judges, as well, could have dismissed these cases for lack of evidence but did not, apparently believing that the man owed the woman support.

The second kind of pseudo-marriage case was similar to the first. The difference was that the couple did not actually live together. Though their relationship spanned several years and included the birth of children, both parties lived independently and the women supported themselves with occasional help from the men. In all of these cases family opposition and class differences precluded marriage. For example, Ellen McCarthy, a mill operative, had a long relationship with Alfred Rowbotham, the mill manager. They became intimate when she first went to the mill at the age of sixteen, and she had two children with him, whom he supported. In 1890 he married someone else, admitting that his mother had always disliked his arrangement with Ellen, and his new spouse was more acceptable. In *Dean v. Hollins* the defendant began a sexual relationship with the plaintiff when she was sixteen. They knew each other because they were neighboring farmers (though he was wealthier), and they had five children over the next fourteen years. Yet both of them remained on their own farms. In other cases the couple had social considerations as well as economic differences that led them to conceal their irregular unions. Thomas Speakerman was a minister and May Hope had been a Sunday School teacher, but, despite a thirteen-year relationship (and two children), they never lived together for obvious reasons.[50] Although these pseudo-marriages worked well as long as both of the couple were content, they turned into grave hardships for the women when the men left. Juries and judges recognized this and provided funds to allow the women to rebuild their lives after the end of relationships longer than some marriages.

Women, then, could collect, but they had to pass certain character tests. Strictures of virtue for successful plaintiffs are all too common to feminist historians of the Victorian courts. Plaintiffs were either "good girls" or "bad girls," a false dichotomy that obscured the array of sexual choices open to women and the wide variety of their responses.[51] All the same, at least the good girls in breach-of-promise cases did not have to be completely chaste; a woman who fell only with her fiancé was considered a victim. In deciding the outcome and setting damages, juries made no distinction between sexually active women and those who had remained chaste; the median awards for both were £100. Only in rare cases did the juries find for the defendants. Judges, too, were largely sympathetic to female plaintiffs. Thus, although the courts persisted in seeing good women as passive, they rewarded them for their aggressive use of the courts.

Backhouse and Anna Clark, among others, have characterized the law courts as hegemonic patriarchal structures, penalizing women and condoning male sexual aggression.[52] Certainly, in cases of rape or criminal seduction the courts belittled or ignored men's violation of women. But in the civil courts judges and juries believed women's claims more readily. Backhouse has argued that seduction suits rewarded fathers rather than women, which explained their higher success rate. But this explanation will not work for breach of promise. Plaintiffs in breach-of-promise suits brought the action in their own names and collected the damages themselves. Women entered the male public space of the courtroom and displayed aggression that flatly contradicted their roles as passive victims of male lust. Yet juries consistently found for them.

Numerous factors explain the peculiar success rate of breach of promise. First, the case was a civil action, which meant that even if found guilty, the defendant would not go to prison. Jurymen were more willing to assess damages than to jail a man for sexual misbehavior. Second, jurors were of the same class as most principals and may well have accepted the courtship norms demonstrated by the cases. They apparently agreed with women that a fall under a promise of marriage was different than promiscuity. Third, breach-of-promise cases were not specifically about the sex act; indeed, 75 percent of them did not involve sexual relationships. Most of the evidence dealt with the courtship, the promise, and the breach, not with sex. The sexual act was a peripheral event to the real issues at hand.

But the most important reason was that the language of the cases insisted on female passivity: the active male seduced the passive female. Over and over, barristers simply said that "she was seduced," or "the defendant succeeded in seducing her," or "the defendant took advantage of her," or "she gave in to him." In one case the plaintiff's barrister characterized the relationship by saying that "the defendant not only made himself master of the plaintiff's affections, but he made himself master of her person."[53] As long as the woman had been a virgin before her liaison with her first lover, then, she was assumed to be seduced rather than an equally willing partner. If she became pregnant, her barrister invariably described this in euphemisms as well, almost always adding the word "unfortunate."[54] "Unfortunately" the plaintiff "found herself in an interesting condition," or "became in the family way" (or he skipped mention of the pregnancy altogether, saying, "a child was born from the intimacy"). In this wording the woman had no active role: she was a vessel and a victim. Though this characterization ignored the plaintiffs' activity and sexuality, it aided them in appealing for damages.

In cases involving sexual intercourse, juries gave women lower awards or found for the defendant in only two scenarios. First, as stated above, in courtships in which the woman was too sexually aggressive, juries reduced the awards. The second reason that juries gave low awards was when they believed that the plaintiffs were mature enough to defend their own honor. Widows or not, older women should know how to fend off improper advances. Mrs. Wheeler, about fifty years old, had sex with her fiancé from the beginning of their acquaintance, and the jury believed the defendant's contention that she did not run a respectable house and so found for him. Similarly, Ann Farrow had no success with her story of seduction since she was a widow with eighteen children.[55]

Other than in these two instances, juries and judges sympathized with seduced women. They assumed that the plaintiffs were passive victims, giving in to their fiancés' demands, as may indeed have been the case in some relationships. Men occasionally tried to paint the women as sexually aggressive, but this ploy had little success. Ellen Roberts, who had let her lover into her home at night, had to defend herself against the defense barrister's claim that her relationship with Hugh Hughes was merely a sexual affair. The judge, too, summed up for the defendant. But the jury found for Ellen with damages of £250. Ellen was twenty years younger than Hugh and had never gone with any other man; this was enough, apparently, for the jury to assume her passivity.[56] Though many of the courtships show a canny use of sexuality by women and indeed some enthusiasm, most men in the courtrooms could not fathom such ambiguity. To them, either the woman was a victim of male aggression and deserving, or she was sexually active and undeserving. Though this division was harmful in the long run, it shielded some plaintiffs against counteraccusations of defendants.

Despite the sexual double standard of the Victorian era, then, juries and judges were largely lenient with fallen women, at least if they had done so for the first time and under a promise of marriage. They believed in female chastity, but they also insisted that men bear part of the burden for sexual activity. In this way breach of promise was part of a large-scale resistance to the harsh aspects of the New Poor Law's bastardy clause. Clearly, as many historians have discovered, there was a limit to men's sexual freedom, despite their advantages. As Dubinsky found, men were lectured about chivalry and self-control, even when they were acquitted of seduction charges.[57] In breach-of-promise cases juries found for women frequently, sometimes with fairly questionable evidence, probably because they believed in male sexual responsibility. For instance, Agnes Richards had a two-year sexual relationship with Robert Palmer that began when she was seventeen (he was ten years older), which she claimed was based upon a promise of marriage. Her only corroboration was the evidence of her brother, who said that he heard Robert say once that he was going to marry Agnes. The defense barrister insisted that this was an immoral relationship and blamed Richards, but the judge said that "he could not see any difference between the immorality of the girl and the immorality of the man." This was a surprisingly egalitarian view of the need for chastity in the sexes, and the jury agreed, awarding Richards £200.[58]

In fact, in a few cases the sexual history of the defendant damaged his case, rather than the more common reverse situation. One of the things that hurt William Hampson in his defense against Mary Wilkinson was his bad reputation. Wilkinson's mother "told him that she did not approve of him. He was not a respectable man, for he had sown a deal of wild oats in his time, and she did not want him to sow any at her door." When Mary became pregnant, William deserted her. After hearing such a tale, the judge summed up firmly against him, and the jury fined him £600. When Eli Bowers asked to court Annie Blakeman, her father was dubious and warned Bowers "that he must be straightforward in his conduct, and the reason was that the defendant was somewhat of a flirt . . . he had shown a disposition to 'flutter from flower to flower.'" When Bowers jilted Blakeman for another woman, she won £2,000.[59] Although men's sexual freedom was greater than that of women, they could not always escape unscathed when they behaved irresponsibly, at least as long as the women could sue for breach of promise. In this way the action undermined the sexual double standard prevalent in trials of rape or seduction.

Ironically, then, though the language in the cases stressed female passivity and lack of agency, the court case actually encouraged women to fight for themselves. When their fiancés broke the unwritten rules of lower middle- and upper working-class courtship, these women demanded, and received, monetary compensation. Seduced women could almost always expect some kind of award, even if they could not achieve marriage. These cases show that there was nothing monolithic about the Victorian demand for chastity and passionlessness in women or indulgence for men's sexual peccadillos, nor were the courts simple hegemonic patriarchal structures. Young women put themselves forward as victims of male lust and thus not really guilty. Widows were calmly assumed to be sexually aware. Men, on the other hand, were roundly criticized and fined for sexual misconduct and even had their pasts examined in a few cases.

Even more important, the relationships of these couples indicate that premarital sexual intercourse was a normal part of courtship in the lower middle and upper working classes; women used their sexuality to negotiate for improved positions in life and quicker marriages. Servants, small business owners, milliners, and teachers could easily lose their jobs and businesses due to an ill-considered romance; their reputations could be ruined; and they might be stigmatized as the mothers of illegitimate children. They appear to be the class of people with the most to lose from an unwanted pregnancy. Thus, the conventions of sexual freedom between engaged couples must have been widely accepted for so many to risk so much. Indeed, women's indignation at men's betrayals is evident from their use of the civil courts when the convention broke down. Breach of promise was not an overturning of sexual mores; it worked like the divorce court, correcting the worst abuses without actually changing the system. But it offered more than most other actions to keep the men from having it all their own way in the "bad time for the girls" of the late nineteenth century.[60]

VII

Four Case Studies, 1846–1916

THE PRECEDING CHAPTERS have dealt with breach-of-promise cases in a broad way. Though revealing, categorization into types sometimes masks the individual tragedies and comedies so many of these suits also illustrate. To correct this skewed perception, we must concentrate on a few well-documented trials. The four case studies explored in this chapter are in no way typical. Selected because their records are unusually explicit, they are about people in the higher classes or deal with legal issues that led to protracted trials. Despite their peculiarities, however, they illustrate several of the themes of breach-of-promise actions, especially the importance of parental consent and the pervasiveness of class considerations. In every case the couple came from different classes and one or both sets of parents objected. Moreover, the cases demonstrate the varied outcomes of trials, including victories for both the plaintiff and the defendant, and successful and unsuccessful appeals. The cases range widely in time: one before 1850, two from the late-Victorian period, and one from the early twentieth century. They show breach-of-promise cases in detail, an opportunity not often available despite the wide press coverage of these actions.

On February 14, 1846, the case of *Smith v. Ferrers* came to trial in the Queen's Bench Division in London under Justice Wightman. The plaintiff was Mary Elizabeth Smith, twenty-one, the daughter of a small farmer in Austrey, Staffordshire. The defendant was Washington Sewallis Shirley, Earl Ferrers, twenty-four, the son and heir of a noble family who owned manors in both Staffordshire and Leicestershire. In many ways this case was peculiar. First, the defendant was of the upper class, and the nobility usually settled such matters out of court. Second, it was highly publicized, yet happened earlier in the century than the boom in breach-of-promise actions. Third, the outcome was unexpected, and, because of the contradictory nature of the evidence, hard to evaluate.[1]

Smith's story was as follows. She first met Ferrers in 1839 when she was fourteen and he was seventeen; he was living with his tutor, a Mr. Echalaz, and the couple saw each other often. They fell in love, but the differences in their station made both of their families uneasy. Ferrers's parents sent him abroad from 1840 to 1842, while Smith went to school in London and France. In 1842 they both returned to Austrey and began to court again, writing to each other frequently. They eventually set a wedding date for May 1844, although they postponed it twice, first to July and then August. In the meantime Mary bought several items for herself, such as books and clothing, all of which she claimed that Ferrers had given her as gifts. He never paid for them, though, and Smith's father and grandfather footed the bills. Nor did Ferrers agree to meet her parents, despite coming to her home on a few occasions. In July 1844, as the wedding date approached, Smith got two letters from Ferrers's brother, warning her that Washington was seriously ill. He was perfectly well, however, and married Augusta Chichester a few days later. Mary learned of the wedding by reading the announcement in the newspaper. She was deeply hurt, and her male relatives urged her to sue.

Smith's primary evidence consisted of twelve letters allegedly written to her by the earl, testimony from a few townspeople who saw the two of them together (although never very close) as well as friends who posted letters to him on her behalf, and a ring she claimed he gave her as a token (he denied this). Since neither of the parties was allowed to testify in breach-of-promise cases before 1869, the burden of testimony for the plaintiff rested on her mother and sister. Mrs. Smith stoutly insisted that all that her daughter claimed was true, although she admitted that she had never met Ferrers and that her daughter kept running up bills with local tradespeople that he never paid. Mrs. Smith also testified that the twelve letters her daughter submitted as evidence were not in Mary's handwriting (and therefore not forged), but she did identify four mysterious letters submitted by the defense counsel as being in the hand of her daughter. Mary's sister Ann, thirteen, claimed to have seen Washington at her parents' house twice during 1843. Mary's case ended with the reading of the twelve letters that Washington had allegedly sent to her in 1843 and 1844.

Ferrers told an entirely different story. He claimed to have hardly known Smith and never to have courted her. His counsel was Frederick Thesiger, the future attorney general, and Thesiger insisted that the entire action was a plot from beginning to end. Smith conceived a hero worship for the earl at an impressionable age and wrote letters to herself to try to prove it. She also bought presents for herself, claiming that Ferrers would pay for them. Of course, he never did so since he did not know her. The lies started out small, but built over time, until Mary could not deny the relationship without humiliating herself. Thesiger pointed out the weakness of much of the evidence: the letters had no postage on them (she claimed they were hand delivered); Mary's parents had never met Ferrers; no one had seen them in any intimate contact; and she had bought every "gift" for herself.

Ferrers's main defense, however, centered on their correspondence, since the twelve letters that he supposedly sent to Smith were totally ridiculous. They contained people that did not exist, discussed political issues on the wrong dates, put Ferrers in places he could prove he had not been, called pets and friends by the wrong names, and were generally nonsensical. The plaintiff's counsel explained the peculiarities of these epistles by saying that Ferrers had a "strangely wild imagination" and an imperfect education.[2] Smith insisted later that Ferrers wrote so much foolishness because he wanted to protect himself and because he wanted to enhance "his own importance in my eyes."[3] The most logical explanation, though, was that they were written by someone who knew nothing about the earl. William Devereaux Shirley, Ferrers's brother, also testified for him; he denied ever meeting or writing to Mary, since the times he supposedly did so he was in Scotland with his regiment.

The climax of the case came on the third day, when Thesiger presented his strongest evidence. He admitted that he had still not explained why so many of Smith's friends testified to sending letters to Ferrers from her. The explanation, he insisted, was that Smith had been sending Ferrers anonymous letters for years. The earl had burned most of them, but he still had four, and these four were the mysterious letters that Mrs. Smith had identified as her daughter's handwriting. The letters clearly came from someone who admired Ferrers but did not know him. A typical passage from one dated March 3, 1844, was as follows: "It is, I am aware, unmaidenly thus to write; but you know not the writer, and it is to that one a solace and comfort to tell you how much she loves you."[4] Smith, in a pamphlet written after the trial, admitted to writing the four letters, claiming that she wrote them "as a mere girlish frolic" to try to induce Ferrers to come to a ball and later to ascertain if he were interested in anyone else.[5] Presented with this new evidence, the plaintiff's counsel withdrew from the case, and Smith was nonsuited. The trial thus ended with a victory for the defendant.

At first sight the case against Smith seems airtight. However, there are several unexplained aspects of both parties' evidence. First, if Smith barely knew Ferrers, how did she acquire a sample of his handwriting with which to forge the letters? They were good enough forgeries to fool five different witnesses who testified to their authenticity. And, if she did forge them, why invent people and places at all? Why not write only of love and keep the times and places vague? Furthermore, if she were plotting to trap Ferrers, why not post at least one letter from the local post office so that it would appear to come from him? Surely someone clever enough to concoct an elaborate plot would have thought of such an obvious ploy. Also, were the townspeople who witnessed the two of them walking together to be completely discounted? What possible motive could they have to lie? Most of them barely knew Smith and had more to gain by keeping on the right side of the local peer. And why did neither side call the main intermediary between the two, a servant named Joseph Adkins? Surely he could say whether or not he delivered the letters. Smith claimed she did not call him because he received a pension from Ferrers and would have lied to keep it, but the defendant gave no explanation at all.[6] Finally, could a fourteen-year-old girl really start a plot to trap a nobleman and continue consistently with this plot for six years? Thesiger claimed that Mrs. Smith was a party to the plot, but since she was ignorant of large parts of her daughter's actions, this was at best unproved.

Susan Edwards has argued that Smith was the victim of an unsympathetic male court system, but probably neither side was being entirely truthful.[7] It was quite possible that in 1839, when both parties were very young, Mary and Washington had a brief courtship (or friendship). Perhaps also during that time Smith obtained samples of Ferrers's handwriting, or he may have written a few of the nonsensical letters himself. They were then separated for two years, and Ferrers forgot all about her, while Smith continued to nurture her feelings. When they met again, he was no longer interested in romance, while she wanted to resume relations. Possibly, the townspeople saw them together during that time because Smith tried to initiate contact on various occasions. It was most likely at this point that Smith began to fabricate her romance with the earl, writing colorful letters to herself (or bringing out the old letters he had composed), sending anonymous letters to pique his interest, and running up expensive bills at local stores. She may have so convinced herself of the reality of the romance that she was genuinely shocked when Ferrers married. And, having committed herself thus far, she could not refuse when her male relatives insisted that she sue. Although this interpretation does not explain everything, it does clear up most of the puzzling points. Smith lied, but Ferrers was also probably less than frank.

Whatever the truth of the matter, *Smith* became a byword among legal writers as an example of the abuses of breach of promise by scheming women. It confirmed every fear these men had of empowering a sex that could not be trusted where matters of marriage were concerned. Indeed, it was one of the few actual cases that bore any resemblance to the picture painted by fictional accounts—Smith was too young to have really been blighted; her engagement was at least partly imaginary; and the victim-hero was the male defendant. *The Breach of Promise,* a novel published in 1845, may even have been inspired by it, since Smith began the case in that year. Cases such as this justified middle-class disdain for the action; they equated all breach-of-promise actions with Smith's. In fact, contemporaries wasted no time in condemning her. In his beginning address Thesiger compared her to a spider, weaving an "intricate web."[8] Mary published a pamphlet in 1846, defending herself, which was so harshly reviewed by *Britainia* magazine that she sued the editors for libel. The jury awarded her only one farthing in damages.[9]

People used *Smith v. Ferrers* to argue against breach-of-promise cases specifically and women in court in general throughout the nineteenth century. Lord Chelmsford, in the arguments over the Evidence Amendment Act of 1869, insisted that female plaintiffs could not be trusted, backing up this assertion with an undisguised reference to *Smith*.[10] The editors of the *Law Journal* refuted his reasoning, though hardly in terms complimentary to Smith: "There [in *Smith v. Ferrers*] the case for the plaintiff was a tissue of lies and forgeries, and the discovery of them would have, in all probability, been accelerated by the cross-examination of the lady." The unanimous condemnation continued into the twentieth century. J. B. Atlay, writing in 1906, called her case a "tissue of absurdities and mis-statements" and wondered at her "most extraordinary ingenuity." As late as 1962 a legal writer commented that "in 1846, both judge and jury realized that girls on the verge of womanhood often do get up to some odd behaviour" (a reference to the beginnings of menstruation).[11] Most men (and probably women until recently) wanted to believe the worst about Smith, to see her as a scheming villainess. Once she was nonsuited, no one considered her side of the story, nor did anyone spare her any sympathy. As in many of these suits, those involved as well as the public saw them only in black and white. Thesiger considered it one of his greatest accomplishments, concluding, "I believe I may venture to say that I never did anything better than this while I was at the Bar."[12] In many ways *Smith v. Ferrers* confirmed sexual stereotypes— women as habitual liars, man-chasers, and creatures controlled by their reproductive organs. In short, they were threats to men. Mary's aggressiveness and her apparent untruthfulness disqualified her from chivalry; she became, in Eric Tudgill's formulation, a "magdalene" rather than a "madonna."[13]

This case reveals more than the sexism inherent in the English legal system, however. It also shows (again) the importance of class differences in Victorian society, even before 1850. One of the reasons that commentators deplored Smith's behavior may well have been the fact that she was lower born than the man she pursued. Moreover, both sets of parents wanted to separate the two young people when they discovered that they were friends. The entire association made the Smiths, in particular, uneasy. They feared that their daughter would be the victim of a trifler. And, in fact, Ferrers did not take the relationship seriously, but instead married a more suitable partner. The case also illustrates the importance in Victorian courtship of the couple meeting each other's families. One of the weakest parts of Mary's case was that her parents had never seen Ferrers. It was simply not credible that a man over twenty-one, whose parents were dead, would not publicize his engagement and meet his fiancée's parents.

The case also shows the surprising freedom that Smith enjoyed in her family. Her father was a middle-class farmer, but he was bedridden much of the time due to illness. Her mother must have made few demands on her eldest daughter, since Mary had enough time to take part in (partly) imaginary trysts, to write numerous letters, to shop for books, clothing, and jewelry, and to plan a wedding. Nor did her parents question her long absences when she claimed to be meeting her fiancé. At the same time her entire family stepped in when there was trouble. They paid Smith's bills, her mother helped her with the wedding, and her male relatives insisted that she sue Ferrers when they believed he had jilted her. In many ways they behaved as families usually did in dealing with courtship, not exercising much control until difficulties began. In this case parental supervision came too late to keep Mary Smith from becoming notoriously unrespectable.

Smith v. Ferrers was a cause célèbre because of its high-born defendant and dramatic conclusion. The case of *Frost v. Knight* received publicity because it involved important legal issues, even though it did not initially seem unusual. Polly Frost was the daughter of a gamekeeper in Staffordshire. She was well educated, despite her humble circumstances, and in December 1861 she went to work as an assistant to a Mrs. Knight, who lived with her husband and son at Milwich Hall. Josiah Knight, the son, soon made overtures to her, declaring his interest in June 1863. The two decided to get married, although Polly was somewhat dubious, since Knight's father was sure to disapprove. Josiah assured her, however, that he would marry her as soon as his father died and he came into his property. In 1865 Mrs. Knight died, and Polly was promoted to housekeeper. Mr. Knight became infirm from an accident the same year, so the couple were able to court freely. Surprisingly, the two apparently did not have sexual intercourse, despite a six-year courtship. In June 1869 Josiah went to Rhyl where he met his cousin and decided to marry her. When he returned, he was indifferent to Polly. She noticed his change in behavior and questioned him; Josiah then told her that he was repudiating his contract.[14]

Polly was only twenty-three years old in 1869 and probably could have found someone else, particularly since she had not lost her virginity. But her secure financial future was gone, as well as a man who had professed love to her. She decided to sue, and the case was heard by Baron Martin in March 1870. Martin heard the first part of the story and at once saw the flaw in Polly's case: Josiah had only promised her conditionally—on the death of his father—and the elder Knight was still alive. Realizing that this could be a matter for much legal wrangling, Martin tried to persuade the couple to settle the case, but to no avail. He then allowed the jury to hear the rest of the evidence, and they awarded Frost £200. Martin chose not to nonsuit her, but he did give leave for the defense to appeal on the grounds that the conditions set for the fulfillment of the promise had not been met. The defendant so appealed at the earliest possible date.[15]

The Exchequer Court, consisting of barons Kelly, Channel, and Martin, heard the appeal in February 1871. The primary arguments in the case centered on *Hochster v. De la Tour,* a contract case that the plaintiff's counsel insisted was a precedent for Frost's action. In *Hochster* the plaintiff had been hired as a courier by the defendant to begin on the first of June and to continue for three months. Before June the defendant told Hochster that he would not honor the contract; as a result, the plaintiff brought an action for damages on May 21. The defendant pleaded that there could be no breach of contract before June 1, but the court ruled that the defendant had ended the contract definitively when he informed the plaintiff of his intentions. In other words, it did not matter that the contract had been conditional; De la Tour broke his word as soon as he announced that he would not fulfill his side of the bargain.[16]

Frost's counsel relied on *Hochster,* arguing that the situations were similar because Knight had made it clear that he did not intend to marry her before *or after* his father's death. The defense, however, raised a more general question about the nature of the marriage contract. They argued that a breach-of-promise case was different from an ordinary contract action: "In the present case not only was the time for the marriage quite uncertain, but it might never arrive, as one or both of the parties to the contract might die before the defendant's father." Since business contracts could not involve such considerations, *Hochster* was not a suitable precedent.[17]

To the surprise of most legal observers, the court agreed with the defense, although Martin dissented. Chief Baron Kelly delivered the judgment, whose main thrust was that *Hochster,* and other mercantile contract cases, did not extend to "a contract of a totally different character . . . a contract to marry." Having brought up a contentious issue, however, Kelly did not explain why a marriage contract was special, contenting himself with saying that this idea was a well-founded one, expressed by Frederick Pollock in *Hall v. Wright* (1859).[18] The court merely seconded the defense in the distinctions between Frost's case and Hochster's, arguing that by the time the elder Knight died, both of the couple, but especially Knight, might be in different circumstances (older or poorer), so damages would be minimal.[19] In other words, the condition was too open-ended; anything could happen before Knight's father died. Thus, judgment was for the defendant.

Although Kelly tried to discriminate between *Frost* and *Hochster,* legal observers felt that the decision had overturned the earlier case; as the *Law Times* said, *Hochster* "has been virtually declared bad law." The editors went on to point out the many flaws in the reasoning of the court's decision, particularly with regard to the position of the plaintiff. Was she to wait indefinitely to sue? What if she married in that time, or must she delay marriage for several more years? Was this not compounding her injury? Knight had told Frost bluntly that he did not intend to marry her, and this ended the contract. As to the question of damages, the jury could consider the same thing they always had, particularly the fact that Frost had lost an establishment above her present station. The editors concluded that "the judgement of the Court of Exchequer in that case cannot be relied on as giving a correct statement of the law."[20]

The editors of the *Law Times* were correct. Polly appealed the judgment to the Exchequer Chamber, and the court decided the case in February 1872. The chamber unanimously reversed the decision of the lower court, finding no significant difference between mercantile contracts and contracts of marriage. Furthermore, the court rejected the idea that a woman's loss of marriage was not as difficult for her as a loss of business. Instead, Baron Cockburn insisted that the loss of marriage was worse: "Independently of the mental pain occasioned by the abrupt termination of such an engagement, the fact of its existence, if followed by such a termination, must necessarily operate to her serious disadvantage. During its continuance others will naturally be deterred from approaching her with matrimonial intentions . . . while the breaking off of the engagement is too apt to cast a slur upon one who has been thus treated."[21] After two years of legal battles, then, Frost finally received her £200.

A chorus of approval greeted the decision. The *Law Times* congratulated itself for having insisted correctly that the earlier decision was incorrect and predicted that "the law on this important subject is not likely to be again unsettled." The *Solicitor's Journal* also approved of the new decision, arguing that "the distinction supposed to be found between a contract for marriage and other kinds of contracts is merely superficial." Some women's advocates also agreed with the decision. Keñingale Cook, writing for *Woman,* called the earlier decision "a striking example of base subtlety" but expressed pleasure with the result of the appeal. He concluded, "This will tend to the better protection of women."[22] In fact, the only negative note about the case came much later, in 1889, when John Popplestone published a satirical poem based on the case for the humorous American legal magazine, *Green Bag.* The poem was full of amusing verses, such as the following:

He took my love, nor recked the cost;
My heart was warm to him, my *Knight*.
He took away the warmth and light,
And left me an unchanging *Frost*.

and

Love did the wrong the law redressed,
I take the gold the jury gave;
No more the love he vowed I crave,
The gold I have, methinks, is best.[23]

Except for this ditty, the decision was greeted with enthusiastic approval.

Frost v. Knight illustrates one of the central paradoxes of breach of promise. In order to bring this action, women had to assume (and hope that the courts did as well) that the marriage contract could be treated similarly to other contracts. They were, in fact, arguing that it did not differ significantly from commercial bargains and that women had a pecuniary loss when they were unable to marry. The men, on the other hand, argued that the marriage contract was unique, a bond based on affection and religion that lasted a lifetime. Therefore, they did not see the breaking of a marriage promise as similar to the flouting of a business contract.

These different approaches were based partly on the legal needs of both sides, but they also mirrored contrasting ideals of courtship by gender. As Gillis has pointed out about the working class, "Though supposedly the more romantic sex, the female actually had the more practical view of marriage." Lower middle- and upper working-class women, because of their lack of economic opportunities, had to look upon marriage as their best opportunity for material, social, and intellectual fulfillment. Also, because of the power of the husband in the marriage bond, a woman had to be pragmatic in her choice of a life partner. Women, therefore, looked for the best possible bargain; while men, although they wanted good housekeepers, also had freedom to marry for affection. Only heiresses and some widows found such liberty for the female sex. It is not surprising, then, that most men supported a view of marriage as a romantic relationship, while most women saw it as a great deal more. Considering their hardships, sometimes gold *was* better than love, and women would have been foolhardy not to consider the material side of matrimony.[24]

Frost v. Knight also illustrates the understanding that juries and most judges had of the peculiar situation of lower-class women. As the Appeals Court decision pointed out, marriage was more important to women, and they lost a great deal when they were left "hanging about" for several years. Nor could Polly have entertained any other admirers without losing Josiah. He, however, broke his word without hurting his matrimonial prospects in the least. They simply were not in the same position; treating them equally in this situation would have been unjust. Frost's actions also demonstrated the amazing success of lower middle- and upper working-class women in asking for redress. Polly was a servant, but she knew her rights and persevered in her case through three trials. There were not many types of cases in which a working-class woman sued a middle-class man successfully, and the experience of finally defeating such a superior in gender and class must have been empowering. Working-class women may have been open game to criminal assaults, but they could at least strike back against jilters.

Frost's experience showed that even a poor woman could win a complicated lawsuit and overcome exploitation. The third case study, on the other hand, was a clear case of victimization, and it demonstrated the legal weakness of women in Victorian society.[25] Frances Jennie Day was the daughter of a postal inspector in Birmingham, and her family was respectable and well known in local society. Frances had a good education and showed an aptitude for music, so by the time she had reached her early twenties, she had received several scholarships from the London Academy of Music. In 1878, when she was twenty-three, she lived at home and tended to her invalid mother. Morris Roberts was a neighbor. His business, the Sherbourne Hotel, was near to Day's home, and he was a frequent visitor. Frances and Morris began to see each other secretly because both knew that her father would not approve due to Morris's lower social standing and his much older age (forty-eight). Furthermore, Roberts had a criminal record. When he came to Birmingham, he had just been released from prison on a perjury charge, and many years before he had served eleven months for passing "base coin" (coins that had been stripped of their valuable metals, a type of counterfeiting). It is unclear why Day was attracted to Roberts, but perhaps she saw him as a way to escape the confines of her parents' home.

The couple courted for two years and eventually decided to elope. They went through a marriage ceremony at Roberts's hotel on March 16, 1880. The man officiating was supposedly a registrar, and Morris produced a ring and a certificate to authenticate the match. They then had a lavish wedding breakfast, and Morris invited all of Frances's servants to make her new status as a married woman clear. The newlyweds lived in Birmingham, and several people saw the wedding certificate that the bride kept among her things. Morris's business partner, however, was a man named George Tibbits, who was already Roberts's brother-in-law. George disliked the deception that his partner had practiced on his young bride, and in 1881 he told Frances that Morris had married his sister

Elizabeth (nicknamed Fannie) twenty years before and that she was still alive. He ended ominously, "Morris Roberts will serve you as he had served the rest."

Understandably, Frances found this news distressing. She hurried to her supposed husband and questioned him about it. Although Morris denied it at first, he finally admitted that he had married her bigamously and with a fake official. He then blamed Fannie for the breakup, saying she had run away from him soon after the marriage, and he claimed that his fraud was motivated by his love for Frances: "I wanted you, and I dared not be married at a registrar's or in church." He tried to comfort Day by insisting that since his wife had deserted him over seven years before, he could legally marry again, a common, but erroneous belief among the lower classes.[26] Frances was not satisfied, but there was little that she could do.

In May 1881 Tibbits visited with the welcome news that his sister had died. Morris was delighted, saying, "That will make our marriage legal, for she was dead at the time I went through the form of marriage with you." But he soon realized that he was wrong; he had known his wife to be alive when he "married" Frances, and the supposed registrar who had married them was a charlatan. He became afraid that he could be prosecuted for bigamy, and he demanded the certificate back. Frances, realizing that the certificate was her only defense, refused to give it up. She told Morris that he could have it back as soon as he had married her "properly." Morris, infuriated, struck her, but Frances was not intimidated. The certificate, she repeated, was her "hostage" until they were legally married.

Thus out-maneuvered, Morris made arrangements to marry his second "wife" a second time. On May 30, 1881, he went to the registrar of marriages and filled out the forms to declare himself a widower. He and Frances moved in December of that same year to Brixton, London, presumably for the privacy, since they would hardly want it known that they were having to repeat their marriage.[27] On May 23, 1882, they married at the Lambeth Registry Office. Morris then succeeded in getting the first certificate from his wife, and he destroyed it. The next year the two returned to Roberts's hotel in Birmingham, and they lived there for the rest of their marriage.

The next few years were miserable ones for Frances. Morris was unfaithful numerous times; when she complained about this, he beat her. More than once she had a miscarriage due to his ill-treatment. Yet she did not leave him, despite the fact that she had plenty of evidence for a divorce (both adultery and physical cruelty). She stayed with him, she claimed, "because she believed she was his lawful wife." In April 1887 the climax to the violence came. Morris assaulted her twice, once at seven in the evening, and again at ten that same night. Although she was pregnant, he "caught her in the passage by the hair of her head and punished her with his right hand, and also kicked her" in the stomach. When she threatened to call the police, he replied, "You ———, you can do your worst and do your best. If you took a summons out against me you should never live to appear." Finally, he locked her out of the hotel completely. One of the guests eventually let her back in, and she spent the night in the scullery. Only one good thing came of her ordeal: "She had now come to the conclusion that she could remain with this man no longer." She returned to her parents' home in Bromegrove.

Frances had no money at all by the time she left Roberts, so she set about trying to get some kind of allowance from him. Apparently, her family would not or could not support her, for she eventually went to the Selly Oak Workhouse for support (where she again had a miscarriage). The governors there tried to force her husband to pay maintenance. At this point Morris brought up his first wife, refusing to contribute to Frances's future because he was not legally her husband. He eventually gave her £20, out of which he deducted £1. 6s. that she had taken with her when she left. She paid £8 to her legal counsel, so she then had only £10 on which to rebuild her life.

Frances decided at this point to go on the offensive. She met with a solicitor and began to formulate a civil court case. She also supported herself by canvassing for an insurance company. Morris, in defense, tried to cover his tracks. First he instituted divorce proceedings against Elizabeth Tibbits, who was indeed still alive in 1889. He also began a campaign of intimidation against Day. For example, he sent her a valentine with a picture of a fat old woman, weeping (meant to represent her), with the inscription: "You see what a brandy-drinking, thieving, lying, fortune-telling painted harlot and crying hag I have become." He also sent her a purse containing more insults, among other items. He sent his last missive to her workplace, threatening, "I have found you out pretending to get your living by your book, and walking the street. Your fate will be like the Whitechapel tragedy"—an unmistakable reference to Jack the Ripper. As Walkowitz has discovered, attempts to control women through fear of the Ripper were common in late-Victorian England, and particularly so if women were "walking the street," as Day had to do for her job.[28]

Day bore up under this new campaign surprisingly well. She persevered in her legal actions, having writs served for assault, breach of promise, fraud, and slander. These charges were heard together in the Spring Assizes at Birmingham in March 1890 before Baron Huddleston. Day's barrister was C. J. Darling, a queen's counsel and M.P.[29] Roberts retained Alfred Young and Mr. Stubbins. The entire first day was taken up with the plaintiff's story and cross-examination; the second day various witnesses supported her statement, although no one in her family testified. Stubbins then began the defense, which lasted into the next day. The judge summed up after the break for lunch, and the jury deliberated for twenty minutes before reaching a verdict. In all, *Day v. Roberts* lasted almost three days.

Frances's testimony followed the story outlined above—the runaway marriage, her husband's deception, the second phony wedding, the beatings, and her final humiliation. Morris's defense centered on two lines: he painted Day as an unchaste woman and denied any physical violence. Roberts contended that he truly believed his first wife to be dead by the early 1880s. Day, he claimed, wanted to run away with him and did not press him to marry until much later. In fact, she had given birth to twins before she met him, and she had sex with him before they ran away together. She forced Morris to go through the first fraudulent ceremony so she could fool her father with the certificate. He only went through the second ceremony because she insisted, and he truly believed Elizabeth had died. He even accused Frances of lying to him by saying that she had proof of Elizabeth's demise.

Moreover, he argued that he was the miserable one in the marriage. Day drank all of the time, and he was finally driven to pushing her out of his room one night because she was making a scene. He denied ever kicking or beating her and claimed that she ran away on her own. He had given her £20, which was supposed to settle all claims she had against him. On cross-examination he admitted that he had sent the valentine and the other letters, though he tried to excuse this behavior by saying that she sent similar things to him (but he could not produce any such items). Various witnesses testified to Day's immoral conduct and to deny her injuries.

Darling had little trouble making a fool of Roberts during cross-examination. He played upon Roberts's previous convictions, particularly the one for perjury. He strengthened his contention that Morris was a liar by bringing up an old barmaid of Roberts's, named Elizabeth Francis. Roberts had accused Francis of theft, and she had sued him for malicious prosecution, winning £150. Ironically, Darling was the junior counsel for Elizabeth, and neither he nor Roberts had forgotten the previous meeting. Roberts's experience in the box was a plain indication of the problems of breach-of-promise defendants. He was shifty and evasive during all of his questioning; he said "I don't recollect" several times, even to innocuous questions like "when did your brother die?" Huddleston grew disgusted with these replies, complaining, "'I don't recollect' is the refuge which witnesses take when they want to avoid being committed for perjury," to which Darling replied, "Especially when they have been convicted, my lord." Not surprisingly, the jury did not believe Morris. After a masterful final speech by Darling, and Huddleston's summation, which was firmly for the plaintiff, they returned with a verdict for Day on all charges. The damages were assessed as follows: £700 for breach of promise, £1,000 for fraud, £700 for assault, and £100 for slander, a total of £2,500. Huddleston also gave her costs, and "the announcement of the verdict was received by applause from the crowded court, a number of the spectators clapping their hands heartily."

Day v. Roberts is a classic example of the protection breach of promise gave to women who had married fraudulently. Even if Day had not been assaulted or sent threatening letters, she could have sued Roberts for failing to keep his word. In this way it was similar to the twentieth-century case *Shaw v. Shaw*. After seven years of living with Roberts, Day had lost her health, her reputation, and any hope of a musical career. She probably would never marry after having cohabited with another man. Apparently, she had also lost the support of her family, since they allowed her to go to the workhouse and failed to testify for her at the trial. Her mother was an invalid, which explains her absence, but her father also did not appear. Perhaps, after having endured a horrible scandal, Mr. Day found his daughter's elopement impossible to forgive. Whatever the reason, Day had lost almost everything important to her by 1887, and breach of promise gave her a way to strike back.

This case is also a classic example of the dynamics of breach of promise in the courtroom. Day's evidence came first and made a powerful impression, and her testimony was received sympathetically. She may have lost her chastity, but this was due to fraud; her only mistake was in choosing such a mate. She had borne Roberts's unfaithfulness and cruelty for many years without protest. She was clearly his moral superior—the heroine menaced by a villain (indeed, a man who had associated himself with Jack the Ripper). Roberts, on the other hand, cut a poor figure in court. He had lied to Frances about his first marriage; he was unfaithful; he was brutal, beating a pregnant woman and sending her threatening notes; he had failed to provide for her by ejecting her from their home; and he had destroyed her chances at motherhood by causing miscarriages. Little surprise then that Huddleston was impatient with him and the jury awarded large damages. There was also nothing odd about the applause from the courtroom when the verdict was read. This was a play with a clear-cut villain, victim, and moral. And the case shows plainly that the courtroom performances were not necessarily fraudulent or cynical. Day had been cruelly treated and earned sympathy primarily through establishing her case, not through legal tricks.

Despite the satisfaction that the crowd in the court must have felt with the verdict, Day's trial highlighted troublesome aspects about Victorian marriage and the sexual double standard. Like many divorce proceedings, this case shows the toll that these institutions took on women. Day felt she had no choice but to remain with Roberts once she had had intercourse with him. When questioned why she went on living with him when she knew he was married, she replied, "What was she to do?" As long as there was a chance that he would make an honest woman of her, she had to stay. Once married (as she thought) she put up with infidelities, threats, and beatings, as well as repeated miscarriages, because she "believed she was his lawful wife." She did not try to separate from him until he had thrown her out. Nothing could speak plainer about women's lack of power within marriage. As James Hammerton discovered in his study of divorce proceedings, the companionate ideal remained subject to patriarchal resurgence throughout the nineteenth century, and women were the primary sufferers from this tension. Indeed, most women were ambivalent about marriage, rather than entirely optimistic or pessimistic. Day's experience, among others, cautions historians to avoid overly sanguine views of Victorian middle-class marriage, based solely on the diaries and autobiographies of those happily wed.[30]

Indeed, ultimately, Day's ability to overcome her powerlessness resulted from the fact that she was actually single, not married. Rather than relying on the pittance Roberts could provide as alimony, she sued him for large damages, and she did not have to worry that he would disappear without paying maintenance. He might have tried to get out of paying the award, but during the trial he had admitted to property worth £20,000 and an income of £500 a year, so escape was difficult. Furthermore, Day humiliated him in court; she was the victim, while he was a cad who earned the disgust of judge, jury, and spectators. Nor did she have to go through the divorce court to be free of him. Day's case certainly made single life seem far more attractive than marriage to such a brute.

At the best, Frances's story was a cautionary tale to young women about the importance of choosing carefully the men to whom they would give their lives. By the late nineteenth century spinsters had begun to develop communities for themselves outside of marriage, and new jobs had opened in nursing, teaching, the retail market, and the civil service. All the same, unmarried women were still figures of ridicule and spite, and jobs for women were notoriously underpaid. Thus, most women, even at the end of the century, expected and desired marriage. But they also recognized the danger of men's power within the institution and the difficulties of divorce. Indeed, this was why so many feminists worked to reform the law of marriage.[31] *Day v. Roberts,* then, showed the ambivalence of marriage for women; many were fulfilled by it, but others were its victims.

The last case study involved a relationship that spanned several years, from the end of the Victorian era to World War I.[32] Minnie Magdalene Quirk was twenty-four years old and lived with her mother, the widow of a businessman in shipping, when she met Arthur William Thomas in 1897. Thomas, forty-two, was also a businessman (although his business was never specified, he was almost certainly wealthier than Quirk). The two saw each other for six months and soon became engaged. Thomas, however, insisted that the engagement be secret because his mother would not approve of Quirk's religion, which was Roman Catholic. In September 1897 Arthur and Minnie began a sexual relationship that continued for the next four years.

In 1900, however, Arthur's mother and brother became aware of the extent of his attachment to Minnie, and they urged him to give her up. Arthur, afraid of being cut off, began to see Minnie less often. After a few months of this unsatisfactory state of affairs, the couple agreed to part, and in 1901 they went their separate ways. Both apparently saw the break as final, and Minnie returned Arthur's engagement ring. A few months after the breakup she went to London and established herself in millinery. Arthur, too, lived in London, although she did not know that. In fact, the two of them did not see each other again until 1908, when Quirk caught sight of her former fiancé. She wrote to him on May 8, trying to renew the acquaintance, though Thomas was not interested. Still, he felt some lingering affection or sense of responsibility, because he sent her £10 when she became ill and could not work, though he did not visit her.

In 1909 the two began to see each other again, and they eventually resumed their sexual relationship. Minnie even gave up her millinery business in 1910 at his request, so she could spend all of her time with him. However, she did not enjoy renewing the position of mistress rather than wife. In fact, she later admitted that the two of them met in unsavory places for their illicit intercourse. In the spring of 1911 she met Arthur for the last time in a "dubious place." The experience was evidently so unpleasant that the couple argued, and Quirk never saw him again. In 1912 she wrote to him, pleading with him to marry her. She pointed out that she was no longer Roman Catholic; furthermore, at his age, he could not claim to be worried about his inheritance. She ended by pointing out to him that since she had sex with him, she could never marry anyone else. Thomas's reply was to offer her £90, which she indignantly refused.

Quirk's position was indeed serious at this point. She was now forty years old and had neither business nor lover to support her. To rectify this situation she turned to the courts, and in 1913 instituted proceedings for breach of promise. But Minnie had waited too long, because early in that year Arthur died. Breach-of-promise actions automatically died with either the plaintiff or defendant, unless "special damages" could be proved (such as loss of business or financial outlay for the marriage). At first Quirk tried to appeal to the executors of the estate. She wrote them a begging letter on August 25, 1913, explaining her difficulties, and adding, "It is apparent to the most casual observer that my life has been spoilt by broken promises." The executors declined to help her. Minnie then sued the estate, and the court gave her leave to amend her claim to try to prove special damages. She maintained that she had lost her business, having given it up in order to marry, and she deserved some compensation.

In the assize trial the jury awarded her £350, but the judge determined that she had not proved special damage, because she divested herself of the business before Arthur's last promise (the only one for which she had corroboration). Quirk appealed, but the King's Bench agreed with Justice Lush, using even broader arguments. Lord Justice Swinfen Eady declared: "The action is really an action for a breach arising from personal conduct of the defendant and affecting the personality of the plaintiff. . . . It is difficult to see how, in such a case, there can be any 'special damage.'"[33] Justices Lush and Pickford agreed. Lush thought that special damage might be successful in some cases, but not in this one; Pickford, on the other hand, agreed with Swinfen Eady that breach-of-promise cases could not survive the death of either party. Although breach of promise was a contract case, it was treated as a tort on this issue because of the personal nature of the injury. Even when the law was amended in 1934, it only allowed for recovery of actual pecuniary loss, not punitive damages.[34]

Minnie's story is a sad one in a number of ways: her experience was one of the few times that a breach-of-promise suit failed to protect a woman from exploitation. Though the jury believed her to be in the right, she gained nothing from her lawsuits except high legal fees. She never felt that she could be with any man other than Arthur, and at forty-two, even if she had been willing to marry someone else, her chances of finding another man were slim. Quirk was the woman with whom Thomas had his most enduring relationship; he had been with her, off and on, for fifteen years. But because she did not have the position of a widow, Minnie received nothing at his death. Her situation was similar to those women who lived with soldiers during World War I but were refused the benefits the government gave to dependents because they could not produce marriage certificates. Relief workers told them "you went into this with your eyes open. You will just have to suffer."[35] Minnie, too, suffered a lack of support just as she entered a difficult age at which to earn money.

Quirk embodied the ambiguities of breach of promise by her own actions. At the court trial the defense counsel cross-examined her on her motives, asking her how she could forgive Thomas's cruelty. How could she be so long-suffering? Minnie replied, "A woman always has to forgive." She thus summed up a woman's disabilities in the late Victorian age, particularly once she had sex with a man. And yet, Quirk did not remain a passive victim forever. She, in fact, did not "always forgive." In 1912 she sued her ex-lover in the civil courts.

She would likely have won, too, except for Thomas's death. Breach-of-promise cases may have shown the powerlessness of women in many romantic situations, but they also show a canny use of the law whenever possible, an aggressiveness, and a willingness to step out of the private domain. Quirk did not walk away from the trials with an award, but she did have the satisfaction of having asserted herself. Certainly, she got more from her lawsuit than Mary Smith had seventy years earlier, since at least the jury sympathized with her.

All of these cases demonstrate legal, social, and cultural themes that breach-of-promise cases highlighted. They also demonstrated changes and continuities in Victorian law and society over the course of the nineteenth century. In particular, they illustrate a crucial change in the use of the law courts. One of the striking aspects of late nineteenth-century plaintiffs was the fact that so many came from the lower middle and working classes. Despite some remaining disabilities, the courts became increasingly open to poorer women in the latter part of Victoria's reign, even though the High Court remained expensive. One can see this even in raw statistics: breach-of-promise cases rose substantially between 1860 and 1900, and the average number of cases per year doubled from thirty-four to sixty-seven.[36] Higher literacy rates and greater opportunities for employment allowed women to know their rights and seek professional help. Even if they could not afford the fees, solicitors and barristers probably became more willing to take cases on spec. Smith's case was against an aristocrat, which was typical of such suits in the late eighteenth and early nineteenth century. Even by the time of Frost's action, however, a middle-class plaintiff was unusually high born; indeed, as early as 1805, a shipwright sued a servant for breach, and the trend continued downward from that time on. The use of courts and solicitors seems to have permeated across class and gender boundaries through the spread of newspapers and popular literature.[37] Such democratization was not limited to single women; as Gail Savage has shown, a surprising number of lower middle- and working-class people also used the divorce court.[38]

There are several reasons for this change, some of which were purely legal. For instance, the Evidence Amendment Act encouraged more women to sue, since they could testify on behalf of themselves. Poorer women might have had few written pieces of evidence, but they could express their side of the story orally. Indeed, the large jump in the numbers of breach-of-promise actions in the 1870s can be directly attributed to that law reform. There was a slight change in the winning percentage, however. In the 1860s plaintiffs won 86 percent of the time; in the 1870s, 84 percent; in the 1880s, 80 percent; and in the 1890s, 80 percent. Defendants' winning percentage, on the other hand, went from 6 percent in the 1860s to over 9 percent in the 1890s. Apparently, as more people brought actions, juries became more likely to weed out dubious or undeserving cases. Many writers stressed the stupidity of juries, but they were plainly discriminating carefully as the action became easier to pursue. Nevertheless, an 80 percent winning margin did not discourage most potential plaintiffs.

Not only did poorer women bring more cases after the change in the law, but older women did as well. Women over the age of forty increased from around 8 percent of the plaintiffs in the 1850s to more than 20 percent in the 1870s. Although these numbers leveled off to around 18 percent in the 1880s, older women continued to bring suits more readily than they had before. Widows had already been married, so they had a harder time pleading for compensation for "blighted feelings" or "loss of marriage." Furthermore, they had no parents living with them to testify for them, and they often had relationships with lodgers or employers, which meant they received few letters. Thus, the Evidence Amendment Act opened a door for older women that had been largely closed before.

Legal changes, then, were significant. However, most of the reasons for the expansion of the action and its change to lower-class women were cultural, social, and economic. As argued in chapter 2, the development of melodrama in the early part of the nineteenth century produced a form for the lawsuit that made victories easier for female plaintiffs. Although there is no way to prove it directly, the influence of the melodramatic motif on the trials may well have encouraged women to sue. Another main reason for expansion was the weakness of women in British society and economy, even at the end of the century. Breach of promise was simply more necessary as the construction of gender hardened around 1830. Women were expected to follow strict rules, and one of their first duties was to get married. A broken engagement was not only a blow to a woman's future but also often a slur against her character, implying that she lost her fiancé through misconduct. Furthermore, the Victorian double standard of sexuality that hardened around 1850 put women in a difficult bind if they had yielded to their lovers before matrimony. Breach of promise, then, both answered a need for Victorian women and masked the cruelties of gender roles, relieving the worst abuses in courtship.[39]

Indeed, changes over time support the idea that breach of promise acted as a way for fallen women to escape the sexual double standard when conditions for them were at their worst. In the 1860s about 33 percent of the cases brought involved a sexual relationship. This was a difficult time for seduced women, because it was before many economic and legal improvements in their status and after only cosmetic changes to the bastardy clause of the New Poor Law. By the 1890s the percentage had dropped to 25 percent, when gender ideology was more in flux, due to the women's movement, radicalism, and legal changes, and when economic and social conditions were slightly healthier for a single woman with a child.[40] This change was reflected in defenses as well: in the 1850s and 1860s over 33 percent of the main defenses of breach of promise were claims of the plaintiff's unchastity, but after 1870 the numbers fell to around 25 percent. Though unchastity was one of the few successful defenses to breach of promise, its stigma had lessened somewhat as the century wore on, and juries tended to disbelieve such charges without firm proof. Indeed, as stated in chapter 3, by the 1890s judges and juries, as well as the defendants themselves, believed that chastity was as important for men as women; thus, the defense of unchastity, though never without influence, lost some of its power.[41]

The necessity of these cases also points out the loss of community and church sanctions in local life. Breach-of-promise cases were seldom brought outside spiritual courts before the Hardwicke Marriage Act of 1753, and those that were concerned property disputes and were often brought by men. Only in the nineteenth century did women become the majority in the number of plaintiffs and also sue for wounded feelings. The loss of protection of the church courts by the act was one blow to women, since those tribunals were notoriously friendly to marriage. With the expansion of industrial towns and the dislocations of the industrial revolution, women also lost village controls over courtship and their own economic viability. The New Poor Law of 1834 stripped away their ability to get support for illegitimate children.[42] The only place to turn was the High Court. These actions filled a void and helped define socially acceptable behavior in courtship at a time when other supports had gone. In addition, breach of promise is yet another example of increasing state intervention in the family: the courts stepped in where the old institutions no longer functioned. State action may have been necessary, but it was not as private or effective as the old ways and lacked preventative power entirely.

This change in the regulation of the family, in particular, relates to the issue of class. Lower middle- and working-class parents lost control over the courtships of their children at just this time. Young working people met those above and below them in station continually—at work, on the street, and at public entertainments. This change can be seen in the statistics on how the couples met from before 1850 to 1900. Before 1860 less than 20 percent of the couples met through the workplace; after 1860 close to 40 percent did so and another 10 percent met casually in pubs, hotels, trains, or on the street. Their parents worked long hours and often had several children to worry about; furthermore, many of the plaintiffs and defendants worked away from home. In the days of the rural economy, most young people were within a tight family structure until their late twenties, so, even though they did not necessarily live with blood kin, they had a master and mistress in charge of their welfare. The economic maelstrom of the nineteenth century ended all of that. Moreover, their social class made delays and separations during the courtship inevitable. This, too, increased from the mid to late century; in the 1860s less than 10 percent of the actions involved either delays or separations, but after the 1870s the amount rose to 14 percent for separations and almost 20 percent for delays.[43] Without the rural community and economy to smooth out these rough patches, women were often deserted. The changing economy of the nineteenth century meant less supervision and more opportunities for breaches.

In addition, the social construction of the middle and upper classes meant that they were reluctant to air their dirty linen in public. If at all possible, they avoided the courts, particularly if intimate relationships were involved. Though the lower middle class may have agreed with such sentiments in theory, in practice women had little choice but to take their injuries to a public forum. Since they did not have as much social standing to lose, they found the risks acceptable. And, indeed, if the woman had fallen, a public vindication served as a positive inducement. Most of the working class had too little money to afford the law courts and may well have felt that any judicial forum was weighted against them. However, those that found the wherewithal to sue did so vigorously.

These are not negligible changes; for whether industrialization was a revolution or an evolution, it certainly changed the way people met, courted, and resolved disputes. Nevertheless, what is more striking even than the changes are the continuities. Most especially, three things changed very little over the course of the century. First, companionate love remained central to people of the lower middle and upper working classes. The single most important reason for broken engagements in every decade was that the defendant decided to marry someone else. Furthermore, other major reasons for the breakups were lack of affection or the belief that the couple would be unhappy together. All of these together explained over half of the broken engagements in every decade under study, except for the 1890s, in which the figure was slightly under 50 percent.[44] It is clear that most people wanted to marry for affection, even if not passionate sexual attraction. Of course, men may have given spurious reasons for their decisions, but it is still significant that they felt that romantic excuses were valid. Indeed, second only to unchastity as a defense was the plea of exoneration—that the two people had realized their mistake and agreed to part mutually. This persistence in finding a true love supports the idea that the lower classes had always married for love. While middle-class romanticism may have deepened this conviction, it did not initiate it or even replace it.

The second great continuity in courtship was the influence of family. Despite the importance of work in how couples met, the family remained a significant factor. Before 1860 families figured in around 18 percent of the matches, but in every decade afterward family influence was felt in close to 25 percent.[45] Couples often met in the homes of relatives when they were visiting; at other times one or the other principal had relatives who worked with their future lovers or lodged with them. In addition, families were instrumental in breakups; indeed, if anything, their influence increased as the century went on. Before 1880 families were the primary cause of the breach in slightly less than 20 percent of the matches, but in the 1880s and 1890s the numbers increased to almost 25 percent. And these were only the cases in which the family was the main influence; they were certainly a subsidiary factor in many others.[46] The importance of family can be explained in part by class. Having few formal social occasions, the lower middle and upper working classes had to meet suitors wherever they could, including work and through relatives. And because so many of the young people had to work and struggle for years, men were often dependant on parents and other relatives who might have property to offer. As England entered a long agricultural depression and a relative industrial decline in the last three decades of the century, families had even more leverage against the young.

The third continuity was the ideology of chivalry the courts employed toward the women bringing breach-of-promise actions. Despite the weakening of gender ideology in the late Victorian period due to the women's movement, radical critiques of marriage, bitter denunciations of the suit, and numerous law reforms, female plaintiffs continued to enjoy large winning percentages. As early as 1871 Mr. Bulwer, a male plaintiff's barrister in a breach-of-promise case, tried to argue that with the increasing equality of women under the law, breach of promise should be a gender-neutral case. He averred that he did not need to justify an action of a man against a woman, since "we found the ladies very forward in asserting their rights, and this was a case in which an attempt was to be made to assert their liability." However, in that suit as well as most other men's actions, the plaintiff received no damages.[47] No matter how much the position of women changed, it was not fast enough to justify the end of chivalry, at least to most of the men in the courts. Considering the relative poverty of the female plaintiffs, their total responsibility for childcare, and their remaining legal disabilities, the juries were probably correct. Discrimination against women is one of the great continuities in all of history, and substantial progress did not come until after the Second World War. Since the law often lags behind social change, then, it is not surprising that it took Parliament and the legal profession until 1970 to abolish breach of promise.

As the courts opened up to those beneath the elite, the complications of their domestic lives stood revealed in far brighter light than the middle- and upper-class leaders wished. Many in the middle class, both men and women, insisted that the action was wrongheaded, bad for marriage, and bad for women. Their arguments reveal the difficulty of elite men and women in understanding the needs of those beneath them on the social scale. They also demonstrate startling ambiguities about marriage, gender, and the law in Victorian England.

VIII

Elite Men Debate

ON MAY 6, 1879, FARRER HERSCHELL introduced a resolution in the House of Commons to abolish the action of breach of promise of marriage except in cases of pecuniary loss.[1] His action gave the debate over the class of suit a national forum, but he was not the first to argue against it. Breach of promise had been parodied as early as the 1830s, and by the 1850s a growing number of M.P.s, legal scholars, and popular writers questioned the action's value. On the other hand, many people in the legal profession and Parliament, including most judges and almost all jurors, defended breach of promise vigorously. The debate centered on the nature of marriage, the roles of men and women in the family and society, and the definition of contracts and promises in the courts. The controversy over breach of promise illustrated tensions in Victorian values and judicial philosophy, both between and within society and the legal profession.

In a large measure those who opposed breach-of-promise actions did so because they saw them as a threat to the values of domesticity in several ways. First, the class of suit violated the middle-class ideal of marriage, since it put an economic valuation on something many people saw as personal, social, and religious. In other words, the contract of marriage was not the same as a commercial contract, despite the ruling in *Frost v. Knight*. The editor of the *Law Times* insisted in 1868 that "there is something very repulsive in the view of marriage as a matter of business instead of affection." Charles MacColla, a barrister and author of a book about breach of promise (published in 1879), insisted that, by allowing this action, the law did not acknowledge the uniqueness of marriage, thereby undermining it and, consequently, society. He wrote, "The welfare of the community can only be attained by elevating men's views of the marriage bond . . . and making it absolutely free from any coercion or avoidable restriction."[2]

More specifically, breach of promise threatened the axiom that companionate love was the main reason to marry and the primary guarantee of a successful marriage. The companionate ideal of marriage had made strong inroads among middle- and upper middle-class men by the late nineteenth century; in consequence, some argued that no one should marry without affection. Mr. Rodwell, an M.P., argued as follows in the 1879 debate: "The contract with which the Resolution dealt was not analogous to other contracts. The first foundation of an engagement of this kind was in 'reciprocity.' There should be mutual return of affection; and his argument was that the moment that affection ceased on one side or on the other, it was for the good of both parties that the engagement should cease." Breach of promise encouraged men and women to take part in loveless matches, even though such unions led to even greater evils—family violence, divorce, and desertion. MacColla speculated that fear of a lawsuit could be one of the reasons there was a shortage of husbands for English gentlewomen: men avoided all appearances of courtship so they would not be forced into marriage. In light of this, it was absurd to punish a man who drew back from making an unwise match. The only way to avoid unhappy marriages was to make an engagement a trial period, not a contract. "There should be, and there should be recognized to be, a 'place for repentance' up to the very moment when the knot is tied," wrote J. Dundas White in 1894.[3]

A second way that breach-of-promise cases offended the Victorian domestic ideal was its use by women. Breach of promise was vulnerable to this criticism since it was almost always brought by women, though theoretically open to both sexes. Women were expected to be modest, chaste, passive, and morally superior to men. Simply by bringing the case they violated these norms. Reformers, then, consistently portrayed plaintiffs as unladylike, insisting that no decent woman would accept money for a broken heart, act so aggressively, or expose herself so shamelessly in court. Their attitude is best exemplified by the reaction of the *Law Times* in 1868: "The really injured woman never seeks pecuniary damages for wounded affections. The very fact that a woman will go into a court and permit her heart's secrets to be exposed to public gaze, and her love's passages made the jest of counsel and the provocation to 'shouts of laughter,' is of itself proof that she is not a woman whom any man ought to be compelled to marry."[4] Most opponents of the action agreed. Female plaintiffs were described by a series of unflattering terms: "clever and cunning," "designing," "unscrupulous," and filled with "perverseness."[5] Even those who in general supported the action admitted that the typical plaintiff "is not the most delicate of her sex, and is frequently not without blame herself in the matter."[6]

The fact that women resorted to this action so frequently was, in part, what damned it in the eyes of many men. In other words, women were too successful; they not only went to court often, but they won most of the time and received substantial awards. It was not just the theatrical nature of these cases but also their almost inevitable conclusion that was troubling. Because of the almost automatic victory for the female plaintiffs, critics concluded that women must somehow be cheating. Law journals were quick to print stories about cases that seemed ridiculous or unfair. For example, the *Law Times* pub-

lished a scathing account of *Haycox v. Bishton,* in which Eliza Haycox apparently
sued her landlord to avoid paying her rent. The editors concluded, "Fortunately
for the defendant, the plaintiff was neither young nor pretty, and therefore did
not . . . excite the sympathy of soft-hearted and soft-headed jurymen." *The
Times* also gave added space to suits that appeared wrongheaded. In May 1880
the editors wrote a leading article on two actions, *Sans v. Whalley* and *Jacobs v.
Wolfe,* characterizing both as "unaccountable." In the former the editors insisted
that the plaintiff tried to hurry the drunken defendant into a quick marriage; in
the latter they asserted that Wolfe had been tricked by his fiancée, who was
younger and greedier than he thought. In *Sans v. Whalley, The Times* may have
been correct; the couple did not know each other well, and Whalley was indeed
too drunk to marry on their wedding day. But there was certainly no reason to
believe the defendant's side in *Jacobs v. Wolfe,* in which a man tried to marry a
stepmother for his children and jilted Jacobs because she was "too young." Nor
did the editors see the significance of the awards in these cases—the juries gave
Sans only £25 and Jacobs one farthing. Surely this moderation showed that the
action was working correctly, not being abused, yet *The Times* demanded that
"some process of discrimination" be applied to stop such frivolous suits.[7]

Furthermore, it did not escape the notice of the critics of the action that
25 percent of the cases involved the seduction of the plaintiff. In arguments that
sounded much like the critics of the Old Poor Law, the reformers contended
that breach of promise rewarded women who had fallen by fining the men who
had seduced them. Women should be morally and spiritually superior to men,
and this class of suit was encouraging them to lose their virtue. The editors of
the *Law Times* declared flatly that the suit "encourages immorality. Many a cunning woman is tempted to entrap a man . . . by the hope, which this action
encourages, that she will be enabled to pick his pocket." Herschell urged abolition in part because it would force women (though, of course, not men) to be
"more careful and more robust in regard to their virtue." The *Saturday Review*
went even farther, demanding that all actions for seduction and breach of promise be eliminated in order to shore up the virtue of the female sex.[8] Instead of
encouraging vice, then, reformers wanted women to guard their own virtue or
else bear the consequences. These arguments show a fear of female sexuality
and power, despite their reference to women as the "weaker vessel."[9]

Such criticisms show an upper middle-class bias and a misunderstanding of
the nature of courtship in the lower middle and upper working classes. Mac-
Colla, in fact, stated bluntly, "The middle and lower middle classes of society
alone can claim the honour of having in their circle persons who are not
ashamed to apply love wholly and solely as an article of commerce and a mercenary snare."[10] The lower middle and upper working classes did not have the

economic security of the middle and upper classes, nor the assured penury of the lower class. They had, therefore, only the most tenuous hold on hard-earned respectability. MacColla, and others like him, failed to see that awards in breach-of-promise cases meant the difference between eking out a respectable living and descending into unrespectability, as well as giving some measure of redemption to women who fell after a promise of marriage. Instead, legal commentators insisted on seeing these actions as simple grabs for money. The *Law Times* pronounced in 1868 that "as a matter of fact, nine-tenths of the actions for breach of promise of marriage are purely mercenary. The woman has first deliberately set a trap for the man, and caught him."[11] None of these men understood the desperate plight of many plaintiffs or acknowledged any wrongdoing on the part of defendants.

All through these comments the writers used criminal imagery. Women were "mercenary," out to "pick men's pockets," and they "trapped" their "victims." Most often, the men who opposed the action felt that breach of promise was little more than a legal form of blackmail. Herschell "regarded it as a perpetual fount of extortion," which was why he tried to abolish it.[12] These men did not regard the awards as justifiable in any sense, since they were earned through threats. Furthermore, many legal writers felt that breach-of-promise actions actively encouraged perjury and fraud (although they failed to object to other actions, such as negligence suits, that also encouraged these transgressions). By criminalizing female plaintiffs, the critics portrayed men as victims and women as aggressors, the opposite of the dynamic at work in most of the trials.[13]

Finally, the opponents of breach of promise also reflected domestic values in their disgust with the public nature of the suit. This seemed to show a growing sense that the home and the family were private and should be separated from the public world. These men defended domesticity not so much against an intrusive state as against the press and nosy neighbors. Their fears of exposure were related to their accusations that plaintiffs in breach-of-promise suits were blackmailers. Through the nineteenth century the perception of blackmail changed from the threat of physical violence to a threat of exposure. As Mike Hepworth has shown, this change was related to the Victorian need for respectability and purity in domestic life; such a value system left those who cherished their reputations all the more open to the threat of scandal.[14] Opponents of the action made their disgust with the press and public clear. John MacDonell quoted Bentham's description of a courtroom as a theatre and lamented that "the theatre, if such the court be, may be one in which unclean things must be talked of." He went on to blast newspaper editors for their role in publicizing the suits, calling such reporting "garbage." The editors of the *Solicitor's Journal* in 1881 ironically pointed out that abolition "would, in many small towns, really be almost a deathblow to the assizes regarded from the dramatic point of view." In addition, the publicity of the class of suit was one reason these writers assumed that no true lady would bring it.[15] These upper middle-class professionals were frankly horrified at the privacy of the home being violated, no matter what the cause.

Opponents of breach of promise were defending the family as they understood it. As Herschell summed up in his opening statement, "If passed, it [the resolution] would elevate men's views about the marriage bond; it would check much that was evil; and his firm conviction was that it would add to the well-being and happiness of the community."[16] Domesticity was more important even than contract and individual responsibility. It is here that opponents like Herschell came into conflict with those who supported breach-of-promise suits. The latter were equally convinced of the importance of the marriage bond but saw this as all the more reason to ensure that it was scrupulously enforced. They tended to argue for the rule of law, even in private life, and from a protective and old-fashioned attitude toward women.

The defenders of the action insisted that the betrothal promise, though a very special one, was still a contract and had to be enforced.[17] Otherwise, all contracts could be called into question. Susan Staves has argued that the contract ideology of marriage developed strongly in the eighteenth century, but then declined again by the early nineteenth.[18] At least to some men in the Victorian period, and at least in regard to engagements, the equation of marriage with a contract held firmly. Sir Hardinge Gifford, the solicitor general, complained in 1879 that abolition was "a complete inversion of our jurisprudence; a breach of any contract, according to our ordinary rules of law, gave a right of action." These men assumed that to disappoint a woman in marriage was a particularly blatant injury because she lost her main opportunity in life, perhaps forever. True justice demanded that a jilted woman find redress. In 1868 the *Law Times* insisted, "The law is bound to take cognisance of any willful injury inflicted by one person on another; and what injury is more willful than that of engaging the affections of a woman, exciting her expectations and hopes, and then disappointing them?" And besides the punitive damages, a woman would have lost the money she spent on the wedding and her trousseau, as well as (usually) her job. Although these losses were not the main concern, they should be taken into account.[19]

Far from undermining marriage, the threat of a lawsuit made the relationship less frivolous. "Young men cannot be too deeply impressed with the serious nature of the step they take in making a marriage engagement; and anything which would induce greater levity in such matters would be a danger to public morals," the editors of the *Law Times* insisted. *Chambers' Journal* agreed, stating that a court case "may sometimes help to teach foolish flirts of either sex that promises of wedlock are too sacred and serious a subject to be trifled with." Those who supported the action clearly saw it as both contractual and sacred, a contradiction that Steven Mintz has shown was common in Victorian culture. Of course, they did not condone loveless marriages, but the action did not either. It merely compensated the wounded party for the breach.[20]

The advocates of this class of suit retained a chivalric view of women. The action was necessary to protect them in a society where men had obvious advantages. Of course, a chivalric regard for women was also part of the domestic ideal, but only if the woman remained in her proper role. The defenders of breach of promise, on the other hand, felt that all women—even those who were not "ladies"—deserved the law's attention. To their minds, women were more likely to be the victims of male perfidy than scheming gold diggers; in other words, they more readily accepted the melodramatic portrayal of most of the suits. An article in the *Solicitor's Journal* of 1881 elaborated on this: "There are a great many men of a selfish and sentimental order of mind, but without much manly sense of responsibility and fidelity." In other words, the men were the ones who were not fulfilling their roles correctly when they reneged on their protective responsibilities. B. L. Mosely, a barrister, wrote several letters to the *Law Journal* defending the action. In 1878 he wrote, "The abolition of actions for breach of promise of marriage will place the weaker sex at the mercy of capricious, vacillating, and treacherous men." Several M.P.s agreed, including Sir Eardley Wilmot, Mr. Cole, and Mr. Morgan Lloyd. In other words, as the *Law Times* succinctly put it in 1884, "The men who find themselves at the mercy of unscrupulous women are not always over-deserving objects for the law's protection."[21]

The supporters of breach of promise did not deny that some women abused the law or were less than ladylike, but they did not think this was the point. As Morgan Lloyd stated: "The argument that high-minded women would not resort to the law in cases of breach of promise had no value whatever, as the same might be said of all rights of action. . . . Parliament did not legislate for high-minded or low-minded people. It legislated on the justice of the case." In other words, the many abuses of the action should not mean that it should be done away with. Indeed, the abuse was in treating this action differently from others. As the earl of Birkenhead pointed out, "That such an action may be brought from improper motives is a comment which may be made on practically all causes of action."[22]

At any rate, the cases that got to court were not nearly as important as the many that did not, for the value of the class of suit was as a deterrent to rash or deceitful promises. The editors of the *Solicitor's Journal* in 1881 argued that "it is all very well to say that it is better to break the promise than keep it in such cases. We say that it is better not to make the promise in such cases, and our suggestion is that the existence of the action causes fewer promises to be made which it is afterwards better to break." G. R. Dodd, a solicitor, seconded that point: "Undoubtedly to some extent the fear of such actions acts as a deterrent to men who might otherwise be disposed to trifle with the affections of women."[23]

What is interesting about this argument is its recognition of the economic weakness of most women. Men, defenders insisted, lost much less than women with the breakup of an engagement. Therefore, the engagement contract was automatically not a contract between equals but instead one in which the male half was advantaged. Abolishing breach of promise would leave women helpless in the face of stronger, more economically secure men. Mosely saw this distinction the most clearly, complaining, "Mr. Herschell would wish to make an exception [to the rule that there is no wrong without a remedy] in the very instance where the protection of the law is most needed, namely, to shelter the weak against the strong." The *Law Times* was even blunter, saying, "It is not only that marriage is a woman's chief, perhaps only, opening in life—that an abortive 'engagement' robs her of the chance of marriage through a longer or shorter period of the best years of her life, and leaves her permanently depreciated (to put the matter in the most practical shape) in the matrimonial market."[24] In short, these men were arguing in favor of a strict definition of contract while at the same time insisting that the contract was not between equals. Usually, as in the case of employment contracts, the argument that contracts were not made between equals was a reason *not* to uphold them. This was why, for example, P. S. Atiyah argues that English courts stopped rigidly enforcing such contracts after the 1870s, for people had come to realize that a contract between a rich industrialist and a poor worker was not a fair bargain.[25] But the process was quite the opposite in breach-of-promise actions. The courts were being asked to hold men to their bargains strictly *because* men had far more power than women. This, then, is another way that breach-of-promise contracts were an anomaly. The rash of actions in the late nineteenth century may have been due to the transitional nature of the period, which fell between early modern community- and church-enforced marriages and modern egalitarian ones. The need to enforce a protective and compensatory contract in the interests of the unfree party was the result.

The defenders of breach of promise better understood the difficulties of lower middle- and upper working-class courtship and the hardships women suffered because of long, fruitless engagements. They also seemed to understand that although many people found these actions humorous, they were not a joke to most of the people involved. One writer in 1884 stated, "Actions for breaches of promise, with their reams of ridiculous correspondence, and their exposure of the secrets of both parties, are generally considered amusing reading; and yet the subject has its melancholy side; and we cannot envy the feelings of the plaintiff when exposed to a severe and protracted cross-examination." Birkenhead agreed, writing, "It is desirable that breach-of-promise actions should be treated seriously, for they are in the nature of tragedies, not comedies."[26]

Nevertheless, though these men were sympathetic, they ultimately took a paternalistic stance about women. In this instance the protective instinct worked in women's favor, but it did not always. As Albie Sachs and Joan Hoff Wilson have pointed out, judges in nineteenth-century Britain often spoke of protecting and respecting women, shielding them "from the harsh vicissitudes of public life." However, this attitude often worked against women, because it was used to bar them from their rights as citizens or to enter the professions.[27] Breach of promise, in fact, was one of the few instances in which this viewpoint was an advantage.

Breach of promise often provoked these kinds of contradictions, both in legal matters and in general Victorian values. The elite males who largely wrote and argued about the action found themselves issuing paradoxical statements on women, marriage, and class in order to shore up one position or the other. Without intending it, they revealed deep divisions in Victorian ideals, as well as the intense anxiety about gender, class, and traditional institutions (such as the common law and marriage) that emerged in the latter half of the nineteenth century. In this process the action itself played a peculiar role, both a tradition and an innovation, a problem and a solution.

Most obviously, the arguments reveal ambivalent attitudes toward both genders; neither side in the debate presented women plaintiffs or men defendants realistically. Like the barristers, judges, and juries in court, they could see only victims and villains, with no middle ground. In particular, both sides objectified women in whichever way suited their arguments. Those who wished to abolish the case painted women as scheming adventuresses, blackmailers, and seducers. They highlighted only the aggressiveness of the female plaintiffs, while ignoring any hardships they might have suffered. Those who wanted to keep the action, on the other hand, portrayed women as passive victims, seduced and used by treacherous men and in need of upper-class male protection. Though more sympathetic, this picture was equally inaccurate. Women who came into court were often amazingly assertive—persisting through long court battles, testifying publicly, and revealing their personal feelings in court. Nevertheless, their supporters ignored these contradictions. Men, too, were hardly presented as complex characters: they were either hapless boobs or evil seducers. Neither side could overcome their stereotypes, despite the evidence that the female plaintiffs and male defendants were complicated human beings. Because of the courtroom's adversarial nature, coming to terms with these complexities was virtually impossible. As in divorce cases, someone had to be the injured party and someone at fault, whether or not these distinctions really fitted.

This controversy took place largely within the tight legal community of Victorian Britain. Because of their professions, the debaters were deeply concerned over the state of the law and particularly the law of marriage. The combatants were uneasy with breach of promise as a legal action but also with the idea of changing it. On the whole, judges tended to be defenders of the action, while barristers and solicitors argued for its abolition or at least reform. But even these categories were not absolute. Some judges, most notably Baron Bramwell, objected to the action, while some lawyers defended it. The only major law journal that consistently supported the action was the *Solicitor's Journal and Reporter.* Though the others wavered with changes in editors, for the most part they wanted change.

One of the reasons for this anxiety was the peculiarity of breach of promise, for it seemed a perfect symbol of the problems of common law reform. The action had always been set apart to some extent, subject to numerous exceptions and unique provisions. It was one of only two executory contracts that were stringently enforced before the nineteenth century.[28] It was one of the few contract actions that did not require written proof; it was exempted from numerous reforms by name, including the 1851 Evidence Amendment Act, the 1933 Juries Act, and the 1949 Legal Aid Act; and it was one of the few cases that required material evidence to support the testimony of the plaintiff. One reason that opponents of the action disliked it so much was its anomalous nature. Particularly, legal critics focused on two aspects: damages for wounded feelings in a contract action, and the lack of a requirement for written proof. Almost all the men who argued against breach of promise were willing to retain it if the damages were limited to pecuniary loss and if such promises required written evidence.[29]

These complaints underline the oddness of breach of promise of marriage in the late nineteenth century, for it was the only major exception to the law's emphasis on "business and consumer transactions."[30] Why make such an exception? Atiyah has argued that breach of promise showed the triumph of individualism and the market even in social relations, and he saw its decline (and eventual abolition) as the result of the decline of contracts and individualism after 1870.[31] However, since breach-of-promise contracts had been enforced long before the triumph of contract in the nineteenth century, and continued to be enforced (and even expanded) in the twentieth century, his explanation is not complex enough. If Atiyah were correct, judges and juries would have limited the success of many of the cases, but quite the opposite was true. Breach-of-promise actions demonstrated instead that judges brought social values to bear on contract issues, rather than relying on mere formalism. They masked their aims in the language of "finding the facts," but they imposed the judgments for moral or social reasons. When supporting breach of promise, they upheld the institution of marriage and offered patriarchal protection to women. Conversely, if they disliked it, they elevated marriage by removing it from the commercial realm. Either way, they used the action to defend the family and the common law.

The mere fact of the debate was proof that legal considerations were not primary. After all, both sides should have realized that they were not really arguing about enforcing or breaking a contract. No one was proposing that the man be forced to marry the woman. Instead, the argument was really about compensation for loss, as in a tort action.[32] The opponents' wish to eliminate the punitive damages, then, was hopeless, since it was asking that the action be turned into a regular contract suit, which it could not be. The concept of what the woman lost in being jilted was the real center of the debate, and that was why worries about gender, marriage, and the family crept into the discussion and into the judgments.

It is not surprising, therefore, that the members of the legal community were confused and ambivalent, splitting into factions and contradicting themselves. The difficulties led many who were otherwise socially conservative to call for reform. The best example of these confused tendencies was Baron Bramwell. Bramwell "opposed virtually every proposed interference with freedom of contract" during his long tenure in the Exchequer Court and as lord justice of appeal. In fact, Atiyah uses him as an example of the extreme individualist, as "something of a fanatic" on issues of individualism and contract.[33] And yet, Bramwell was the most consistent critic of breach-of-promise actions during the nineteenth century. He made frequent remarks both in and outside the courtroom about the action, and his words were widely reported in legal journals. The *Law Times* quoted him from 1865 as follows: "I cannot help thinking . . . that these are actions which ought not to be encouraged. If people change their minds, it is better that they should do so before marriage than when it is too late." Bramwell was known to question plaintiffs on why they wanted to marry men who did not like them; he also announced in court that the action was "dishonest" and "mischievous."[34] Bramwell persuaded some juries to his point of view. In six of the nine cases in the database in which he was the trial judge, the jury found for the defendant or gave nominal damages.[35] And in two of the three cases in which the plaintiff won, it was in spite of, rather than in agreement with, his summation.[36]

Bramwell's reasons for disliking the action were noteworthy. He did not argue that breach of promise was not a contract or that it violated legal doctrines. Instead, he argued that it damaged marriage, and that people should not marry unless they cared for one another. In the appeal of *Nightengale v. Perry,* Bramwell expressed his contempt for the plaintiff because of the lack of forethought she had shown in her choice of a husband: "It was fortunate the bargain was not concluded, as the woman wished to enter into a solemn engagement with as little precaution as she would use in taking a week's lodgings." The judge felt that both parties should think long and hard about whom they planned to marry, and breach-of-promise actions penalized men for doing just that.[37] In short, despite his insistence that men be kept to commercial bargains, Bramwell had an entirely different set of assumptions about marriage contracts. In his case the tension was more than simply the conflict of domesticity and individualism; Bramwell was trying to inculcate different morals in different situations. He wanted the courts to tell the business world that they would force people to keep their word, but to the domestic scene he wanted the message to be that the courts would promote companionate love. In other words, Bramwell supported the middle-class ideal of separate spheres, and he believed that the private sphere did not belong in the courtroom.

To Bramwell, breach of promise was part of the problem with marriage law and should be abolished. Like many critics of the action, Bramwell argued that breach of promise destroyed the companionate base for marriage and thus harmed it as a whole. For most judges, though, breach of promise was a much needed part of an old system that required protection from the seemingly endless attempted reforms. By the end of the nineteenth century, marriage law was under attack from radicals, feminists, and legal reformers, even though it had been changed a great deal, such as in the Divorce and Matrimonial Causes Acts and in the Married Women's Property Acts. Most judges blamed these changes, rather than the lack of them, for a perceived decline in respect for marriage. Those who supported the action were also likely to fight the liberalization of divorce laws or feminist reforms for married women. Such changes, they felt, had done marriage irreparable harm and threatened worse. It is instructive how a simple action for damages could prove both a harbinger of the decline of marriage and as one of its last bastions. Yet, despite their distance from one another, both sides of the debate agreed on one thing—the law of marriage was in serious trouble.

The best example of the more conservative tendency was Lord Coleridge. He was widely reported in law journals in 1881 as saying, "It was too much forgotten that these actions were often extremely useful in keeping people within the bounds of duty, which, if there were not such laws, they would avoid." In 1889 he went farther in defending the action, saying that "the very existence of such an action had a great deterrent influence . . . and many marriages, fairly happy, took place in consequence."[38] Coleridge, apparently, had a different expectation of marriage, at least for those in the lower middle and working classes. In his eyes a good marriage could result from a match based on convenience as well as from affection. He continued to defend the action into the 1890s, declaring, "Such actions were often the only legitimate means of bringing a scoundrel to book."[39]

Again, Coleridge's reasons were not strictly legal; he particularly stressed deterrence of bad behavior from men and protection of women as reasons to keep the class of suit. In fact, Coleridge did not support heavy damages for women who had been engaged only a short time, although he felt they should get the judgment. And he was horrified at the plaintiff in *Austin v. Harding,* who sued the estate of her ex-fiancé even though he had left her £400 in his will and had committed suicide after she had threatened the suit. Coleridge commented that "his desire to sustain that form of action had received a severe shock."[40] Even more interestingly, Coleridge did not support the right of a man to sue for breach of promise. In George Hole's case against Minnie Harding, for example, he urged the jury to find against the male plaintiff since "the circumstances were different" between men and women.[41]

Coleridge was with the majority of his colleagues on the bench on that point; breach of promise was clearly seen as an action that protected women, not men, because of their different economic and social positions. Judges frequently justified their support of the action in such terms, insisting that women had more stake in marriage than men and that their whole futures were compromised by broken engagements. In *Berry v. Da Costa* in 1866 Justice Willes upheld a large jury award (£2,500) by arguing, "We cannot shut our eyes to the fact that not only has the plaintiff lost the opportunity of marrying a gentleman in a position of life far superior to her own, and been deprived by the loss of her virtue of the opportunity of contracting a happy marriage with another man, but by the course taken at the trial imputations upon her character were unsparingly showered upon her." Willes's opinion is significant, since he was threatened with a breach-of-promise suit himself right after his appointment to the bench; fearing a scandal, he married Miss Jennings, and had an unhappy marriage. He eventually committed suicide, primarily because of ill health, but his family life offered little comfort.[42] Despite his own misery, Willes believed that the action should be maintained.

When the controversy began to rage, other justices spoke out during trials, usually in favor of the case. In 1870 Undersheriff Burchell pronounced, "After a long experience, in his opinion, great mischief would arise if it [breach of promise] were done away with." At the conclusion of a case in 1875, Justice Brett treated the jury to a long discussion on why women were particularly vulnerable to jilting and thus deserved the protection of the law. Men were different: "A man was a more robust creature than a woman; he had enjoyed her society for years, and simply enjoyed it no more, but still he could work for himself as well as he did before." Many other judges, including Grantham, Field, and Matthew, supported the action, even when they did not refer to the controversy itself.[43]

The only Victorian justice who was an outspoken critic of the action was Baron Bramwell, but others argued against seeing marriage as a commercial bargain. Sir Frederick Pollock protested a judgment for the plaintiff in *Hall v. Wright* by saying, "I think that a view of the law which puts a contract of marriage on the same footing as a bargain for a horse, or a bale of goods, is not in accordance with the general feelings of mankind, and is supported by no authority," an opinion also quoted in *Frost v. Knight*.[44] Early in the twentieth century Justice McCardie announced his opposition to breach-of-promise actions at the end of a trial, but nineteenth-century justices usually confined themselves to limiting the scope of the action. Justice Manisty and Baron Huddleston for instance, could be quite strict on plaintiffs if they believed their motives for bringing the action were insufficient.[45] Most of the time, however, if a justice supported a defendant it was due to the peculiarities of the case and not to a disapproval of the action as a whole.

What I am arguing here is similar to what Stephen Hedley has argued in other contexts.[46] Victorian judges ostensibly made decisions solely based on interpretation of law, but many other factors, moral and social, came into their decisionmaking, and their conclusions resulted from all of them. That is why sometimes their judgments seemed contradictory. In the instance of breach of promise, judges often went to great lengths to help women plaintiffs. They invoked the Evidence Amendment Act sparingly, gave a wide interpretation of new promises in the Infants Relief Act, seldom lessened awards, and allowed women to sue men in other countries under English law. Male plaintiffs, on the other hand, did not receive the same consideration. This different treatment was based on the values that the judges had, particularly their paternalistic and protective regard for women.

Comparing two international cases of the Victorian period illustrates this point. In 1872 an officer in the Indian Army named Cherry brought an action against his fiancée, named Thompson, who was also a British subject. The two became engaged in Germany where he was stationed. After he had gone back to England, she wrote to him, breaking off the engagement. Cherry sued under the provisions of the Common Law Procedure Act of 1852, which allowed British subjects to sue in the British courts, even if they were residing "out of the jurisdiction of the said superior courts," as long as the cause of action occurred in Britain. Thompson refused to appear and argued that the cause of action had occurred in Germany, so the action could not be pursued in British courts. Justices Cockburn, Blackburn, Lush, and Quain found for the defendant. Blackburn wrote the opinion, basing the decision on a strict interpretation of the 1852 act. Blackburn insisted that the whole cause of action had occurred in Germany, not Britain, and the letter that Thompson had sent to Cherry was simply evidence that she had renounced him. "Had his letters followed him to Ireland he would have received the evidence in Ireland. But the act which he had the option to treat as a breach took place in Germany, and in Germany alone."[47] Thus, Cherry's suit failed.

In 1900 a similar case, *Franklyn v. Chaplin,* occurred, although in South Africa rather than in Germany. The plaintiff and defendant became engaged in South Africa, where the latter had promised that he would marry Franklyn when the two returned to England. Chaplin later changed his mind, and Franklyn sued him in the English courts. His barristers tried to stop the writ from being served, arguing that the plaintiff should not be allowed to serve it out of jurisdiction. They argued that she should be barred because she produced no material evidence to back up her accusation, and "it was settled law that an action for breach of promise of marriage could not be maintained unless the plaintiff produced some corroborative evidence of the promise beyond her own word." At the lower court level Justice Day ignored this argument and allowed her to issue the writ, and he was upheld by the Court of Appeal. The court insisted that "it could not be held as a matter of law that this was necessary in order to entitle the plaintiff to obtain leave for service out of the jurisdiction."[48]

Although there were several differences between *Cherry* and *Franklyn,* the primary difference was the sex of the plaintiff. In *Cherry* the justices seemed to be looking for a reason to dismiss the appeal, while in *Franklyn,* though they had a reason to do so, they refused to use it. And, in fact, justices were often also generous to foreign women who hoped to sue men technically out of the jurisdiction of the British courts.[49] Clearly, gender bias influenced breach-of-promise cases, even though the judges used legal language to legitimate their findings.

The confusion of the judges, then, was heightened by their refusal to acknowledge that they were not just arguing about legal issues, precedent, and contract. It is obvious that their concern was broader than just marriage law—

they were deeply concerned over marriage as a whole rather than just its legal aspects. As many historians such as Mary Lyndon Shanley and David Rubenstein have pointed out, the late Victorians had a general anxiety about marriage and a variety of ways of viewing it, although most writers have concentrated on the feminist critique of the institution. Like many of their contemporaries, most male debaters were convinced that marriage needed help, and they, too, saw the institution in splintered ways.[50] The opponents of the action implied that marriage was a relationship of two individuals and must be voluntary. The community was involved, but the needs of each of the partners were paramount, and if one was unhappy, he or she must not be forced into a union by legal disincentives. The point, however, was not just individual unhappiness, but the fact that forced marriages were likely to be unsuccessful ones and that marriage as a whole was damaged by these failures. This was the companionate ideal in its purest form, urged both for the happiness of the individual home and for the good of all.

The view of the supporters of the action was different. To them, marriage was an institution, not only a relationship, and the good of the community was more important than the needs of one individual. They disputed the romantic notion that there was only one perfect person for each man and woman. Particularly for those of the lower classes, there were many other considerations besides personal attractiveness or sexual chemistry. To allow a flouting of a promise to marry was to lessen the value of the institution as a whole, inducing levity and frivolity in a serious and holy business. Such behavior was the real danger to marriage, not unions that might lack that perfect degree of mutual affection. Hammerton has argued recently that divorce petitions demonstrate that the companionate ideal had not totally triumphed even in the upper middle classes in the nineteenth century, particularly among men. This judicial clash of views supports his contention. It also demonstrates the great anxiety about marriage in the middle classes, supposedly the class most influenced by the companionate ideal.[51]

Of course, justices were not alone in speaking out about breach of promise, although their opinions had the most influence. Many lawyers, including Herschell and MacColla, disliked the action heartily. Sir Henry Hawkins called such cases "sorry specimens of advocacy." Moreover, after Herschell gave up the fight, Mr. Lockwood and Sir Roper Lethbridge introduced bills to have the action abolished, though without success.[52] Despite the fact that Herschell's 1879 resolution had passed, no bill to abolish the action ever got a second reading. Possibly the reason for the failure was that the ministries had too much to do to spend time on such a minor reform. Also, Gladstone's attitude might have influenced the turn of events, since he came out against the change in 1880.[53] For whatever reason, breach of promise remained actionable until late in the twentieth century.

The arguments over the class of suit were not confined to the legal community. The opinions of the general public also split on definite lines, but in this case, the difference was class-based. Those of the upper and middle classes disliked the class of suit, while those of the lower middle and working classes supported it. Most newspapers, particularly *The Times,* found the action disgusting, although none of them hesitated to print the most salacious details possible when the opportunity arose. The *Gloucester Mercury,* for example, proclaimed (after thoroughly discussing a case) that "in all the immorality of the day there is nothing so immoral as the business-like estimate of what a hand is worth, when there was or is no heart to be given along with it." The editors went on to castigate the plaintiffs involved as "traffickers in affection" who "bring their dirty linen out and wash it publicly." The *Birmingham Gazette* called the action "absurd," and "a very ugly unroofing of English homes."[54] The irony of juxtaposing such sentiments with their own reports of breach-of-promise cases was apparently lost on newspaper editors. Only the *Daily Telegraph* took the opposite view, arguing that the action was of value to women and pointing out the potential good side of publicity. "Above all," the editors insisted, "the girl has the opportunity of publicly proving beyond slander that she is not in fault."[55]

Other literate sections of society also found the action distasteful, although most of the commentators on women and the law in England ignored single women because of the glaring disabilities of married women. The only articles that dealt with the class of suit were those written about marriage in general. Radical critics of nineteenth-century marriage, who found its contractual basis and indissolubility offensive, also disliked breach of promise as part of the archaic system. Their views tended to coincide with those who felt that marriage could only be improved by further reform. Frederic Harrison in 1892 advocated a system of one-year trial marriages, one of its advantages being that "the absurd agreement to agree, promise to promise, now called an engagement, would probably disappear, and with it the even more anomalous action for breach of promise." Other critics of marriage agreed, at least insofar as they thought that only mutual affection should be a basis of marriage. Clementina Black, though she did not mention breach of promise, wrote in 1890, "Surely, at the worst, the broken courtship will cause less pain than the unhappy marriage."[56]

Despite the bias to abolition in the law journals, newspapers, and magazines, the general public appeared to give breach-of-promise actions strong support. At the very least, the constant criticism from the elite sections of society had little practical effect on the outcome of the many cases brought in the late Victorian period. Although at the beginning of the 1890s breach-of-promise actions appeared to be dying down, in actual fact the 1890s were one of the busiest decades for the actions.[57] Moreover, juries continued to find for the plaintiffs and give large awards far more often than they found for the defendants. As the *Law Times* admitted in 1884, "In spite of ridicule, and in spite of argument, juries, common and special, persist in treating breach of promise as a substantial wrong, and, what is more, the great British public gives no sign of dissenting from the views of its representatives in the jury-box."[58] There is, in fact, no reason to suppose, as Rosemary Coombe has about Canadian suits, that the action was unpopular with the average person. On the contrary, the lower middle-class men who sat on the juries consistently demonstrated their support by their verdicts. Only the upper classes, offended by the action's assault on Victorian domesticity, objected. Some of them recognized the class difference, but few understood the reason for the division. Only one writer, in 1890, pointed out the difficulties of lower middle-class women in finding husbands and upholding their respectability when an engagement fell through:

> It prevents whole classes of very decent young women from being victimised by men who make an amusement of love-making, and who would, but for the law, delight in a succession of "engagements," after each of which the girl would be deserted, often with circumstances of insult, and always with a distinct injury to her social position and her chance of a pleasant settlement in life. The women in the class we speak of are enormously in the majority, quite a third of the men emigrating, or, in their eagerness to get on, postponing marriage till late in life. The men can practically pick and choose, and they prefer, like everybody else, girls younger than themselves.[59]

The tensions between domesticity and individualism, between law reform and tradition, and between companionate marriage and marriage as an institution were thus further complicated by a difference between the classes. This does not necessarily mean that the lower classes were more individualistic than their superiors; more likely, they were probably not as wedded to the companionate ideal. They often looked for roles rather than personalities when they tried to find spouses. They did want a companion, but practical needs were also important. And, in fact, some of the advocates of breach of promise pointed out that the companionate ideal was not sacrosanct. The editor of the *Spectator* insisted that "most men and women, once seriously attracted by each other, can love one another if they please, and break off engagements not so much from distaste as in hope of still greater satisfaction from a new venture."[60] Particularly for lower middle- and upper working-class women, marriage involved more than romance, but there were few upper-class people who recognized this. These considerations influenced jurors, however, since they were closer in social standing to the women bringing these suits.

It is noteworthy that the one class that seemed to support breach of promise across gender lines was the lower middle class.[61] (The working class may well have approved of the action, but since most were unable to afford to pursue a case, their position is impossible to know.) One reason may be the peculiar nature of their courtship, with its blend of romanticism and practicality. Lower middle-class women had sustained an emotional loss, while at the same time they were threatened with a slide into the lower working class, due to lost marriageability, businesses, and (at times) chastity. Another reason for this support was their view of proper manly behavior. To jilt a woman after even a short engagement was to break a promise and fail to provide, two taboos of Victorian masculinity. Finally, the influence of the melodramatic mode was also present. The lower middle and working classes were the main audiences of these entertainments, and they carried their sympathy for the victims of the plays into the courts.

Breach-of-promise cases illustrated the popular nature of English justice, since the juries had their way, despite the complaints of the bulk of the legal establishment. Even disapproving judges never overruled the verdicts of the juries, and higher courts hesitated to change the awards, even when they seemed excessive. And, for the most part, judges and juries agreed in their sympathy for the plaintiffs in these cases, against the feelings of the barristers and solicitors. The action was an illustration of the way that old paternalism blended into new class and gender assertiveness. David Roberts has argued that the paterfamilias of the governing classes had a more old-fashioned approach to marriage and manliness than those of the middle class. Their institutional view complemented the practical needs of the lower middle and upper working classes. It is not surprising, then, that judges banded with the lower middle-class jurymen to enforce marriage promises.[62] Again, this bonding should caution against a simple linear view of the rise of companionate marriage. Though affection was not absent from lower middle- or working-class unions, such couples and their superiors on the bench were not wedded to the idea, and their decisions often ignored it.[63]

Juries, in fact, were even more sympathetic to women than judges. They often sided with women even when the judges did not, especially in cases of seduction. Jurors also showed little consideration to male plaintiffs. The vast majority of plaintiffs were women, but twenty-two men in my sample brought cases.[64] Few male plaintiffs got high damages; indeed, seven of the twelve cases that went to the jury got £20 or less. Although six plaintiffs got more than this, they were almost all before 1850; furthermore, most of these men had suffered large pecuniary losses due to their engagements.[65] Men won only 57 percent of their cases (compared to 80 percent for women) and their median award was a mere £12 10s., compared to £100 for women. Clearly, juries had little sympathy with men who sued for wounded affection, which goes along with their ideas of the proper behavior for Victorian men. Juries evidently felt that complaining about broken hearts was a female preserve.

Not surprisingly, juries were much more lenient toward female plaintiffs, finding against them in only sixty of my sample. Jurors accepted the idea that a woman needed to be provided for and had a greater emotional stake in relationships. Indeed, juries found against women plaintiffs for only three reasons. The main action that disqualified a female plaintiff was sexual nonconformity, which accounted for 25 percent of the lost actions.[66] Second, juries found for the defendant if they felt that the relationship had simply been courtship with no promise of marriage or if the break had been mutual. A final reason was if the defendants could prove fraud or that the plaintiff had plotted to get money from him.[67] This last, again, was a character test for the plaintiff, an attempt to enforce female passivity in courtship and in earning. Other than these exceptional circumstances, women had the overwhelming sympathy of juries, and many defendants had to over-prove their cases to win.

That women's advantages were overwhelming at least helps explain the upper middle-class fear of female power. Many of them felt that the action encouraged women to make a habit of suing, or threatening to sue, any man they happened to know for breach of promise.[68] In fact, there were few women who sued for breach of promise more than one time (of course, it is impossible to know how many threatened the action more than once). Only eight women out of my sample sued two different men. In half of these cases the fact that the woman had sued before hurt her second action. For instance, Emma Read got £200 the first time she sued for breach of promise against the father of her illegitimate child, but her second action against Ralph Bennion netted only £20.[69] In the other four cases the women won both times because the juries believed they had sustained real wrongs twice. For example, Harriet Roper was engaged for four years to Samuel Hill before he decided not to marry at all. She sued him in 1871 and settled during the trial for £100. Three years later she began courting a Mr. Bagley, but this engagement also came to nothing because of his father's opposition. Roper, furious, sued again, and although she was twelve years older than the defendant, she won £80.[70] These cases, however, were the exceptions. Few women used breach of promise cynically, making a career of threatening hapless men with lawsuits, and juries showed discernment in weeding out dubious claims. Unlike their superiors, lower-class jurors did not assume that jilted women were mercenary, and the evidence tends to support their conclusions.

The argument over breach of promise illustrated a division within the Victorian elite as well as between the elite and the lower classes. The ideals of romantic love conflicted with the continuing desire to shore up individual responsibility, while the upper-class view of marriage did not comprehend the needs of the lower classes. The argument did not promote simple dichotomies either, since the elite was divided against itself; even the tight legal community was not in agreement about the advisability of maintaining the class of suit. The only fact all the debaters agreed upon was that they should feel great anxiety about men, women, marriage, and the common law. Such a conclusion was hardly comforting. A similar problem existed among the Victorian women who wrestled with the question of abolishing breach of promise. They, too, argued among themselves about the correct view of the controversy, and their arguments were just as revealing about Victorian feminism as the men's were about Victorian values.

IX

Elite Women Debate

In June 1879 the editors of the *Woman's Suffrage Journal* began a short editorial with the remark that "there is much difference of opinion among women themselves to the expediency of abolishing the action for breach of promise of marriage."[1] And, indeed, the editors were correct; liberal or conservative, within the women's movement or without it, Victorian women found themselves divided over what to do about the class of suit. The nascent women's movement of the late nineteenth century particularly faced a dilemma when confronted by the contradictions of an action that violated the very notion of women's equality, yet also protected poorer women from exploitation. Despite a few tentative suggestions, a solution to the dilemma evaded Victorian women, but their arguments illuminated important differences within nineteenth-century feminism and between economic classes of women.

A wide variety of women's publications addressed breach-of-promise cases. Some, such as the *Lady's Own Paper* and *Woman* gave reports of trials as well as making editorial statements. Others, including the *Englishwoman's Review* and the *Woman's Suffrage Journal,* gave the voice of the organized women's movement. Middle-class domestic journals also addressed issues of courtship and marriage, particularly in *Woman at Home, Young Woman,* and the *Englishwoman's Domestic Magazine.* Nor were working voices ignored, since *Work and Leisure,* a working woman's journal (although admittedly slanted to the lower middle class), also commented on the controversy.[2] Obviously, however, the people who wrote and edited these journals were primarily middle class. They were commenting, then, on an action with which they had little personal experience. In addition, this issue was not as important to most of these publications as suffrage or, for domestic magazines, the home. Nevertheless, although breach of promise was never as contentious as such issues as the Married Women's Property Acts or divorce reform, it still garnered a substantial amount of attention.

As with the men, the women basically fell into two groups, those who agreed with abolition and those who did not. Those who wanted to be rid of breach of promise did so for a variety of reasons. One strand of the women's movement felt strongly that women should be working for complete legal equality.[3] Breach-of-promise cases were based on the premise that women's only lot in life was in marriage, and therefore women should be compensated when deprived of it. This premise offended these women's ideals of equality between the sexes, particularly their dislike of women's dependence on and in marriage. The editors of the *Englishwoman's Review* came out in favor of abolishing the action, for the following reason: "It has been maintained in the same spirit of 'protection' which dictated the Factory Acts of last year, which goes upon the theory that a woman is not competent to act or judge for herself, that she is in a degree a 'perpetual infant,' or at best a weak, confiding, half-witted creature, who must have trustees to look after her property and laws to enforce that she does not work too many hours at a time, and lawyers to see that her feelings are not injured by being deprived of a husband and protector."[4] The reference to the 1878 Factory Act is especially noteworthy because the issue was similar. In both instances egalitarians protested the practice of putting women in a special category, which protected them to some extent but ultimately blocked them from exercising the full rights of English subjects.[5]

Another reason for some women's distaste for the action was that it undermined the view of marriage they hoped to promote. Shanley and Philippa Levine, among others, have documented the importance of marriage reform to leading women: they hoped for equality and mutuality, an ideal that could only be achieved in marriages based on affection.[6] Other women, even though they did not work for women's rights, still believed firmly in domesticity. Rather than punishing an errant lover, many women felt that a woman should be glad he did not marry her if he could not love her as a husband should. Annie Swan, who for many years edited the "Love, Courtship, and Marriage" column for *Woman at Home,* felt that breach-of-promise cases were "pitiful reading," since "it has always been to me a source of wonder that the jilted ones had room for any feeling but that of gratitude for their escape from the misery of a loveless marriage." A letter to the editor of the *Lady's Own Paper* made a similar point in 1870, arguing that marrying without love was "at once a blunder and a crime."[7] Loveless matches would prove disastrous, and no one deserved compensation for having been saved from that fate.

Most nonfeminist women's publications blamed the woman whenever an engagement failed; as Rowbotham noted in her study of girls' literature, "If the man was a rogue or she had mistaken her heart, or his, she had failed in her womanly responsibilities to judge well before accepting any offer."[8] Nevertheless, most of the women's journals and magazines insisted that breaking the engagement was better than marrying without love. In two articles in *Young Woman,* girls were cautioned to be sure of their feelings before marrying. Rev. H. R. Hawies insisted that "the girl who has the presence of mind to say 'no' in time, after she has either conscientiously, deliberately, or hastily said 'yes,' has my respect; for I believe that in so doing she is consulting her own and her lover's best interests." The editors also cautioned in 1893, "Better a broken engagement than an unhappy union."[9]

Ladies' domestic journals also supported this view, reflecting the beliefs of their largely upper middle-class readership. Evelyn Lang, in the *Lady's Realm,* stated flatly, "It is better to break off an engagement than to be miserable for life." In early 1900 the journal *Womanhood* published a series of articles asking the question "Should Men Break Engagements?" Each was written by a woman, and each supported men's right to break engagements, although two writers felt it was acceptable only in certain circumstances (for example, if there were physical or mental deficiencies in either partner).[10] For the most part, though, marriage was too important and serious to take lightly; if breach of promise threatened the institution, it should go.

All the same, two of these women advocated breach-of-promise cases in exceptional situations. Beatrice Lewis, who wrote the leading article in the *Womanhood* series, supported the action when it was used against men "who, taking a fleeting fancy to some girl, would become engaged to her, with the sole object of obtaining a lover's privileges, and with neither wish nor intention of marriage." She also felt that in cases where "actual financial harm" could be proved it should be allowed, but emphatically *not* when the motive was simply "salve for wounded feelings." Mabel J. J. Blott, in her article, argued that the action could be valuable if the proceedings were made private (not reported in newspapers), but not otherwise. Occasionally, too, Swan heard of jiltings so cruel that she angrily wrote, "It is cases like these which would seem to justify the bringing of a breach of promise action." All the same, except for these exceptions, domestic writers disapproved of the action, since monetary rewards were not suitable to love affairs.[11]

On the whole, then, broken engagements were preferable to bad marriages. And these women assumed that a bad marriage was one that was not voluntary or predicated on love; only a match based on affection could succeed. Considering the importance of class and status in the choice of the mates of most middle-class families in the late nineteenth century, these protestations about marrying only for love rang somewhat hollow. In addition, middle-class women could afford such disinterestedness only because they knew they would be cared for if they never married. Nevertheless, they insisted that their vision of marriage was appropriate to all classes.

In addition to their concerns about marriage, these women were uneasy with the effect of breach-of-promise suits on women as a whole. The editors of the *Englishwoman's Review* disliked the dependency that the class of suit bred into women and insisted that "the abolition of breach of promise damages will, as far as it goes, foster a healthier feeling of independence in women." Even worse, only unscrupulous, brazen women went to court for redress. A writer on the "Woman Question" for the *Examiner* insisted that "the women who bring such actions are mercenary adventurers, who seek revenge for baffled intrigues."[12] Most leading women hoped to raise the status of the female sex and to promote the view of women as gentle, morally superior, and worthy of respect. Breach-of-promise plaintiffs were the opposite of this ideal. In this regard, women's movement leaders agreed with many upper middle-class women who did not support equal rights. The *Lady's Own Paper* was not a feminist publication, yet the editor's view was similar: "A woman whose love is true not only shrinks from publicity into the closest reticence, but she is incapable of even a just resentment. Nay, more—betrayed, abandoned, insulted, she loves the traitor still, as only a woman can love."[13] The plaintiffs in breach-of-promise cases hardly exercised the kind of self-sacrifice that the cult of domesticity demanded. In other words, women who brought breach-of-promise cases were criticized by women reformers for being too dependent and by domestic writers for being too independent, all at the same time.[14] Neither group questioned the men's behavior in these cases or considered that they may have been at fault. Like the men who opposed the action, egalitarians focused on the women plaintiffs, comparing them unfavorably with their more refined middle-class sisters.

The women who opposed the class of suit found pleasure in only one type of breach-of-promise case—that in which a man sued a woman. To legal reformers this showed a true equality between the sexes; to other women, it was a lesson on what equality would bring should women achieve it. In 1892 a young male farmer brought a successful action against his rich ex-fiancée, winning £50. The daily press trumpeted such remarks as, "Sauce for the Gander," and "Aha for the women's righters!" but many of the latter were not dismayed. The *Woman's Herald* replied stoutly, "For why should a man *not* have as much justice meted out to him as a woman? To wish the contrary would be to want to fling England back into the barbaric ages, of which ages justice to women mostly smacks."[15] If the action could not be abolished, the next best thing was to apply it equally.

Despite their firm views, and unlike most of the male commentators, women writing on this subject were not dogmatic. Even those publications that in general disapproved of the class of suit recognized that there might be unpleasant consequences for women should it be abolished outright. The *Lady's Own Paper,* a consistent foe of the action, nevertheless admitted that "the law is bound to take cognisance of any wilful injury inflicted by one person on another." The editors went on to say that breach-of-promise cases did at least instill in young men a respect for the seriousness of promises to marry and that "anything which would induce greater levity in such matters would be a danger to the public morals." The editors of *Woman's Opinion* also waffled on the question, criticizing the use of money to soothe broken hearts but also realizing that monetary compensation was a practical way to help jilted women. They admitted that "when men throw up a woman merely for caprice, the pocket is perhaps the best thing to make them feel it." The *Englishwoman's Review* cautioned that abolishing breach of promise should "only be looked upon as a step towards the assertion of the complete social equality of men and women." The editors urged Parliament not only to remove the protections of women but also to equip women to make their own way in the world, by, for example, granting them suffrage.[16]

If even those opposing the action recognized its value, it was not surprising that other women felt it should be maintained. These women also included leaders of the women's movement, but this strand realized that to do away with breach of promise was to deprive women, particularly those with little income, of valuable protection. They saw that women who had been left on the shelf for years or who had been seduced and deserted would have no redress if the action were abolished. The leaders on this side of the debate were the editors of the *Woman's Suffrage Journal,* who opposed the numerous attempts to abolish the class of suit in the late nineteenth century. In 1881 they gave their primary objection to an attempt at abolition: "The Bill if passed would deprive women of such protection as the law can give against a very cruel wrong. It is too common for men to pursue a girl with attention, engage her affections, induce her, under promise of marriage, to leave some occupation whereby she was earning a livelihood, and having obtained all they wanted to cast her off with blighted affections and ruined prospects in life." The class of suit, in fact, had proved its worth in protecting the interests of the female sex. The editors realized that the action was gender-biased, but the reason for that was "obvious and natural," since women gained an income primarily through marriage and men did not. As long as these economic differences remained, women needed some recourse when they were unfairly jilted. As a writer in *Work and Leisure* put it, "There is no doubt that its abolition would be the cause of much practical injustice."[17]

Those women who supported the action resented the fact that the all-male Parliament with its all-male constituency was trying to abolish an action with peculiarly female plaintiffs. The *Woman's Suffrage Journal* was particularly bitter about their exclusion. The editors pointed out the inconsistency of refusing to give women suffrage and yet abolishing breach of promise because of its inequality, contrasting Parliament's "alacrity" in taking away women's legal rights with "the slowness and difficulty they exhibit when they are asked to entertain any proposition for extending the rights or improving the legal status of women." The editors of the *Journal of the Vigilance Association,* not always in agreement with feminist leaders, emphatically concurred: "This is one of the questions that might in common decency be postponed until women have a voice in making the laws."[18]

Nor did it escape the notice of these feminists that laws protecting men from injuries were accepted without a murmur. In 1879 the *Woman's Suffrage Journal* pointed out, "There is an action for damages in the Divorce Court, in cases where there is no presumption that pecuniary loss has been sustained, but through which men seek and receive pecuniary compensation not only for wounded feelings, but also for wounded honour." The *Journal of the Vigilance Association* was even blunter, pointing out that the men working to abolish breach of promise had little problem with the action for seduction. The editors speculated that the reason was that men received the damages in seduction suits, while "in this case [breach of promise] they go in the very great majority of instances into the pockets of a woman."[19] Rather than seeing breach of promise as unfairly biased, they insisted instead that the movement to abolish it showed sexual discrimination; men were using their exclusive political power to help their own sex against the other.

Although admitting that the women who brought breach-of-promise suits were not refined, these feminists had more sympathy with poorer women's economic weakness. They faced the class issue squarely, realizing that upper middle-class women did not always understand the needs of the less wealthy. As one editorial put it, "Those women who desire the abolition are precisely those who would not bring the action themselves." The article went on to point out that women in the upper classes had the protection of their families and adequate support for life, whether or not they chose to marry. Many others, however, were not so blessed: "It would be the height of injustice to withdraw from women not so fortunate, not so sheltered, even if we admit that they are not so refined in feeling, compensation for a wrong to which they are infinitely more exposed than the former class." Edward Marshall, in an article published by *Work and Leisure,* also saw this class bias and appealed to a sense of fair play: "Girls in the lower ranks of life are often put to much expense in preparing for their marriage, and often have to give up situations. . . . [I]t is but common fairness that some pecuniary compensation should be allowed them."[20] Such remarks show a tentative attempt to close the class gap, though still with ambivalence. These writers were sympathetic but nevertheless considered poorer women unrefined. This tension is indicative of the difficulties of the women's movement in forging gender solidarity in a class-conscious society.

All the same, the protectionists certainly tried to put class issues below gender concerns on the scale of importance. Indeed, unlike the egalitarians, the more cautious strand of reformers felt that men bringing breach-of-promise suits were scoundrels. *Woman,* a newspaper whose motto was "Forward! but not too fast," reported on the same 1892 Chester case as *Woman's Opinion,* but with the opposite reaction.[21] The editors entitled the article "More than We Bargained for," and, though admitting that strict equality demanded that the man win his £50, they argued that many women would "complain that the law has presented them with the husks and has reserved the corn for itself." In short, these women saw breach of promise as a way to protect their sex until the economic and political situation in Victorian England was less weighted against women's independence. Men did not need this protection, so their suits were wrongheaded.[22]

An article that summed up all the ambiguities and difficulties of women in dealing with this question was published in the *Examiner* in 1871 as part of a series of articles on the "Woman's Question." The anonymous author expressed in no uncertain terms his or her disgust with the action as it was then tried, including the type of woman who usually brought it. The writer disapproved of courts dealing in love affairs, even if the women plaintiffs were without fault, but was sure that only the most undeserving actually resorted to the law. Furthermore, he or she insisted that the juries that were so sympathetic were actually expressing *male* solidarity rather than helping women, since "their hearts bleed for the father, who is mortified by the loss of an expected son-in-law."[23]

Yet, almost uniquely among opponents of the action, this writer understood the economic necessity that compelled poorer women to sue. They may wish not to go through a public humiliation like an open trial, but they had no choice in the matter: "Without property, with no breadwinning knowledge or art, they can choose only between marriage and dependence on their relatives, if they have any. The position is deplorable, but it is not of their seeking; it is prescribed by custom, and must be recognized by law." Therefore, even when the man no longer loved the woman, she remained eager to marry him, for otherwise she was destitute. The preference that judges and juries showed for women was fully justified, since society placed only women in the position of requiring matrimony to survive. The author further realized that simply abolishing the action was not the answer, because "a simple repeal of the law would not affect the real evil. . . . The disgraceful thing is, not that the law should give a pecuniary *solatium* to a woman for the loss of a husband, but that the circumstances in which society places her should allow, nay almost compel, her to demand it."[24] The writer placed the dilemma of women squarely at the center of the article: without economic and political equality, legal equality was meaningless.

Herein lay the chief difficulty for the leaders of the Victorian women's movement, and all of their arguments touched on the ambiguities of women's roles in breach-of-promise suits. The female plaintiffs in these actions appealed to a paternalistic court system to protect them from the loss of marriage; they even mirrored the pathetic heroines of the popular stage. Many of the justifications of the action centered on the weakness of women in comparison to men and the continued perceived responsibility of men to protect the weaker sex. Much of the ire of feminists, indeed, centered on this aspect of the trials. Yet, like the judges and juries who insisted on seeing women as part of a melodramatic role, neither side of the debate realized that the women who were actually taking charge of their lives were the plaintiffs, not women who bravely suffered in silence. Women bringing breach-of-promise cases chose to go beyond victimization and took action against those who had wronged them. As Mary Coombs has pointed out about American twentieth-century cases, these women proved to be strong feminists. Indeed, in a way they were stronger than those who believed in formal equality but refused to sue.[25]

Any number of examples from the previous pages could be brought to support this contention. Breach of promise offered women the opportunity to take the initiative and empower themselves rather than remain passively on the sidelines, letting their futures be decided by others. They were, in fact, using the patriarchal courts to their own advantage, playing on the stereotypes about women as the weaker sex to gain monetary compensation. In a sense they forced men to draw the logical conclusions from their own insistence that women were not equal. Of course, the vast majority of the time patriarchy worked against women in the courts. In particular, as Conley and others have shown, the criminal courts were cruelly unsympathetic to women bringing charges of sexual exploitation.[26] But breach-of-promise cases provided an exception to this general rule, and women were not slow to take advantage of it.

In other words, the women who brought these cases asked the male judges and juries to react with chivalry to their difficult plights. They put themselves forward as weak, passive, modest creatures, used by cruel, active, and powerful men. They played on the common motif of the seduced maiden, victimized by a male villain. Yet, by their very presence in the courtroom, these women belied the stereotypes. They were active, strong, and willing to speak publicly about their lives. Many of them admitted to having sex with the defendants, violating the most sacred taboo of Victorian womanhood, chastity. They denied not only the opinion of other women as to the way women should behave, but also that of the men from whom they asked justice. Furthermore, a large number of female plaintiffs were independent women in the sense that they owned their own businesses, or at least had steady employment. Admittedly, women earned precious little even in the respectable professions, but many of these plaintiffs could and did support themselves. And, as Martha Vicinus has shown, women became increasingly more likely to earn their own living in the late nineteenth century, even banding together to do so.[27] Yet plaintiffs continued to present themselves as requiring male assistance to survive. And they were successful, winning close to 65 percent of the cases between 1859 and 1921 (and 80 percent of those that made it to court). Most jurymen were forced by their own conservative ideals to support breach-of-promise plaintiffs, even though they were thereby penalizing their own sex.[28]

Some of the male opponents of the class of suit did recognize this difficulty and used potentially feminist arguments against the action in response. They were incensed, for instance, that men got derisory awards and public ridicule when they sued. The editor of *Law* complained, "It is a new doctrine that men do not love as strongly and feel as deeply as women; and if a recompense in money is any good to the one, so is it to the other." MacColla argued that since women had (by 1879) advanced economically even into the professions, the greater protection given to them was less and less necessary.[29] Such arguments were self-serving, however, since none of these men were willing to grant women suffrage or equal economic and educational opportunities. Thus, their high moral statements about equality failed to convince enough of the public to do away with the class of suit. They, too, faced a dilemma: if women were equal, then they should be able to vote; if not, then breach of promise should remain as a protection against the relatively stronger male sex.

Women's leaders, caught in similar difficulties, recognized the usefulness of the action, but they offered few concrete solutions to the problems it presented. Because so many had no real understanding of the women who brought the cases, their solutions were unspecific and impractical. The writer to the *Examiner,* for instance, gave only vague proposals that women be made "independent of wedlock" through economic gains. The *Woman's Suffrage Journal,* predictably, called for women to be given the vote before any other reform attempts were made, which was certainly a worthy goal, but not one that was likely to occur soon. The editors of *Woman* were even more impractical in 1891: "It is desirable that men who have trifled with the affections of a woman, and have failed to carry out an engagement *without good reason for doing so,* should be liable to a fine in *reasonable* proportion to their means." The editors went on to say that only promises supported by written evidence should be brought to court. They did not specify how women were to get such evidence, how a jury would decide what a good reason for jilting was, or who would determine a reasonable proportion of a man's means.[30]

Only nonfeminists came up with more specific ideas on how to keep the best parts of the action while jettisoning the distasteful aspects of it. Though these suggestions were precise, however, they were equally impossible to put into effect. The editors of the *Englishwoman's Domestic Magazine* suggested as early as 1869 that men be asked to put down earnest money according to their position and means whenever they made an offer of marriage. If the man later reneged on his promise, he automatically lost his deposit, and his ex-fiancée would have the sum on which to start over without resorting to an ugly public trial.[31] A similar scheme was devised by the *Spectator* in 1893. The writer suggested that all men sign written and stamped proposals of marriage before being accepted as serious suitors. "If it once became an understood thing that the ardent lover should offer such a proof of his good faith, then a girl would know well what to expect from a lover who withheld it." Such a guarantee (or lack thereof) would also alert parents to the intentions of any beaux of their daughters.[32]

These schemes did away with the necessity of public trials, but they were no more realistic than those of feminists. Lower middle- and working-class women were hardly in a position to demand guarantees from their lovers, nor would they think it necessary at the time that they were most likely to receive them. Lower-class courtship was simply too informal to adapt easily to written promises or earnest-money deposits. Nor did parents have the control over their children's courtship that these writers assumed. For better or worse, breach of promise was a single woman's primary recourse when jilted, seduced, or abused.

The action continued to be a source of difficulty for women into the twentieth century, although the improved legal and economic conditions of women made abolition more attractive.[33] And, in fact, because of these political and social gains, few women in Parliament or out complained when the action was finally abolished in 1970.[34] After a few years without breach of promise, however, some women expressed doubts about the wisdom of doing away with its protection. Leonard pointed out in 1980 that, although being jilted was not as devastating as in the past, a woman still spent large amounts of money on her wedding. She may also have lost all chances at marriage to someone else. Furthermore, "the girl is left holding the baby, or is at least no longer a virgin; and marriage remains of great *economic* importance to women—most women's work is still menial and low paid, and this is justified on the basis that most women are married." Leonard's point corresponds with those of women who have realized the potential hazards of women's legal equality with men, even in the late twentieth century. As Julia Brophy and Carol Smart wrote in 1982, "The problem for feminist politics with a concept of rights is that it leaves untouched structural inequalities and makes demands at the level of formal equality. . . . There is nothing inherently progressive in this concept."[35] Thus, women continued to wrestle with the dilemma of demanding equal rights in a society that had moved only slowly toward correcting women's economic handicaps. Breach of promise was an imperfect tool, but it did offer Victorian women a chance to take the initiative in their lives, an opportunity that came far too seldom overall. It was an opportunity that, as of 1970, women in England lost.

Conclusion

The End of Breach of Promise?

BREACH-OF-PROMISE CASES remained an important part of the common law until the Second World War. After 1945 the wholesale expansion of old age pensions, unemployment, health care, and other state welfare projects changed the basis for contracts relating to marriage. Although women certainly could still be hurt by a jilting, their economic position was not as desperate as in earlier centuries, and the number of cases declined. Those that were brought often involved an unusual point of law, such as fraudulent marriages.[1] Still, the British governments of the 1950s and 1960s showed no inclination toward abolition. For one thing, more important business crowded out such a minor matter; for another, the primarily Conservative leaders saw no reason to change a law that had provoked little opposition from the general public.

Periodically, from the 1930s to the 1960s, independent members questioned the attorneys general about the possibility of abolition, but they had little success. Mr. Lipton, for example, queried the need for the action several times in the 1950s and 1960s. He insisted, "This kind of action is sordid, stupid, and not in line with modern ideas of sex equality" and that it was a "Victorian relic."[2] On the occasion of the second remark, the attorney general replied, "I am not aware of any change in public opinion with regard to breach of promise . . . [and, as to sex inequality,] it is open to a man to sue for breach of promise as well as for a woman." This was a typical response for the time.[3] Even when a woman member, a Miss Bacon, insisted that "the majority of the women in the country find the whole business most distasteful," the government remained unresponsive.[4]

Conditions finally became more conducive to change in the late 1960s. In part this was the result of a growing women's movement that again emphasized equality over protection, seeing the latter as a tool to bar women from their full rights. The abolition of breach of promise was one of many legal reforms that equalized the position of the sexes. Although still not equal economically, women could vote, run for public office, and could resort to various legal remedies for overt sexual discrimination in the workplace. The idea, then, that a woman's primary career was marriage was out-of-date. Another factor in the change was the general codification of family law in the late 1960s and early 1970s in areas such as illegitimacy and divorce law. Indeed, at least some of these earlier changes made breach of promise less necessary. The Maintenance Orders Act in 1968, for instance, removed limits on the amount of maintenance women could receive from the putative fathers of their illegitimate children. This, undoubtedly, was a great gain to women, as was the National Health Service in defraying the expenses of pregnancy. Thus, an illegitimate child was no longer a social or economic disaster, and the need to sue for support lessened.

A final reason for the desire for change was the permeation of the companionate view of marriage throughout society. The idea that marriage was a contract like any other was abhorrent to most late twentieth-century men and women. Although women were still more careful about the choice of a spouse and slower to agree to marry, they were not as dependent on a provider as before. Romantic attachment became the most important reason for marriage, so if either party felt that her or his affection was not deep enough, most people felt that she or he should not be forced into a permanent union. This argument remained virtually unchanged from Victorian times; the difference was that more social classes could indulge in romantic love as the century wore on. Insisting that women marry only for love made more sense in 1970 than in 1870, since their choices were no longer as circumscribed.

In 1965 Parliament authorized the formation of the Law Commission, which studied laws that required codification and recommended changes. The commissioners were Justice Scarman, L. C. B. Gower, Neil Lawson, N. S. March, and Andrew Martin (all men). The Law Commission dealt with numerous family law changes, and in 1969 published their study of breach of promise.[5] The commission argued that breach of promise should be abolished outright, not even allowing damages for pecuniary loss. They listed four reasons: breach of promise encouraged gold-digging women; marriage should be based on affection alone; the marriage contract was not the same as any other contract; and the courts should not be involved in arguing about the embarrassing details of romantic breakups. The commission had consulted with a number of lay organizations, including the Co-operative Women's Guild, the Fawcett Society, the British Council of Churches, and the National Women Citizens' Association, as well as numerous legal organizations. The commission claimed that the lay organizations overwhelmingly voted for total abolition, while the legal organizations argued for some provision for exceptional circumstances. Until its abolition, then, breach of promise retained support from some law officers who had firsthand experience with women's difficulties. It is also instructive to realize that the lay organizations were largely middle class, whatever their purported constituencies. Since most middle-class men and women had disapproved of breach of promise for one hundred years, their vote for abolition was hardly surprising.

The commission suggested total abolition with a summary procedure for property disputes. This last addition was primarily to help men, since it involved compensation for investments in joint property (the example used was that of a man putting £500 into a house). Furthermore, the Law Commission insisted that all gifts conditional on the marriage be returned, no matter who had jilted whom. In other words, under their recommendations a man could jilt his fiancée and then sue her for the engagement ring, and she would have no legal right to the property. They justified this provision by arguing that if the courts began questioning who was at fault, they would simply be reviving breach-of-promise cases in another form. Of course, they could easily have avoided this difficulty by saying that all gifts were absolute, thus always awarding the engagement ring to the woman. This, however, was not even suggested. A final provision of the proposed legislation dealt with cases such as *Shaw v. Shaw*, in which a fraudulently married woman used breach of promise to recover part of her husband's estate. The commissioners recommended allowing such widows or widowers to sue for support under an amended version of the Inheritance (Family Provision) Act of 1938.

The Law Reform (Miscellaneous Provisions) Act of 1970 was the result of the commission's work. Julius Silverman oversaw its passage, and the bill was substantially as the commission had suggested, except for a slight amendment to the provision for engagement rings, the only part of the bill that caused any debate. The ideas that marriage should be voluntary and based on affection and that the marriage contract should not be treated as any other contract were accepted without comment. Renée Short made a brief remark about the all-male commission and the all-male parliamentary committee that wrote the statute, but she did not oppose any part of it except for the provision for engagement rings.[6] In the third reading Silverman insisted that "the breach of promise action is an anachronism which cannot be justified in this day and age." He went on to make the now hackneyed argument about marriage being a special contract, as well as insisting that though gold diggers were not common, they still existed and might use this action to their advantage. He ended his remarks by saying, "It is good that the law is beginning to shrink from acting as if it were a 'nosey parker' instrument, meddling in what are essentially personal relationships of adult men and women," thus linking the abolition of breach of promise with the relaxation of birth control limitations, laws against sodomy, and abortion rights.[7] In an age when the state had overwhelming control of people's lives, many found it comforting to have some areas free from litigation. The bill passed easily, and breach of promise ceased to exist later that year.

The view of the action in 1970 was not that far removed from that of the five fictional cases in the introduction or from that of most Victorian opponents of the action. The only difference was that in the twentieth century women had more resources and thus did not need the legal remedy as much. Still, even in 1970, the idea of gold diggers persisted. It is instructive to realize how long these misogynist readings persisted. The power of the fictional plaintiffs overwhelmed the actual women in the courtrooms, at least in the elite. To them, breach-of-promise cases, by implication, were helping largely unscrupulous plaintiffs. The typical fictional case was an engagement of short duration (if at all) between middle- or upper-class people, a mutually beneficial breakup, followed by a vindictive retaliation by the unreasonable female. This type of case was considered typical even in 1969 and helped to abolish the action. It is not surprising, then, that parts of the Victorian elite believed the myth and entirely missed the reality.

The typical genuine case was between two lower middle-class people who had been engaged over three years and broke up due to the strains of long waits and separations. The typical plaintiff had been devoted to one man for many years; in addition, in one of four cases, she had engaged in sexual intercourse. She had often given up her job or business in order to marry and had made expensive preparations for the ceremony. She had certainly suffered a great deal from the termination of her romance, practically and emotionally. To insist, as middle-class critics did, that female plaintiffs be treated equally with the clearly advantaged male defendants, or that women marry only for love in an age that denied them economic opportunities, was to ignore women's material existence.

In any number of ways, then, breach-of-promise cases were a class-biased phenomenon in the Victorian period. The (mostly) women who brought these actions were those who worked for respectability but who did not have economic security. Therefore, they stood to lose the most at the loss of an engagement, yet had the resources and knowledge to use the common law to their advantage. They also were most likely to marry across class lines and therefore courted men with enough money to be worth suing. The fact that they risked their respectability by exposing themselves in the law courts in itself demonstrates the peculiarities of lower middle- and cross-class courtships. The amounts the plaintiffs won were not astronomical, but they were enough to mean the difference between poverty and a decent living, particularly when illegitimate children were involved.

Nevertheless, breach-of-promise cases were also gender-biased; spinsters and widows had definite advantages over bachelors and widowers. It was a uniquely female civil action, and women used it frequently. In part because of their ability to play the part of melodramatic heroines, and in part because of strong gender expectations, women dominated this action. The ambiguities of its relation to Victorian values was reflected in the ambivalence of most women in using and observing it. Women escaped powerlessness by suing, but at the same time they risked a backlash from both men and other women. The action protected and separated them, for, like many legal actions, it was both feminist and antifeminist at the same time. The egalitarians who criticized it were technically correct in their assessments, but their lack of understanding underscores the difficulty of middle-class feminists in resolving family issues to the satisfaction of all women.

It was largely because of this class and sex base, then, that the action provoked an angry reaction from the elite. In breach of promise, class and gender were both important factors, in its success as well as in its dubious reputation. The cases largely succeeded because of the gender of most plaintiffs, but the reasons the engagements that led to these cases failed were complicated mixtures of class difficulties and ideology. Because of their class problems, lower middle- and upper working-class women used both romance and pragmatism in their courtships, and, because they were women, they had peculiar difficulties when their romances failed. In particular, they could not face with equanimity the prospect of losing their positions, spending precious savings on weddings that did not take place, raising illegitimate children alone, and, perhaps, never marrying at all. Marriage for romantic love was the hallmark of middle-class domesticity, but it could not simply be imported to the lower classes because it required the financial security that the middle classes could give to aging spinsters. Until women's structural economic inequality changed, their need for marriage pushed them to legal remedies that those who were wealthier disdained.

Upper- and upper middle-class commentators seldom understood these difficulties, and they sharply criticized the action for its view of marriage. Furthermore, they found its use by women nefarious, since they recognized the power that it gave to the female sex. Yet the action was not without its defenders, since the urge to protect women was another strand in Victorian ideology. Though these protectionists were sympathetic, they did not fully understand the lives of the women they defended, nor could they resolve the ambiguities of the suit. Women played on the chivalric ideal shamelessly, while contradicting it by their presence in the courtroom. In breach of promise, and the varying reactions to it, the contradictions and ambiguities of the Victorian mind become increasingly clear. The contrast between the experience of breach-of-promise plaintiffs and the perception of them by upper middle-class writers is also a reminder of the many different views of love and marriage that existed into the twentieth century. And, as Hammerton has pointed out, it is also a reminder of the importance of studying the actions of ordinary women, as well as the discourse of the feminist movement, in order to understand the process of legal change for women.[8]

Breach of promise has not been actionable in Britain for twenty-five years, yet the issues that it raised are still current. Particularly, the problem of equality under the law is still frequently debated by feminists. It also points to the differences that exist in the reasons men and women marry to the present day: women still have more practical reasons, since they remain more economically vulnerable and retain the primary responsibility for children. The companionate ideal, even in the late twentieth century, is the province of those who can afford it. In that sense, the action of breach of promise of marriage is not out-of-date and may never be.

Abbreviations

Notes

Bibliography

List of Cases

Index

Abbreviations

The following is a list of the Public Record Office Assize Court abbreviations. Only the abbreviations are in the text.

Public Record Office Number	Records
ASSI 1/1–38; 40–45; 48–68	Oxford Circuit Minute Books
ASSI 8/1–4	Oxford Circuit Pleadings
ASSI 15/3–4	Midland Circuit: Miscellaneous Papers and Books—Northants. Lent Assizes List of Cases with Various Particulars
ASSI 15/5–6	Midland Circuit: Letterbook kept by A. D. Coleridge, Deputy Clerk of Assize
ASSI 15/8	Midland Circuit: Judges Notes (1864)
ASSI 22/4–43	Western Circuit Minute Books, Civil
ASSI 24/19	Western Circuit Miscellaneous Books
ASSI 28/1–13	Western Circuit Pleadings
ASSI 32/14, 29–35	Nisi Prius Minute Books
ASSI 32/3–11	Home Circuit Associate's Minute Book (Civil Cases)
ASSI 32/12	Middlesex: Minute Book of the Court of Common Pleas Sitting as Nisi Prius Court for Middlesex (1827–28)
ASSI 32/16–24	Home Circuit Minute Book (Civil Cases)
ASSI 32/25	South Eastern Circuit: Home Division Minute Book (Civil Cases)
ASSI 32/26	South Eastern Circuit: Home Division Associate's Minute Book (Civil Cases)
ASSI 32/36	South Eastern Circuit: Norfolk Division Nisi Prius Minute Book
ASSI 32/37	South Eastern Circuit: Nisi Prius Minute Book
ASSI 32/38	South Eastern Circuit: Associate's Minute Book (Civil Cases)
ASSI 32/39	South Eastern Circuit: Nisi Prius Minute Book

ASSI 34/18–21	South Eastern Circuit: Miscellaneous Books—Norfolk Division, South Eastern Circuit—Certificates of Judgment (Civil Proceedings)
ASSI 34/24–25, 28–31	South Eastern Circuit: Miscellaneous Books—Certificates of Judgment (Civil Proceedings)
ASSI 34/32	South Eastern Circuit: Miscellaneous Books—Associate's Books, 1791–1812
ASSI 34/73	South Eastern Circuit: Miscellaneous Books—Norfolk Circuit Cause Book (Civil Proceedings)
ASSI 37/1–7	South Eastern Circuit Pleadings
ASSI 39/26	South Eastern Circuit Miscellanea: Miscellaneous Papers
ASSI 39/27	South Eastern Circuit Miscellanea: Norfolk Circuit—Nisi Prius Records (1867–75) and Associate's Entry Book (1866–72) of Causes
ASSI 43/9	North Eastern Circuit Miscellaneous Books: Note Books
ASSI 47/15	North Eastern Circuit Miscellanea: Miscellaneous Pleadings
ASSI 54/1–17	Northern Circuit Minute Books (Associate's Minute Book)
ASSI 55/1–2	Northern Circuit Miscellaneous Books: Judgment Book (Civil Only)
ASSI 57/3–7	Chester and North Wales Circuit Records of the Civil Court: Minute Books
ASSI 59/1–33	Chester and North Wales Circuit: Records of the Civil Court—Pleadings, Cause Lists, Jurors Lists
ASSI 59/89–151	Clerk of Assize: Chester and North Wales Circuit—Pleadings, Cause Lists, Jurors Lists
ASSI 63/32	Chester and North Wales Circuit Miscellaneous Books: Rough Note Book
ASSI 67/1	Chester and North Wales Circuit Miscellanea: Miscellaneous Papers
ASSI 67/6	Chester and North Wales Circuit Miscellanea: Miscellaneous Documents
ASSI 73/3	South Wales Circuit Miscellanea: Miscellaneous Pleadings and Papers
ASSI 75/1–4	South Wales Circuit Minute Books (Civil Court)

Notes

Introduction

1. Dickens, *The Pickwick Papers*.
2. Buzfuz may have been based on a real barrister, Sergeant Bompas, K.C., who was called to the bar in 1815 and died in 1844. Fitzgerald, ed., *Bardell v. Pickwick*, 41–43.
3. These letters may have been based on those in the notorious 1836 trial *Norton v. Melbourne*. See Fitzgerald, *The History of Pickwick*, 144–46.
4. Stareleigh, too, may have been based on an actual judge, Sir Stephen Gaselee. Fitzgerald, *Bardell v. Pickwick*, 32.
5. Fitzgerald estimated that the costs would have amounted to around £220. See *Bardell v. Pickwick*, 107.
6. Hollingshead, *Bardell v. Pickwick*; Barrymore, *Bardell v. Pickwick*; and Cosmo Hamilton and Reilly, *Pickwick: A Play in Three Acts*, 179–216. See also Young, *Mr. Pickwick*, 129–56; Fitzgerald's remarks in *Bardell v. Pickwick*, 1, 43; the preacher quoted in Fitzgerald, *The History of Pickwick*, 150 n. 2; and the *Oxford English Dictionary*, quoted in Fitzgerald, *Bardell v. Pickwick*, 111.
7. Law books quoted in Fitzgerald, *Bardell v. Pickwick*, 63; *Gregory v. Beach*, ASSI 22/ 33; *Dorset County Chronicle*, Mar. 13, 1873, 8; *Owen v. Williams*, ASSI 59/142; *Caernarvon and Denbigh Herald*, July 19, 1879, 7; and *Jones v. Chapman*, ASSI 22/40; *Cornish Telegraph*, Mar. 7, 1889, 6.
8. *Law Times* 48 (1870): 407; 44 (1868): 484; and *Law Notes* 11 (1892): 69. See also *Solicitor's Journal and Reporter* 25 (1881): 791.
9. MacColla, *Breach of Promise*, 15; Odgers, *A Century of Law Reform*, 216; Parry, *The Law and the Woman*, 37; Ashley, *My Sixty Years in the Law*, 199; Nokes, "Evidence," 143–44; and *Hansard's Parliamentary Debates*, (hereafter abbreviated to *Hansard*) 5th series, 799 (1970): 928. See also Lockwood, *The Law and Lawyers of Pickwick*, 55–62, 70–103.
10. Buckstone, *Breach of Promise; Or Second Thoughts Are Best*. First performed in London, it was revived in New York in 1853 and 1855.
11. *The Breach of Promise* was a novel published in 3 volumes.
12. Robinson, ed., *Trial by Jury*, 42–57.
13. *A Strange Case of Breach of Promise of Marriage*.
14. "A Breach of Promise," *Chambers' Journal* 33 (1860): 257–60.
15. "A Breach of Promise," *Bow Bells* 6 (1867): 428–29.
16. "Our Engagement," 132–40; "A Breach of Promise," *All the Year Round* 28 (1881): 297–302; and Holmes, *A Breach of Promise*. See also Gorham, "The Ideology of Femininity," 39–59, especially 40–52; and Mitchell, "The Forgotten Woman of the Period," 29–51.
17. Kuehn, "Reading Microhistory," 512–34; and Hammerton, *Cruelty and Companionship*, 170–76.

I. The Legal History of Breach of Promise

1. *Hansard,* 3d series, 245 (1879): 1869.
2. See especially Sir Hardinge Gifford, ibid., 1884.
3. Bacon, *A New Abridgement of the Law,* 4:460–61; and "Breach of Promise," *Justice of the Peace* 56 (1892): 563.
4. "Some Early Breach of Promise Cases," *Pump Court* 11 (1891): 592.
5. 2 *Croke's Reports* 66 (n.d.). See also *Pump Court* 1 (1883): 100; and MacColla, *Breach of Promise,* 3–4.
6. Ingram, *Church Courts, Sex, and Marriage in England,* 192–95. See also Amussen, *An Ordered Society,* 104–17.
7. Ingram, *Church Courts, Sex, and Marriage in England,* 205–9; Houlbrooke, *Church Courts and the People,* 66–67; Milsom, *Historical Foundations,* 289; and Amussen, *An Ordered Society,* 109–11.
8. For a late example of such intervention, see *Fuller v. Sheppard,* Lambeth Palace Library, Court of Arches Depositions, D797, Case 3544, 105–341 (fiches 4400–4408; 1750).
9. Quoted in White, "Breach of Promise of Marriage," 135; case found in *Carthew's Reports,* 233 (1674). See also Jenks, *A Short History of English Law,* 310.
10. Bacon, *A New Abridgement of the Law,* 4:461.
11. White, "Breach of Promise of Marriage," 135–36; case found in *Carthew's Reports,* 469 (1698). See also Jenks, *A Short History of English Law,* 310.
12. Jenks, *A Short History of English Law,* 311; and MacColla, *Breach of Promise,* 13.
13. See *Annual Register* 9 (1766): 75; 11 (1768): 97, 155; 19 (1776): 200–201; 21 (1778): 187; 23 (1780): 218–19. See also Gillis, *For Better, For Worse,* 179–89, 231–47; and David Levine, *Family Formation,* 131–45.
14. 98 *English Reports* 543 (1772). The jury awarded her £500.
15. See *Annual Register* 19 (1776): 138, 200–201; 22 (1779): 203.
16. 170 *English Reports* 217, 209 (1796).
17. *Annual Register* 23 (1780): 218–19.
18. See nn. 12, 14 above.
19. Lawrence Stone, *Road to Divorce,* 85–95; and Hill, *Eighteenth-Century Women,* 140.
20. Grossberg, *Governing the Hearth,* 33.
21. The preeminent law treatise on the subject was that of Joseph Chitty on Contract. I have also drawn this section from the following: Cleveland, *Woman under the English Law,* 222–24; Crofts, *Women under English Law,* 15–16; John William Edwards, *The Law of Husband and Wife,* 1–16; Emery, *The Law Relating to Husband and Wife,* 1–4; Eversley, *The Law of Domestic Relations,* 111–18; Geary, *The Law of Marriage and Family Relations,* 410–13; Grant, *Marriage, Separation and Divorce,* 18–21; Jenks, *Husband and Wife in the Law,* 4–7; Johnson, *Family Law,* 15–27; MacQueen, *The Rights and Liabilities of Husband and Wife,* 224–31; Parry, *The Law and the Woman,* 37–39; Thicknesse, *The Rights and Wrongs of Women,* 37–39; Travers, *Husband and Wife in English Law,* 8–11; and Wharton, *An Exposition of the Laws,* 213–18.
22. See *Frost v. Knight,* 7 *Law Reports, Exchequer Cases* 111–18 (1872); *Albany Law Journal* 3 (1871): 133–37; 5 (1872): 152–53; *The Times,* June 22, 1871, 11.
23. 120 *English Reports* 695–706 (1859), quote from 703.
24. See *Baker v. Cartwright,* 142 *English Reports* 397–98 (1861).

25. *Hansard*, 3d series, 54 (1840): 967–75, quote from 971. See also Higginbotham, "The Unmarried Mother and Her Child," 21.

26. "Proposed Mode of Redress for the Poor in Cases of Seduction, under Breach of Promise of Marriage," 234.

27. *Jurist* 4 (1840): 305–6, quote from 306.

28. Head, *Report on the Law of Bastardy*, 26–31.

29. *Hansard*, 3d series, 54 (1840): 971–75; and Henriques, "Bastardy and the New Poor Law," 117–20.

30. *Hansard*, 3d series, 116 (1851): 1–20; 118 (1851): 838–49.

31. Waddilove, "The Law of Evidence," 136.

32. Wilson's and Forsythe's arguments are in "Summary of Proceedings," 241, 247.

33. *Hansard*, 3d series, 195 (1869): 1801–2.

34. Quoted from *Bessela v. Stern*, 2 *Law Reports, Common Pleas Division* 266 n. 1 (1877).

35. *Hansard*, 3d series, 195 (1869): 1801, 1807.

36. *Law Journal* 4 (1869): 180.

37. 2 *Law Reports, Common Pleas Division* 265–72 (1877), quote from 266; and *The Times*, Feb. 8, 1877, 10.

38. *Wiedemann v. Walpole*, 2 *Law Reports, Queen's Bench Division* 537–42 (1891); *The Times*, June 11, 1891, 13; June 12, 1891, 4; June 13, 1891, 18; June 15, 1891, 3; June 16, 1891, 3; June 17, 1891, 3; June 18, 1891, 4.

39. *Watkins v. Davies*, ASSI 57/7; *Caernarvon and Denbigh Herald*, Mar. 30, 1872, 3; *The Times*, Apr. 20, 1872, 11; *Weekly Notes*, Pt. 1 (1872): 146; *Callan v. Price*, ASSI 54/2; *Liverpool Daily Post*, Feb. 9, 1880, 6; *Fishwick v. Barrow*, ASSI 54/14; *Liverpool Mercury*, July 29, 1896, 7; *Potter v. Fox*, ASSI 54/4; *Manchester Evening News*, July 17, 1885, 3; *Hirst v. Waddington*, ASSI 54/7; *Manchester Guardian*, July 13, 1889, 11; *Nicholson v. Maclachlan*, ASSI 75/3; *Haverfordwest and Milford Haven Telegraph*, Jan. 22, 1896, 4; *Jardenes v. Oppler*, *Illustrated Police News*, June 25, 1898, 8; *Owen v. Moberly*, *Justice of the Peace* 64 (1900): 88; and *Spooner v. Godfrey*, *The Times*, May 6, 1908, 17–18.

40. "Parties as Witnesses in Breach of Promise," 390. See also *Law Times* 47 (1869): 311; 48 (1870): 407.

41. *Law Journal* 26 (1891): 414; and *Haycox v. Bishton*, ASSI 1/65; *Staffordshire Sentinel and Commercial and General Advertiser*, Mar. 19, 1870, 8.

42. "Parties as Witnesses in Breach of Promise Cases," 271.

43. The examples used by the supporters of the bill were commercial contracts by seamen and students. See *Hansard*, 3d series, 219 (1874): 1225–26.

44. *The Times*, Mar. 19, 1878, 6; and 3 *Law Reports, Common Pleas Division* 439 (1878).

45. *Northcote v. Doughty*, 4 *Law Reports, Common Pleas Division* 385–91 (1879), quote from 386; *Ditcham v. Worrall*, 5 *Law Reports, Common Pleas Division* 410–23 (1880), quote from 421. See also *The Times*, Mar. 12, 1880, 4; May 10, 1880, 6; June 24, 1880, 6.

46. See *Whitehead v. Hall*, ASSI 54/5; *Solicitor's Journal and Reporter* 31 (1886–87): 445; *Manchester Examiner and Times*, Apr. 29, 1887, 8; *Jurist* 1 (1882): 164; and *Holmes v. Brierly*, *Law Times* 59 (1888): 70–72. See also *Pump Court* 7 (1888): 117; 8 (1889): 32.

47. See *Copley v. Ottley*, brought in the Holmfirth County Court in 1871, *Lady's Own Paper* 8 (Oct. 14, 1871): 253.

48. *Hansard*, 3d series, 245 (1879): 1867, 1887.

49. MacColla, *Breach of Promise*, 51–52.

50. *Prevost v. Wood, Times Law Reports* 21 (1905): 684–85; and *Siveyer v. Allison,* 2 *Law Reports, King's Bench Division* 403–8 (1935).
51. *Fender v. St. John-Mildmay,* 1 *Appeal Cases before the House of Lords* 1–56 (1938). See also *Skipp v. Kelly, Times Law Reports* 42 (1926): 258–59.
52. 2 *Law Reports, Queen's Bench Division* 429–43 (1954).
53. Olive Stone, *Family Law,* 24. See also *Beyers v. Green,* 1 *All England Law Reports* 613–15 (1936).
54. *Hanson v. Dixon, Law Times* 96 (1907): 32–34; and *Kremezi v. Ridgeway, Solicitor's Journal and Reporter* 93 (1949): 287–88.
55. *Chana v. Chana, The Times,* May 20, 1969, 2; *Modestou v. Yeannopoulis, The Times,* Mar. 31, 1954, 11.
56. Bromley, *Family Law,* 16; *Hansard,* 5th series, 302 (1934–35): 173–75; 312 (1935–36): 2012–13; 536 (1954–55): 174–75; 621 (1959–60): 1053; 653 (1961–62): 586–87; 666 (1962–63): 1126; 704 (1964–65): 1209–10; Law Commission, *Breach of Promise of Marriage;* and *Hansard,* 5th series, 799 (1969–70): 913–39.

II. The Court as Public Theatre

1. *Bardens v. Amey,* ASSI 28/8, Thomas Parker to J. H. Amey, June 26, 1892, 1–2.
2. *Bardens v. Amey,* ASSI 28/8, Correspondence, 1–9. See also ASSI 22/41; *Western Times,* Mar. 9, 1893, 3. Bardens eventually won £100.
3. Dubinsky, *Improper Advances,* 90–94. See also Gay, *The Bourgeois Experience,* vol. 2, *The Tender Passion,* 203.
4. See *Richardson v. Anderson,* ASSI 54/12; *Manchester Examiner and Times,* May 2, 1893, 7; *Jones v. Chapman;* and *Ibbetson v. Strickland,* ASSI 22/40; *Western Times,* Mar. 5, 1889, 3.
5. *Vickery v. Strawbridge,* ASSI 22/42; *Devon Weekly Times,* Feb. 1, 1895, 6; and see also *Gore v. Sudley, Cardiff Times,* June 13, 1896, 6.
6. *Lewis v. Jenkins,* ASSI 75/4; *Swansea Herald and Herald of Wales,* Aug. 13, 1898, 2; *Kelly v. Bell,* ASSI 54/2; *Carlisle Express and Examiner,* July 3, 1880, 8.
7. *Parker v. Stockwell,* ASSI 54/17; *Manchester Guardian,* Apr. 26, 1899, 10.
8. Peter Brooks, *The Melodramatic Imagination,* 28–49. See also Booth, *Hiss the Villain,* 9–40; Poovy, *Uneven Developments,* chapter 3; and Walkowitz, *City of Dreadful Delight,* chapters 3, 6.
9. Dubinsky, *Improper Advances,* 128–30.
10. Because the vast majority of plaintiffs in the nineteenth century were women (97 percent in my sample), this chapter will assume that plaintiffs are female. For early correspondence after a breach, see *Searing v. Newton,* ASSI 37/1, Correspondence, letters 9–11, 13–14, 17–19 (1878). Also found in ASSI 32/36 and ASSI 39/1. Eventually, the case was withdrawn.
11. Peter Brooks, *The Melodramatic Imagination,* 33.
12. See, for example, Bullock, *Courtship and Marriage,* 24–25.
13. *Jukes v. Lloyd,* ASSI 1/67; *Shrewsbury Chronicle,* July 28, 1882 (Second Sheet), 9; *Allmand v. Forrester,* ASSI 1/67; *Shrewsbury Chronicle,* Feb. 3, 1882, 6; and *Blackham v. Simpson,* ASSI 1/68; *Staffordshire Advertiser,* Feb. 19, 1887, 6.
14. Anna Clark, "Queen Caroline," especially 52–54.
15. *B. v. R.,* Greater London Record Office, Foundling Hospital Petitions, A/FH/A8/

1, Rejected Petitions 1 (1841); and a letter from Emily Klingelhorfer to Guardians of the London Foundling Hospital, 2.

16. For a case with a contingency fee, see *Thatcher v. D'Aguilar, Chronicles of Breaches of Promise* (n.d.), 137–42.

17. Thirteen barristers appeared 10 or more times in the 300 cases for which the barristers were listed. They include Addison (13); Bullen (14); Bulwer (11); Coleridge (10); Gully (10); Huddleston (15); Matthews (15); MacIntyre (12); McKeand (15); Metcalfe (12); O'Malley (13); Powell (11); and Shee (16).

18. *Bardens v. Amey*, ASSI 28/8, Albert Akaster to Thomas Parker, June 27, 1892; and Albert Akaster to Olive Bardens, June 27, 1892, 1.

19. Ibid., Thomas Parker to Albert Akaster, June 28, 1892.

20. *Frampton v. Veeley*, ASSI 28/12 (1897); and *James v. Phillips*, ASSI 75/3; *Cardigan and Tivy-Side Advertiser*, Mar. 1, 1889, 4. See also *Fawkes v. Harding*, ASSI 54/11; *Carlisle Journal*, Feb. 20, 1893, 3.

21. For an example, see *Price v. Brooks*, ASSI 8/3, "Statement of Defense." Case also found in ASSI 1/66; *Worcester Chronicle*, Mar. 16, 1878, 8.

22. Some pleadings were more detailed, particularly when they involved multiple actions or countersuits. See *Orman v. James*, ASSI 22/43; ASSI 28/13 (1898); and *Corio v. Salmon*, ASSI 32/38; ASSI 37/7 (1886).

23. Judicial Statistics, *Parliamentary Papers*, 1859–1922, passim.

24. See *Wilkinson v. Rylands*, ASSI 54/3; *Liverpool Mercury*, May 4, 1882, 8; *Liverpool Daily Post*, May 4, 1882, 6; *Pepperell v. Grills*, ASSI 22/33; *Devon Weekly Times*, Aug. 1, 1878, 8; and *Williams v. Mathias*, ASSI 75/3; *South Wales Daily News*, June 25, 1894, 7.

25. See judge's remarks in *Williams v. Mathias*, *South Wales Daily News*, June 25, 1894, 7; and *Haun v. Bradford*, *The Times*, July 29, 1872, 11; July 31, 1872, 11.

26. Searing's barrister went through her correspondence and underlined crucial passages. He also put reminders in the margin, either double vertical lines or simply "Read!" *Searing v. Newton*, ASSI 37/1, letters 1–5, 9–12 (1878). See also *Jones v. Griffiths*, ASSI 59/144; *Chester Chronicle*, July 31, 1880, 5.

27. Peter Brooks, *The Melodramatic Imagination*, 36.

28. Ibid., 35–36.

29. Polson, *Law and Lawyers*, 2:266.

30. Walton, *Random Recollections*, 2:145. See also *The Bench and the Bar*, 1:218.

31. *Solicitor's Journal and Reporter* 22 (1878): 741.

32. For an exception, see *Stanton v. Paton and Wife*, *Annual Register* 85 (1843): 383–88. The defense went first, but only because the defendant was female.

33. *Barrow v. Twist*, ASSI 54/5; *Manchester Examiner and Times*, July 17, 1886, 3.

34. Peter Brooks, *The Melodramatic Imagination*, 37.

35. *Brown v. Barnfather*, ASSI 54/4; *Carlisle Express and Examiner*, Jan. 23, 1886, 8.

36. *Pettit v. Tough*, ASSI 54/16; *Lancaster Gazette*, July 9, 1898, 6. See also *Bull v. Robinson*, ASSI 32/31; *Cambridge Independent Press*, Aug. 6, 1870, 6–7.

37. *Ashton v. Scholes*, ASSI 54/14; *Manchester Evening Mail*, Dec. 9, 1895, 3; and *Harvey v. Foard*, ASSI 1/65; *Gloucestershire Chronicle*, Apr. 5, 1873, 5.

38. See, for example, *Ashton v. Scholes*.

39. *Penny v. Rees*, ASSI 22/32; *Western Times*, Mar. 18, 1872, 4; whole case on 3–4; Mar. 19, 1872, 5.

40. *Penny v. Rees, Western Times,* Mar. 19, 1872, 5.

41. See *Richards v. Palmer,* ASSI 22/40; *Taunton Courier,* Feb. 22, 1888, 7.

42. Richard Harris, ed., *The Reminiscences of Sir Henry Hawkins,* 2:88–90.

43. *Burrow v. Lovell,* ASSI 22/41; *Western Times,* Mar. 9, 1893, 3. See also *Black v. Sparling,* ASSI 54/16; *Liverpool Daily Post,* Feb. 16, 1898, 3.

44. Peter Brooks, *The Melodramatic Imagination,* 88.

45. *Shickell v. Warren,* ASSI 32/39; *Norwich Argus,* July 26, 1890, 4. See also *Seed v. Caldwell,* ASSI 54/12; *Manchester Examiner,* Mar. 7, 1894, 2.

46. *Humphries v. Gain,* ASSI 22/39; *Hampshire Chronicle,* Aug. 9, 1884, 7. The jury awarded the plaintiff £125.

47. For remarks on defendants' difficulties, see *Capron v. Denning,* ASSI 22/28; *Exeter and Plymouth Gazette,* July 27, 1866, 6. For an exoneration defense, see *Railton v. Wilcox, Manchester Evening News,* Apr. 12, 1880, 3.

48. *Jones v. James,* ASSI 75/2; *Carmarthen Journal,* Mar. 6, 1868, 2. Jones won £250, and the judge recommended the three witnesses be tried for perjury.

49. See remarks in *Owens v. Horton, Birmingham Daily Gazette,* Mar. 22, 1890, 6; and *Dainty v. Brown,* ASSI 32/31; *Northampton Mercury,* July 23, 1870, 7.

50. See *Pattinson v. Heslop,* ASSI 54/14; *Carlisle Express and Examiner,* July 4, 1896, 6; and *Williams v. Dodd,* ASSI 54/16; *Manchester Evening Mail,* Apr. 25, 1898, 4.

51. Peter Brooks, *The Melodramatic Imagination,* chapter 3.

52. Ibid., 31.

53. *Roberts v. Jones,* ASSI 59/142; *Caernarvon and Denbigh Herald,* July 19, 1879, 7.

54. *Hancock v. Davies,* ASSI 73/3; *Swansea Herald and Neath Gazette,* Aug. 7, 1889, 3; and *Clough v. Southern,* ASSI 54/11; *Liverpool Mercury,* Apr. 14, 1892, 7.

55. *Langley v. Trickett,* ASSI 54/2; *Manchester Evening News,* Feb. 3, 1880, 4. The jury gave the plaintiff £25.

56. *Lamb v. Fryer, Liverpool Daily Post,* Aug. 9, 1881, 7.

57. *Adams v. Leach,* ASSI 22/42; *Taunton Courier,* Jan. 23, 1895, 6. For older plaintiffs, see *Owen v. Williams;* and *Norris v. Burnett, Somerset County Gazette and Bristol Express,* Aug. 10, 1872, 7–8.

58. Most jurymen were lower middle class, except in cases with "special" juries, which were of higher station. Defendants sometimes requested special juries, perhaps fearing that lower middle-class men were influenced by melodrama or class solidarity. Crispe, *Reminiscences of a K.C.,* 250; Jenks, *The Book of English Law,* 79; Peter Brooks, *The Melodramatic Imagination,* xii; and Booth, *Hiss the Villain,* 15–16.

59. Ruth Harris, "Melodrama, Hysteria and Feminine Crimes," 31–63. See also Conley, *The Unwritten Law,* 72.

60. See *Jones v. Lloyd, Maddocks v. Bennett,* and *Clark v. Daintith,* ASSI 59/14; *Chester Chronicle,* Mar. 14, 1891, 2 (respectively, 2 hours, 6 hours, and 1 hour); and *Williams v. Roberts,* ASSI 59/9; *Caernarvon and Denbigh Herald,* July 20, 1888, 8, slightly over 2 hours.

61. See *Allit v. Bradley,* ASSI 1/66; ASSI 8/1; *Oxford Times,* July 7, 1877, 2; *Allen v. Hutchings, The Times,* Mar. 22, 1878, 10; *Hairs v. Elliot, The Times,* Apr. 18, 1890, 3; Apr. 19, 1890, 5–6; and *Otte v. Grant, The Times,* Nov. 27, 1868, 11.

62. See *Bowden v. Tucker,* ASSI 22/40; *Western Times,* July 23, 1889, 5.

63. For denial of costs, see *Lewis v. Molyneux, Liverpool Mercury,* Nov. 7, 1878, 8. For

stays, see *Lamb v. Fryer;* and *Theophilus v. Howard,* ASSI 75/2; *Cardiff Times,* Aug. 1, 1874, 6.

64. *Chilton v. Hawkes,* ASSI 1/68; *Shrewsbury Chronicle,* Mar. 15, 1889, 6; and *Gibson v. Moore,* ASSI 59/3 (1885).

65. On juries' discretion, see *Hickey v. Campion, Weekly Reporter* 20 (1872): 752–54. For unsuccessful appeals, see *Miller v. Joy, The Times,* Jan. 25, 1884, 3; *Blackham v. Pratt, The Times,* Mar. 7, 1864, 11; *Law Times* 39 (1864): 217–18; *Roberts v. Denham, Law Times* 4 (1844): 118; *Nightengale v. Perry, The Times,* Apr. 20, 1875, 11; and *Thomas v. Shirley, Weekly Reporter* 11 (1862): 21; *The Times,* Nov. 6, 1862, 8; Nov. 7, 1862, 9.

66. *Holt v. Hamer,* ASSI 54/2; *Manchester Evening News,* July 22, 1881, 3; *Parker v. Wilkins,* ASSI 32/38; *Norwich Argus,* July 25, 1885, 8; *Whittaker v. Haythornethwaite,* ASSI 54/17; *Manchester Guardian,* July 21, 1899, 3; and *Bowden v. Tucker.*

67. *Cowper v. Holden,* ASSI 54/7; *Manchester Examiner and Times,* Mar. 6, 1889, 3; and *Drake v. Blake,* ASSI 22/32; *Winchester Herald,* Mar. 9, 1872, 3. See also *Softley v. Thompson, The Times,* Feb. 19, 1883, 10.

68. Barret-Ducrocq, *Love in the Time of Victoria,* 157.

69. *Kennedy v. McCann,* ASSI 54/13; *Manchester Evening Mail,* Apr. 17, 1895, 3; Apr. 18, 1895, 2.

70. Ibid., *Manchester Evening Mail,* Feb. 14, 1896, 2. See also *Leathers v. Marshall, Lady's Own Paper* 8 (Sept. 16, 1871): 187.

71. *Knowles v. Duncan,* ASSI 32/39; *The Times,* Aug. 13, 1890, 8. Most of the details are from Wyndham, "Romance That Failed," *Dramas of the Law,* 169–205.

72. Crispe, *Reminiscences of a K.C.,* 132–35.

73. *Pump Court* 1 (1883): 98. Holloway was probably depressed because the jury based the low award on the fact that "they thought the plaintiff had had a very lucky escape" in not marrying him, *The Times,* Nov. 8, 1883, 3.

74. *Hamilton v. Jacobs, Illustrated Police News,* Jan. 16, 1897, 8.

III. Gender Roles

1. Davidoff and Hall, *Family Fortunes;* Gillis, *For Better, For Worse;* Stearns, *Be a Man!* and Tosh and Roper, eds., *Manful Assertions,* 1–24.

2. McClelland, "Masculinity and the 'Representative Artisan,'" 74–91; and McClelland, "Time to Work, Time to Live," 180–209. For middle-class studies, see Mangan and Walvin, eds., *Manliness and Morality;* Vance, *Sinews of the Spirit;* and most of the articles in Tosh and Roper, eds., *Manful Assertions.*

3. Most of the people who brought breach-of-promise cases were lower middle class. From the 493 cases in which the classes of both parties are known, 153 are between 2 lower middle-class people, 105 are between a lower middle-class plaintiff and a middle-class defendant, and 80 are between a working-class plaintiff and a lower middle-class defendant. Although 53 percent of the cases involve cross-class matings, then, they do not involve wide margins.

4. *Brookfield v. Wilcock, Lady's Own Paper* 8 (Aug. 19, 1871): 125.

5. *Foote v. Hayne,* 171 *English Reports* 1310–11 (1824); *The Times,* Dec. 22, 1824, 1–4; Dec. 23, 1824, 2; Dec. 27, 1824, 3; and *Adams v. Jeeves,* ASSI 32/34; *Bedfordshire Times and Independent,* July 25, 1874, 6–7. See also *Dainty v. Brown.*

6. See *Addison v. Scoular, Norwich Argus,* Aug. 12, 1870, 7; *Hickey v. Campion;* and *Nightengale v. Perry,* in which the plaintiff had been engaged twice before and still won £500.

7. *Brookes v. Cox, Chronicles of Breaches of Promise* (n.d.), 173–76, quote from 176.

8. Warren, "Popular Manliness," 199–216, especially 200; and *Morris v. Leigh,* ASSI 54/11; *Manchester Examiner and Times,* Mar. 2, 1893, 7.

9. *Alderton v. Hunt,* ASSI 1/67; *Oxford Chronicle and Berks and Bucks Gazette,* July 10, 1880, 7; and *Kitteridge v. Crowe,* ASSI 32/29; *Cambridge Independent Press,* Mar. 24, 1860, 6. See also *Lewis v. Franklin,* ASSI 75/2; *South Wales Daily News,* Mar. 28, 1878, 3; and *Jillard v. Ryder,* ASSI 22/43; *Western Times,* June 21, 1899, 2.

10. *Bebbington v. Hitchen,* ASSI 57/7; ASSI 59/130; *Chester Chronicle,* Aug. 9, 1873, 3; *Williams v. Hughes,* ASSI 59/146; *Chester Chronicle,* July 30, 1881, 6; McClelland, "Masculinity and the 'Representative Artisan,'" 82–83; and Davidoff, "'Adam Spoke First,'" 237.

11. *Orford v. Cole,* 171 *English Reports* 670–71 (1818); *The Times,* Apr. 6, 1818, 3; and *Fleming v. Thompson, Lady's Own Paper* 4 (Aug. 28, 1869): 98. See also *Turner v. Jackson,* ASSI 54/16; *Manchester Evening Mail,* Apr. 26, 1898, 4.

12. McClelland, "Masculinity and the 'Representative Artisan,'" 85–87; and Sonya Rose, *Limited Livelihoods,* 53, 127–35. See also Lystra, *Searching the Heart,* 129–36; and Hall, *White, Male, and Middle-Class,* 219.

13. *Harworth v. Taylor,* ASSI 54/4; *Manchester Examiner and Times,* Feb. 4, 1886, 8; and *Ibbetson v. Strickland.* See also *Bell v. Jackson, Chronicles of Breaches of Promise* (n.d.), 131–33; Walker, "'I Live but Not Yet I,'" 92–112; Ross, "'Fierce Questions and Taunts,'" 575–602; and Anna Clark, "Queen Caroline," 53–54. For virile masculinity, see Norma Clark, "Strenuous Idleness," 25–43; and MacKenzie, "The Imperial Pioneer and Hunter," 176–98. See also Gregory Anderson, *Victorian Clerks,* 33; Conley, *The Unwritten Law,* 72; and Hammerton, *Cruelty and Companionship,* 29–33, 149–63.

14. *Wood v. Irving,* ASSI 54/9; *Carlisle Express,* July 11, 1891, 6; and *Nates v. Heap,* ASSI 54/9; *Manchester Examiner and Times,* Nov. 30, 1891, 6. For "hysteria" see *Penny v. Rees.*

15. Davidoff and Hall, *Family Fortunes,* 108–13, 180–92; and Tosh, "Domesticity and Manliness in the Victorian Middle Class," 46.

16. Conley, *The Unwritten Law,* 91.

17. *Windeatt v. Slocombe,* ASSI 22/32; *Western Times,* Mar. 15, 1872, 6.

18. *Carter v. Stowe,* ASSI 54/9; *Liverpool Mercury,* Mar. 24, 1891, 7; and *Wilkinson v. Hampson,* ASSI 54/5; *Liverpool Daily Post,* June 2, 1886, 3.

19. Springhall, *Youth, Empire and Society;* Rosenthal, *The Character Factory;* and Warren, "Popular Manliness." I am not arguing that this "virile manliness" approved of male unchastity, but that the aggressive aspects of late Victorian training for boys overcame some of its Christian features.

20. *Hairs v. Elliot, The Times,* Apr. 19, 1890, 5; *Herron v. Mort,* ASSI 54/8; *Liverpool Mercury,* July 28, 1890, 7; and *Fawkes v. Harding.*

21. *Green v. Ramwell, The Times,* Apr. 2, 1866, 11; and *Lewis v. Franklin.*

22. This was even true in the lower working class to some extent. See Ross, "'Not the Sort That Would Sit on the Doorstep,'" 49–51.

23. See *Davies v. Jenkins,* ASSI 75/2; *Cardiff Times,* July 24, 1869, 8. For more on re-

spectability, see the following by Ellen Ross: "'Fierce Questions and Taunts,'" "'Not the Sort That Would Sit on the Doorstep,'" "Survival Networks," 4–27, and *Love and Toil.*

24. *Dales v. McMaster,* ASSI 54/3; *Liverpool Mercury,* May 22, 1884, 6; May 23, 1884, 5, 8. See also *Roberts v. Hughes,* ASSI 57/7; ASSI 59/135; *Caernarvon and Denbigh Herald,* Mar. 25, 1876, 8; and *Williams v. Roberts,* ASSI 54/12; *Liverpool Daily Post,* Mar. 18, 1894, 3.

25. See *Orford v. Cole;* and *Martin v. Secker,* ASSI 22/41; *Western Times,* July 26, 1892, 7.

26. *Turner v. Jackson.*

27. *Chedzoy v. Woodbery,* ASSI 22/33; *Somerset County Gazette and Bristol Express,* Aug. 10, 1872, 7–8, quote from 8.

28. *Wilkinson v. Kelsall,* ASSI 57/7; ASSI 59/128; *Chester Chronicle,* Aug. 17, 1872, 7.

29. *Harbert v. Edginton, Law Times* 3 (1844): 51; *The Times,* Apr. 1, 1844, 6; Apr. 20, 1844, 8, quote from Apr. 1; and Conley, *The Unwritten Law,* 90.

30. See *Adams v. Jeeves.*

31. *Hagger v. Bush, Chronicles of Breaches of Promise* (n.d.), 169–73, quote from 170; and *Davies v. Harris,* ASSI 1/63; *Hereford Journal,* Mar. 26, 1864, 3.

32. *Williams v. Roberts* (1894).

33. Sonya Rose, *Limited Livelihoods,* 154–84.

34. See, among many others, Davidoff and Hall, *Family Fortunes,* 335–43; Gay, *The Bourgeois Experience,* vol. 1, *The Education of the Senses,* 88, 240, 259.

35. *Wilkinson v. Hampson;* and *Williams v. Mathias.* See also *Haynes v. Haynes, Chronicles of Breaches of Promise* (n.d.), 178–80; *Nangle v. Bamford,* ASSI 54/12; *Manchester Examiner and Times,* July 13, 1893, 8; and Sonya Rose, *Limited Livelihoods,* 99.

36. Conley, *The Unwritten Law,* 102.

37. *Bull v. Robinson.*

38. Tosh and Roper, eds., *Manful Assertions,* 1. See also Springhall, "Building Character in the British Boy," 59–61, 68–70; and Davidoff, "'Adam Spoke First,'" 246–47.

39. *Hole v. Harding,* ASSI 22/38; ASSI 28/6; *Exeter and Plymouth Gazette Daily Telegram,* Jan. 30, 1882, 3.

40. See *Robinson v. Cumming,* 26 *English Reports* 646–48 (1742); and *Morris v. Leigh.*

41. Tosh and Roper, eds., *Manful Assertions,* 15.

42. Of course, I am not arguing that men were the oppressed sex in Victorian times in a general way. Their disadvantages were peculiar to this lawsuit.

43. Hammerton, "Manliness and Marriage."

IV. Courtships and Weddings

1. Jane Lewis, *Women in England, 1870–1950,* 148; Michael Anderson, *Family Structure,* 124–32; Michael Anderson, "The Emergence of the Modern Life Cycle in Britain," 84; Jalland, *Women, Marriage, and Politics,* 21–22, 45–54; and Davidoff, *The Best Circles,* 36–52.

2. Hall, *White, Male, and Middle-Class,* 175.

3. Davidoff and Hall, *Family Fortunes,* 219–22, quote from 219; and Barret-Ducrocq, *Love in the Time of Victoria,* 74–86.

4. *Lewis v. Jenkins;* Davidoff, "The Separation of Home and Work?" 68–92. See also *Pope v. Staples,* ASSI 32/31; *Ipswich Express and Essex and Suffolk Mercury,* Mar. 29,

1870, 7; *Stringer v. Oldham,* ASSI 54/17; *Manchester Evening Mail,* July 12, 1900, 4; and *Walker v. Owen,* ASSI 54/9; *Liverpool Mercury,* May 5, 1891, 7.

5. Gillis, "Servants, Sexual Relations, and the Risks of Illegitimacy," 142–73; and Barret-Ducrocq, *Love in the Time of Victoria,* 51–73.

6. *Pearce v. Boardman,* ASSI 22/27; *Bristol Daily Post,* Aug. 16, 1867, 3; and *Haynes v. Haynes.* See also *Berry v. Hurst,* ASSI 54/1; *Manchester Evening News,* Jan. 21, 1872, 2; and *Swain v. Brinn, Newgate Calendar and Divorce Court Chronicle,* issue 9 (July 8, 1872): 138–40.

7. *Crosswell v. Hearn, The Times,* Nov. 13, 1893, 3; Nov. 14, 1893, 13; and *Morris v. Bonville,* ASSI 75/2; *Carmarthen Weekly Reporter,* July 21, 1876, 3. See also *Girling v. Allsop,* ASSI 32/29; *Suffolk Chronicle,* Aug. 3, 1861, 7; and *Copeland v. Hopkins,* ASSI 54/13; *Manchester Evening Mail,* Nov. 2, 1894, 2.

8. *Matthews v. Miller, Cornish Telegraph,* Feb. 16, 1882, 3; *Hancock v. Clifford,* ASSI 22/39; *Bristol Mercury,* Feb. 6, 1886, 6; and *Orman v. James.*

9. *Clark v. Daintith; Edwards v. Roberts,* ASSI 59/151; *Caernarvon and Denbigh Herald,* Feb. 2, 1884, 6; *Crookshank v. Farrow,* ASSI 54/7; *Manchester Examiner and Times,* Feb. 28, 1889, 3; and *Knowles v. Duncan,* ASSI 32/39; *The Times,* Aug. 13, 1890, 8. See also *Cooper v. Hyatt,* ASSI 22/42; *Bristol Mercury and Daily Post,* July 4, 1895, 2.

10. *Brown v. Friend,* ASSI 39/27; *Norwich Argus,* Mar. 29, 1873, 7. See also *Hampton v. Boalsh, Chronicles of Breaches of Promise* (n.d.), 183–84; and *Berry v. Da Costa,* 1 *Law Reports, Common Pleas Division,* 331–36 (1866); *The Times,* Jan. 15, 1866, 11; Jan. 26, 1866, 11.

11. *Abbot v. Harrison, Manchester Examiner and Times,* July 13, 1889, 8; and *Roberts v. Williams,* ASSI 59/3; *Caernarvon and Denbigh Herald,* July 25, 1885, 8.

12. Sudden proposals were apparently known in all classes, since William Gladstone proposed to two women he barely knew. See Magnus, *Gladstone,* 24–31. See also Stephen Gladstone's sudden infatuation in Jalland, *Women, Marriage, and Politics,* 76–77.

13. These figures vary by class. Lower middle-class couples averaged 11 months with a median of 4; working-class couples averaged 17 months with a median of 3.

14. Lower middle-class couples' average and median were almost identical to the overall figures (17 and 10); working-class couples saw each other an average and median of 8 times per month.

15. Michael Anderson, "The Emergence of the Modern Life Cycle in Britain," 82.

16. Crossick, "The Petite Bourgeoisie in Nineteenth-Century Britain," 78–79; and Jalland, *Women, Marriage, and Politics,* 54–55. See also Hill, *Women, Work, and Sexual Politics,* 179–80; and Elizabeth Roberts, *A Woman's Place,* 72–73.

17. *Jones v. Southworth,* ASSI 54/2; *Lancaster Observer and Morecambe Chronicle,* Jan. 21, 1881, 6. Jones, a weaver, received £100 from her plumber fiancé. See also *Wood v. Humphreys,* ASSI 1/68; *Gloucester Mercury,* Aug. 11, 1883, 3; and *Roberts v. Williams,* ASSI 59/29; *Chester Observer,* July 30, 1898, 6.

18. Hall, *White, Male, and Middle-Class,* 145.

19. *Curtis v. Olden,* ASSI 22/39; *Hampshire Chronicle,* Aug. 8, 1885, 8; and *Kerfoot v. Marsden,* 175 *English Reports* 1005 (1860); *The Times,* Aug. 25, 1860, 12. Kerfoot was the daughter of a farmer, and Marsden was a manufacturer. See also *Mallett v. Sutton, Illustrated Police News,* Apr. 1, 1871, 4.

20. *Green v. Patey, Jurist* 1 (1887): 324; *The Times,* Oct. 12, 1887, 7. See also *Lever v.*

Dobson, ASSI 54/7; *Liverpool Mercury*, May 21, 1889, 8; *Gregory v. Beach;* and *Taylor v. Entwistle*, ASSI 54/17; *Manchester Evening Mail*, Apr. 24, 1899, 4.

21. *Hawkridge v. Dommet*, ASSI 22/42; *Devon and Exeter Gazette*, June 29, 1897, 3; and Bullock, *Courtship and Marriage*, 24–25, quote from 25. See also Hill, *Women, Work, and Sexual Politics*, 191.

22. Sonya Rose, *Limited Livelihoods*, chapter 6; Thompson, *The Rise of Respectable Society*, 84; and Hall, *White, Male, and Middle-Class*, 143–45. See also Ross, "'Fierce Questions and Taunts,'" 575–602.

23. See *Dennis v. McKenzie*, ASSI 32/32; ASSI 39/27; *Law Times* 24 (1871): 363; *Cambridge Independent Press*, Mar. 25, 1871, 6–7. For the working class, see Burnett, ed., *Destiny Obscure*, 255; and Barret-Ducrocq, *Love in the Time of Victoria*, 113–23; 141–48. See also Lystra, *Searching the Heart*, 19–20.

24. Lystra, *Searching the Heart*, 157–91; and Rothman, *Hands and Hearts*, 56–84.

25. *Alderton v. Hunt;* and *Jones v. Williams*, ASSI 75/3; *Swansea and Glamorgan Herald and the Herald of Wales*, Nov. 28, 1896, 1 (the defendant was an office worker, the plaintiff the daughter of a farmer).

26. *Wood v. Irving* (Irving was a property owner, Wood the daughter of an innkeeper); and *Hancock v. Davies.* See also *Pullock v. Allard*, ASSI 1/64; *Gloucester Mercury*, Apr. 6, 1867, 2; and Lystra, *Searching the Heart*, 20–26.

27. *Roper v. Hills*, ASSI 32/32; *Suffolk Chronicle*, Apr. 1, 1871, 7; *The Times*, Mar. 31, 1871, 11; and *Wynn v. Hurst*, ASSI 1/66; *Shrewsbury Chronicle*, Mar. 26, 1875, 7.

28. *Jones v. Williams;* and *Jones v. Griffiths.*

29. *Reeves v. Powell*, ASSI 32/34; *Buckinghamshire Herald*, Mar. 15, 1873, 6–7.

30. *Bell v. Jackson*, 131; and *Roberts v. Williams* (1898). See also *Elder v. Brearly*, *Illustrated Police News*, Feb. 20, 1897, 6. In *Sutton v. Aronsberg*, ASSI 54/12; *Manchester Examiner and Times*, July 18, 1893, 5; July 19, 1893, 5, the defendant made an anagram of the plaintiff's name (Amy Sutton) and wrote a 9-line poem to go with it.

31. *Hall v. Taylor*, ASSI 1/65; *Oxford Chronicle and Berks and Bucks Gazette*, Mar. 1, 1873, 5. See also *Williams v. Haines*, ASSI 1/66; *Monmouthshire Merlin*, Apr. 2, 1875, 2; *Jones v. Boumphrey*, *Gloucester Mercury*, Apr. 11, 1863, 5; and *Jukes v. Lloyd.*

32. *Mason v. Mason*, ASSI 54/2; *Westmorland Gazette*, July 27, 1878, 7. See also *Pryke v. Smith*, ASSI 32/32; *Norwich Argus*, Aug. 12, 1871, 7; *Pepperell v. Grills;* and *Pullock v. Allard.*

33. McClelland, "Masculinity and the 'Representative Artisan,'" 74–91; and McClelland, "Time to Work, Time to Live," 180–209.

34. *Micklewright v. Bryning*, ASSI 54/3; *Liverpool Mercury*, Feb. 11, 1882, 8.

35. *Eldridge v. Rees*, ASSI 22/42; *Bristol Mercury*, July 1, 1895, 6; and *Barter v. Lawrence*, ASSI 22/37; *Western Times*, Jan. 26, 1880, 3–4.

36. *Appleton v. Scotter*, ASSI 54/5; *Liverpool Daily Post*, July 30, 1886, 3, between an engineman and a jeweler; and *Spender v. Orchard*, ASSI 22/36; *Hampshire Chronicle*, Mar. 9, 1878, 7. For a judge's view, see *Benson v. Durrant*, *Jurist* 2 (1888): 180; *The Times*, June 6, 1888, 4.

37. In 47 of the cases under study, both of the participants were 40 or above.

38. *Taylor v. Hardman*, ASSI 54/5; *Manchester Examiner and Times*, Jan. 31, 1887, 3; *Smith v. Strickland*, ASSI 54/1; *Liverpool Mercury*, Aug. 8, 1877, 8; *McLeod v. Horrocks*, *Illustrated Police News*, Mar. 30, 1872, 3; and *Wheeler v. Jones*, ASSI 57/7; *Chester Chronicle*, Aug. 21, 1869, 7. Widowers were more often involved in cases than widows: in 46

cases the plaintiff had been married before; in 82 the defendant had. Both parties had been previously married in 23 cases.

39. *Lacy v. Frankeiss,* ASSI 22/36; *Winchester Observer and County News,* July 6, 1878, 8. See also *Ashton v. Scholes;* and *Owen v. Jones,* ASSI 59/23; *Caernarvon and Denbigh Herald,* June 14, 1895, 7.

40. *Halliwell v. Rigby,* ASSI 54/3; *Manchester Evening News,* Feb. 3, 1885, 3.

41. *McLeod v. Horrocks;* and *Smith v. Strickland.* See also *Evans v. Jones,* ASSI 59/21; *Caernarvon and Denbigh Herald,* June 8, 1894, 8; and *Elliot v. Stranger, Bristol Mercury and Daily Post,* Apr. 15, 1878, 3.

42. *Wheeler v. Jones;* and *Thomas v. Edwards, Manchester Evening Mail,* Apr. 21, 1898, 2.

43. Gillis, *For Better, For Worse,* 299.

44. *McLeod v. Horrocks;* and *Thomas v. Edwards.*

45. For a long list, see *Wynn v. Hurst.*

46. *Carter v. Stowe,* between a shop assistant and a tailor; and *Brown v. Friend.* See also Jalland, *Women, Marriage, and Politics,* 37–38.

47. *Owen v. Williams* (the defendant was a farmer, the plaintiff's occupation unknown); *Higgs v. Trow,* ASSI 32/33; *Leicester Advertiser,* Mar. 2, 1872, 8, between a lodging-house keeper and a farmer and publican; *Bebbington v. Hitchen,* between a housekeeper and publican; *Brown v. Friend;* and *Adams v. Ireland, Cornish Telegraph,* Mar. 10, 1892, 2, in which the defendant was a farmer and the plaintiff's job was unknown.

48. *Pryke v. Smith;* and *Owen v. Williams.*

49. See *Higgs v. Trow;* and *Wynn v. Hurst.*

50. *Hill v. Proctor,* ASSI 32/34; *Norwich Argus,* Aug. 9, 1873, 7, in which the defendant was a farmer (plaintiff's occupation unknown); *Williams v. Thomas,* ASSI 75/4; *Brecon County Times,* Mar. 11, 1898, 8, between the daughter of a railroad foreman and a minister; and *Wilkinson v. Kelsall,* between the daughter of a hotelkeeper and a farmer.

51. *Smith v. Woodfine,* 140 *English Reports* 272–77 (1856); *The Times,* July 8, 1856, 11; *Wade v. Rae,* ASSI 32/34; ASSI 39/27; *Norwich Argus,* Aug. 9, 1873, 7; and *Alderton v. Hunt.*

52. See *Trainor v. Radcliffe,* ASSI 54/14; *Liverpool Mercury,* Nov. 23, 1895, 6; and *Tamikin v. Wilson,* ASSI 54/7; *Carlisle Express and Examiner,* July 6, 1889, 8.

53. *Hill v. Proctor.* See also *Wynn v. Hurst; Robinson v. Atkinson,* ASSI 54/3; *Carlisle Express and Examiner,* July 19, 1884, 6; *Penny v. Rees,* ASSI 22/32; *Western Times,* Mar. 19, 1872, 4; Davidoff and Hall, *Family Fortunes,* 407–8; and Elizabeth Roberts, *A Woman's Place,* 77.

54. *Pattinson v. Heslop;* and *Williams v. Thomas* (1898). See also *Ball v. Spickett, South Wales Daily News,* July 14, 1893, 4; and *McLeod v. Horrocks.*

55. See *Brown v. Friend; Higgs v. Trow;* and *Jukes v. Lloyd.* See also Perkin, *Women and Marriage in Nineteenth-Century England,* 21.

56. *Burton v. Howlett,* ASSI 32/37; *Supplement to the Norwich Argus,* Feb. 18, 1882, 1 (Howlett was a merchant; Burton's occupation was unknown); *Williams v. Thomas* (1898); and *Allmand v. Forrester,* between the daughter of a farmer and a farmer. For carriages, see *Hill v. Proctor.*

57. *Graves v. Cutforth, Illustrated Police News,* Jan. 25, 1896, 2; *Langley v. Trickett;* and *Williams v. Hughes.*

58. Ross, "'Not the Sort That Would Sit on the Doorstep,'" 39–59; and Perkin, *Women and Marriage in Nineteenth-Century England*, 126.

59. *White v. Aird*, *Newgate Calendar and Divorce Court Chronicle*, issue 3 (May 20, 1872): 46, between the daughter of an innkeeper and a master tailor; and *Ibbetson v. Strickland*, between the daughter of a farmer and a corn factor. See also *Pendlebury v. Doody*, ASSI 54/9; *Manchester Examiner and Times*, July 16, 1891, 3.

60. *Blakeman v. Bowers*, ASSI 1/68; *Staffordshire Advertiser*, Aug. 2, 1881, 6; and *Dainty v. Brown*.

61. Hill, *Women, Work, and Sexual Politics*, 185–86; Barret-Ducrocq, *Love in the Time of Victoria*, 87–91; and Leonard, *Sex and Generation*, 99–118.

62. *Bingley v. Barnes*, ASSI 54/11; *Manchester Examiner and Times*, Mar. 8, 1893, 7; and *Scrine v. M'Kay*, *Illustrated Police News*, Feb. 28, 1880, 2. See also *Rees v. Powell*, ASSI 75/3; *South Wales Daily News*, Mar. 13, 1888, 2; and *Theophilus v. Howard*.

63. *Shickell v. Warren*; and *Wood v. Humphreys*. See also *Powers v. Battersby*, ASSI 54/17; *Manchester Evening News*, Feb. 5, 1900, 4; and *Gee v. Entwistle*, ASSI 54/2; *Liverpool Mercury*, July 27, 1878, 8; July 29, 1878, 6.

64. *Bath v. Williams*, *South Wales Daily News*, Apr. 7, 1876, 6; and *Roberts v. Jones*. See also *Houghton v. Thompson*, ASSI 54/14; *Manchester Guardian*, Apr. 14, 1896, 9; and *Williams v. Harman*, ASSI 75/3; *Swansea and Glamorgan Herald*, Nov. 28, 1876, 1.

65. *Hole v. Harding*; and *Eden v. Ormand*, ASSI 32/31; *Buckinghamshire Herald*, Mar. 20, 1869, 3. See also *Heap v. Morris*, *The Times*, Mar. 8, 1878, 11.

66. *Sutton v. Aronsberg*; and *Owen v. Williams*. See also *Roberts v. Hughes*, ASSI 75/2; *Cardiff Times*, Feb. 25, 1882, 2; and *Pope v. Staples*.

67. *Smith v. Woodfine*; and *Hart v. Clinker*, *Staffordshire Times and Newcastle Pioneer*, Mar. 23, 1861, 3, between the daughter of a wheelwright and a clerk in an ironworks. See also *Kennerley v. Boulton*, ASSI 54/14; *Liverpool Mercury*, July 28, 1896, 6; and *Grafton v. King*, *Chronicles of Breaches of Promise* (n.d.), 161–63.

68. Thompson, *The Rise of Respectable Society*, 95. See also Wheeler, *Whom to Marry or All About Love and Matrimony*, 77.

69. Lawrence Stone, *The Family, Sex and Marriage*, 666–73; Jalland, *Women, Marriage, and Politics*, 46–51; Thompson, *The Rise of Respectable Society*, 109–12; and Rothman, *Hands and Hearts*, 25–28, 213–23. See also Michael Anderson, *Approaches to the History of the Western Family*, 49–53.

70. Thompson, *The Rise of Respectable Society*, 103; and Davidoff and Hall, *Family Fortunes*, 353–56.

71. *Nixon v. Moss*, ASSI 1/63; *Staffordshire Sentinel*, July 25, 1863, 7.

V. Broken Engagements in Victorian England

1. Joyce, *Work, Society and Politics*; Joyce, *Visions of the People*; Walkowitz, *City of Dreadful Delight*; and Scott, *Gender and the Politics of History*.

2. Perkin, *Women and Marriage in Nineteenth-Century England*, 61–62, 236; Thompson, *The Rise of Respectable Society*, 92–108; and Crossick, *An Artisan Elite in Victorian Society*, 119–27. See also Robin, *Elmson*, 135–55.

3. Howatt, "The Art and Science of Courtship, II," *Young Woman* 5 (1896–97): 112; Swan, "Love, Courtship, and Marriage," *Woman at Home* 2 (1895): 472, 237; and Bowen-Rowlands, *In Court and Out of Court*, 304.

4. Ryan, *The Philosophy of Marriage*, 61–89. Ryan advised marriage for love but also urged that the couple have "age, disposition, rank, and fortune" (89) in common. For the religious aspect, see de Bertouch, "Should Men Break Engagements? III," 376. See also Hall, *White, Male, and Middle-Class*, 173–74.

5. Thompson, *The Rise of Respectable Society*, 95; and Hall, *White, Male, and Middle-Class*, 181.

6. *Fitzpatrick v. Curling, Illustrated Police News*, Feb. 6, 1897, 2. See also Gay, *The Bourgeois Experience*, 1:390–91.

7. *Foote v. Hayne*. See also *Watkins v. Marjoribanks, Illustrated Police News*, Jan. 25, 1896, 8; Feb. 15, 1896, 3; *Gould v. Ingram*, Woman, issue 10 (Mar. 8, 1890): 1; *Hairs v. Elliot*, Woman, issue 17 (Apr. 26, 1890): 1; *The Times*, Apr. 18, 1890, 3; Apr. 19, 1890, 5; Apr. 22, 1890, 10; *Finney v. Garmoyle*, Wyndham, "Case of Viscount Garmoyle," 127–48; *The Times*, Nov. 21, 1884, 4; Kent, "Image and Reality," 94–116; and Rowbotham, *Good Girls Make Good Wives*, 241–45.

8. Walkowitz, *Prostitution and Victorian Society*, 24–31; and Bailey, "Parasexuality and Glamour," 148–72. See also Perkin, *Women and Marriage in Nineteenth-Century England*, 158–60.

9. *Ford v. Strongitharm*, ASSI 54/14; *Manchester Evening Mail*, Mar. 5, 1896, 2; and *Haun v. Bradford, The Times*, July 29, 1872, 11. See also *Seymour v. Gartside, The Times*, Aug. 19, 1822, 3.

10. Apparently, Gardner's work as a machinist was on small machines (probably in the textile trades), since she worked in private homes. *Gardner v. Thomas*, ASSI 22/27; *Bristol Mercury*, Aug. 23, 1873, 3.

11. Ibid. See also *Langford v. Tonge*, ASSI 54/5; *Manchester Examiner and Times*, Jan. 28, 1887, 3.

12. *Watkins v. Davies*; and *Hadad v. Bruce, Times Law Reports* 8 (1891–92): 409–10; *Cornish Telegraph*, Mar. 10, 1892, 2. See also *Wilkinson v. Rylands; Ibbetson v. Strickland; Mather v. Royston*, ASSI 54/17; *Liverpool Mercury*, Aug. 7, 1899, 7; and *Aggett v. Elliott*, ASSI 22/33; *The Times*, July 29, 1872, 11.

13. Barret-Ducrocq, *Love in the Time of Victoria*, 51–73.

14. *Allen v. Hutchings*; and *McGrath v. De Valve*, ASSI 54/8; *Liverpool Mercury*, July 29, 1890, 7. See also *Wood v. Irving; Pattinson v. Heslop*; and *Warwick v. Pownall*, ASSI 54/3; *Liverpool Mercury*, May 24, 1884, 8; *The Times*, May 26, 1884, 14. In Allen's trial the jury could not agree; McGrath settled for £300.

15. *Wharton v. Lewis*, 171 *English Reports* 1303–4 (1824); *The Times*, Dec. 7, 1824, 2–3; and *Brice v. Pemberton*, ASSI 54/11; *Manchester Examiner and Times*, Mar. 1, 1893, 3. See also *Bingley v. Barnes*, ASSI 54/11; *Manchester Examiner and Times*, Mar. 8, 1893, 7; Mar. 9, 1893, 7.

16. Vincent, *Bread, Knowledge and Freedom*, 48–49; and Gillis, "Servants, Sexual Relations, and the Risks of Illegitimacy," 155.

17. These numbers are based on cases in which the parties are of the same class; 2 of the upper class; 36 of the middle class; 153 of the lower middle class; and 39 in the working class. The upper and middle classes were separated 10 times and delayed 7; the lower middle and working classes were separated 34 times and delayed 70.

18. Jalland, *Women, Marriage, and Politics*, 27–30; and Romilly, Armytage, Dixon, and Lang, "Symposium on the Desirability of Long or Short Engagements," 445, 447–49. See also Braby, *Modern Marriage and How to Bear It*, 78–79; and Mrs. Joseph

Parker, "Should Long Engagements Be Encouraged?" 39–40. Those who argued for long engagements include Lang, in Romilly, Armytage, Dixon, and Lang, "Symposium on the Desirability of Long or Short Engagements," 449–50; and Swan and Lady Gilzean Reid, "Should Long Engagements Be Encouraged?" 37–39. However, even those in favor did not expect an engagement to last longer than two years. See Swan, "Love, Courtship, and Marriage," 155.

19. Mrs. Joseph Parker, "Should Long Engagements Be Encouraged?" 39. See also Harry Davies, "The Courtship of Ezra," 969–75; and Penn, *Manchester Fourteen Miles*, 30.

20. *Nelson v. Taylforth*, ASSI 54/16; *Westmorland Gazette*, Jan. 21, 1899, 6; and *Kennerley v. Boulton.* See also *Redfern v. White*, ASSI 1/68; *Staffordshire Advertiser*, Aug. 1, 1885, 5; *Davies v. Jenkins*, ASSI 75/2; *Swansea and Glamorgan Herald*, July 31, 1878, 8; *May v. Rotton*, ASSI 22/36; *Somerset County Gazette*, Apr. 13, 1878, 7; and *Armstrong v. Gray*, ASSI 1/66; ASSI 8/1 (1876).

21. *Roper v. Bagley*, ASSI 32/36; *The Times*, Aug. 2, 1880, 11; and *Brookes v. Cox.* See also *Allmand v. Forrester.*

22. *Burgoyne v. Oldrieve*, ASSI 22/33; *Western Times*, Mar. 18, 1873, 5; and *Ditcham v. Worrall.* See also *Addison v. Scoular;* and Nicholson, *Wednesday Early Closing*, 195–96.

23. *Pierce v. Smith, Newgate Calendar and Divorce Court Chronicle*, issue 9 (July 8, 1872): 146; and *Dods v. Woollett, Liverpool Daily Post*, May 15, 1882, 7; *Liverpool Mercury*, May 15, 1882, 8. See also *Southwood v. Arscott*, ASSI 22/42; *Devon Weekly Times*, Feb. 1, 1895, 6.

24. *Martin v. Secker; Lewis v. Franklin;* and *Hancock v. Thomas, Newgate Calendar and Divorce Court Chronicle*, issue 3 (May 20, 1872): 45–46. See also *Davis v. Latham*, ASSI 1/63; *The Times*, July 13, 1863, 11.

25. *Walker v. Owen; Parker v. Wilkins.* See also *Barker v. Birkett*, ASSI 54/4; *Liverpool Daily Post*, Feb. 10, 1886, 7.

26. *Adams v. Jeeves;* and *Jones v. Lloyd.* See also *Robinson v. Atkinson.*

27. *Otte v. Grant;* and *Mitchell v. Hazeldine, Lady's Own Paper* 5 (Mar. 12, 1870): 146; *The Times*, Mar. 4, 1870, 11. See also *Paris v. Jackson, The Times*, May 7, 1879, 6; May 10, 1879, 6; and *Weir v. Costello*, ASSI 54/9; *Liverpool Mercury*, Dec. 7, 1891, 6.

28. Pooth-Clibborn, *Love and Courtship*, 57; *The Etiquette of Courtship and Matrimony*, 39–40; "The Etiquette of Courtship and Marriage," 114; and Turner, *A History of Courting*, 154.

29. *Redhead v. Huddleston, Law Journal* 8 (1873): 674–75; *The Times*, Aug. 2, 1873, 11; and *Langford v. Tonge.* See also *Davies v. Williams*, ASSI 57/6; *Caernarvon and Denbigh Herald*, Aug. 3, 1867, 6; and *Hewitt v. Mowis, Lady's Own Paper* 1 (Apr. 6, 1867): 317; *The Times*, Mar. 28, 1867, 11.

30. *Kelly v. Routledge, Liverpool Daily Post*, Dec. 11, 1897, 3; and *Chapman v. Rushman*, ASSI 32/29; *The Times*, Mar. 27, 1862, 11. See also *Brewett v. Humber*, ASSI 75/3; *Swansea and Glamorgan Herald and the Herald of Wales*, June 29, 1895, 3.

31. *Williams v. Jones*, ASSI 75/2; *South Wales Daily News*, July 14, 1883, 4; and *Davis v. Goddard*, ASSI 22/35; *Somerset County Gazette and Bristol Express*, Mar. 17, 1877, 6. See also *Holt v. Hamer; Davies v. Harris;* and *Duxbury v. Smith*, ASSI 54/9; *Manchester Examiner and Times*, Apr. 29, 1891, 3.

32. *Lewis v. Davies*, ASSI 1/62; *Star of Gwent*, Aug. 11, 1860, 7; and *Lee v. Wright*, ASSI 32/37; *Supplement to the Norwich Argus*, Feb. 16, 1884, 1. See also *Cottam v. Scott,*

ASSI 54/4; *Manchester Evening Mail,* Apr. 17, 1885, 3; and *Readhead v. Hyatt,* ASSI 22/38; *Hampshire Chronicle,* July 15, 1882, 3.

33. *Brett v. Stone, Annual Register* 85 (1843): 180–81; *Chamberlain v. Weston, Chronicles of Breaches of Promise* (n.d.), 159–61; and *Tittle v. Hooper,* ASSI 75/2; *South Wales Daily News,* Feb. 14, 1883, 4.

34. *Appleton v. Morse, Chronicles of Breaches of Promise* (n.d.), 152–55; *Richards v. Palmer;* and *Hayes v. Cox,* ASSI 54/12; *Liverpool Mercury,* Mar. 15, 1893, 7. See also *Desforges v. Hibbert, The Times,* July 30, 1877, 11; and *Berry v. Dunn, Manchester Evening Mail,* Feb. 2, 1898, 2.

35. Gay, *The Bourgeois Experience,* 2:410–11.

36. *Berry v. Dunn;* and *Brown v. Barnfather.* See also *Tilliott v. Wrightup,* ASSI 32/31; *Norwich Argus,* Mar. 27, 1869, 1.

37. *Owens v. Horton.*

38. *Smith v. Mitchell,* ASSI 54/9; *Manchester Examiner and Times,* Mar. 17, 1892, 7; *Copeland v. Hopkins;* and *Elder v. Brearly.* See also *Vaughan v. Robinson,* ASSI 54/15; *Liverpool Mercury,* May 19, 1897, 10; and *West v. Sales,* ASSI 32/37; *Kent Messenger and Maidstone Telegraph,* July 21, 1883, 5.

39. *Edwards v. Roberts; Halliwell v. Rigby;* and *Smith v. Strickland.* See also *Redfern v. White.*

40. *Bath v. Williams.*

41. *Killick v. Wilkinson, Chronicles of Breaches of Promise* (n.d.), 149–52.

42. *Williams v. Harman;* and *Woodward v. Clarke, The Times,* Feb. 7, 1865, 11; Feb. 14, 1865, 9.

43. "The Perils of Paying Attention," 123; De Pomerai, *Marriage, Past, Present, and Future,* 244; and Thompson quoted in Horn, *The Rise and Fall of the Victorian Servant,* 108.

44. Gay, *The Bourgeois Experience,* 2:45.

45. Jalland, *Women, Marriage, and Politics,* 79–84, quote from 79; and Peterson, *Family, Love, and Work,* 81. See also Ryan, *The Philosophy of Marriage,* 74; and Leonard, *Sex and Generation,* 73. Over 40 percent of defendants were in their thirties and forties, compared to 25 percent of plaintiffs.

46. See *Roberts v. Hughes* (1876); and *Gordon v. Woolridge, Chronicles of Breaches of Promise* (n.d.), 176–78.

47. *Rice v. Hall,* ASSI 75/2; *Brecon County Times,* Jan. 31, 1880, 2; and *Wade v. Radford, Chronicles of Breaches of Promise* (n.d.), 144. See also *Hubbert v. Copping, Bristol Daily Post,* Aug. 15, 1871, 13; *Dyer v. Hare,* ASSI 22/41; *Bristol Evening News,* Apr. 6, 1892, 4; *Berry v. Hurst; Haines v. Lawrence,* ASSI 1/66; ASSI 8/2; *Gloucester Mercury,* Apr. 10, 1875, 4; *Redshaw v. Wilman, Annual Register* 85 (1843): 87–88; and *Blackham v. Pratt.* See also "Breach of Promise," *Law Journal* 6 (1871): 209. Juries gave lower awards to age differentials of thirty or more years; otherwise, they apparently saw nothing odd about a much older male suitor.

48. *Fitzpatrick v. Curling; Ford v. Strongitharm;* Gorham, *The Victorian Girl and the Feminine Ideal,* 53–54; and Jalland, *Women, Marriage, and Politics,* 79–84. See also *Jones v. Lloyd;* and Swan, "Love, Courtship, and Marriage," 473.

49. Elizabeth Roberts, *A Woman's Place,* 73–75; Thompson, *The Rise of Respectable Society,* 101; and Jalland, *Women, Marriage, and Politics,* 87. See also Gilbert, *Religion and Society in Industrial England,* especially chapter 7.

50. *Jones v. Williams;* and *Chamberlaine v. Cave,* ASSI 32/39; ASSI 37/7 (1888). See also Lovett, *The Life and Struggles of William Lovett,* 30–31.

51. *Owens v. Horton;* and *Vibert v. Hampton,* ASSI 22/35; *Cornish Telegraph,* Mar. 13, 1877, 4. See also *Davies v. Jones,* ASSI 75/2; *Brecon County Times,* Aug. 2, 1873, 7; *The Times,* Aug. 2, 1873, 11; and Gillis, "Servants, Sexual Relations, and the Risks of Illegitimacy," 154.

52. *Blinkinsop v. Chapman,* ASSI 32/37; *Norwich Argus,* Aug. 11, 1883, 8; and *Walker v. Boocock,* ASSI 54/14; *Manchester Evening Mail,* July 16, 1896, 3. See also *Amm v. Hill,* ASSI 22/42; *Devon Weekly Times,* Feb. 1, 1895, 6.

VI. Premarital Sex in Victorian England

1. Walkowitz, *Prostitution and Victorian Society;* Weeks, *Sex, Politics and Society,* 19–80; Smith, "Sexuality in Britain," 182–98; Gay, *The Bourgeois Experience,* vols. 1, 2; Jalland, *Women, Marriage, and Politics,* 105–6, 115–16, 120; Thompson, *The Rise of Respectable Society,* 259; Dyhouse, *Feminism and the Family in England,* 157–74; Peterson, *Family, Love, and Work,* 73–78; and Ross, *Love and Toil,* 56–90.

2. For other countries, see Coombe, "'The Most Disgusting, Disgraceful, and Inequitous Proceeding,'" 84 n. 59; and Coombs, "Agency and Partnership," 10–11.

3. Barret-Ducrocq, *Love in the Time of Victoria;* Stansell, *City of Women,* 86–89; and Dubinsky, *Improper Advances,* 72.

4. Dubois and Gordon, "Seeking Ecstasy on the Battlefield," 7–25.

5. Thompson, *The Rise of Respectable Society,* 307–8; Weeks, *Sex, Politics and Society,* 60–64; Turner, *A History of Courting,* 168; Hill, *Women, Work, and Sexual Politics,* 180–86; and Barret-Ducrocq, *Love in the Time of Victoria,* 74–113. For contemporary views, see Chinn, *They Worked All Their Lives,* 145–46; Penn, *Manchester Fourteen Miles,* xxiii; and "Breach of Promise and Marriage Morals," 314.

6. *Capron v. Denning;* and *Bailey v. Rolph,* ASSI 32/36; *Suffolk Chronicle,* Aug. 4, 1877, 10. See also Barret-Ducrocq, *Love in the Time of Victoria,* 97–108.

7. McLaren, *Birth Control in Nineteenth-Century England,* 125–29, 215–30. See also Thompson, *The Rise of Respectable Society,* 55–84.

8. *Bebbington v. Hitchen; Windeatt v. Slocombe; Duxbury v. Smith;* and Gillis, "Servants, Sexual Relations, and the Risks of Illegitimacy," 156.

9. *Hooper v. Stokes, Cornish Telegraph,* Feb. 16, 1882, 3; and *Jones v. Griffiths.*

10. *Morris v. Bonville; Rees v. Powell; Wilkinson v. Hampson;* and *Dales v. McMaster.* See also *Mallett v. Sutton.*

11. *Owen v. Lawley,* ASSI 1/68; *Shrewsbury Chronicle,* Mar. 9, 1888, 7; *Curtis v. Olden;* and *Barrow v. Twist.*

12. Gillis, "Servants, Sexual Relations, and the Risks of Illegitimacy," 159–63; Gillis, *For Better, For Worse,* chapters 4, 6; and Barret-Ducrocq, *Love in the Time of Victoria.*

13. *Hopley v. Hurst,* ASSI 57/6; *Chester Chronicle,* Apr. 5, 1862, 2–3; and *Wood v. Irving.* See also *Levens v. Hutton,* ASSI 54/3; *Manchester Evening News,* Apr. 29, 1884, 3; *Manchester Evening Mail,* Apr. 29, 1884, 3; Apr. 30, 1884, 3.

14. *Capron v. Denning; Sherratt v. Webster, Law Times* 8 (1863): 254–55; *Jurist* 9 (1863): 629; *Nixon v. Moss; Swift v. Rhodes,* ASSI 54/2; *Liverpool Mercury,* Aug. 5, 1878, 3;

Gillis, "Servants, Sexual Relations, and the Risks of Illegitimacy," 165–66; and Barret-Ducrocq, *Love in the Time of Victoria*, 123–27.

15. For less beneficial help (such as abortions and adoptions), see *Nangle v. Bamford; Haynes v. Haynes;* and *Wilkinson v. Hampson.* See also Barbara Brooks, *Abortion in England*, 33–34; Barret-Ducrocq, *Love in the Time of Victoria*, 127–31; McLaren, *Birth Control in Nineteenth-Century England*, 231–53; and Conley, *The Unwritten Law*, 114–15.

16. *Sheppard v. Forder*, ASSI 22/36; *Exeter and Plymouth Gazette Daily Telegram*, July 22, 1878, 3; *Heal v. Nicholls*, ASSI 22/42; *Bristol Mercury*, July 17, 1897, 6; and *Owen v. Lawley.*

17. *Hamer v. Jennings, Liverpool Mercury*, Aug. 1, 1885, 3; and *Eldridge v. Rees.* See also *Mallett v. Sutton;* and *Mather v. Royston.*

18. Barret-Ducrocq, *Love in the Time of Victoria*, 131–35.

19. Stansell, *City of Women*, 87–88.

20. *Hutley v. Master, Illustrated Police News*, Feb. 1, 1896, 7; and *Kelly v. Bell.* See also *Holt v. Hamer.*

21. *Mallett v. Sutton;* and *Mather v. Royston.*

22. Dubinsky, *Improper Advances*, 78.

23. *Brookfield v. Wilcock;* and *Matthews v. Miller.* See also *Holmes v. Preston, Illustrated Police News*, May 23, 1896, 8.

24. *Lewis v. Jenkins;* and *Grave v. Mitchell*, ASSI 54/2; *Supplement to the Carlisle Patriot*, Jan. 21, 1881, 1. See also *Kelly v. Bell;* and *Heal v. Nicholls.*

25. Stansell, *City of Women*, 87.

26. *Spink v. Lloyd*, ASSI 32/33; *Suffolk Chronicle*, Aug. 3, 1872, 7; *Bennett v. Smith*, ASSI 54/12; *Manchester Evening Mail*, July 24, 1894, 2; *Grave v. Mitchell;* and *Heywood v. Yeomans*, ASSI 54/12; *Manchester Examiner and Times*, Dec. 9, 1893, 5. See also Leffingwell, *Illegitimacy and the Influence of Seasons*, 141–42; and Elizabeth Roberts, *A Woman's Place*, 77–79.

27. Higginbotham, "The Unmarried Mother and Her Child," 182; Gillis, "Servants, Sexual Relations, and the Risks of Illegitimacy," 155–57; and Anna Clark, *Women's Silence, Men's Violence*, 79–87. See also Higginbotham, "'Sin of the Age,'" 319–37.

28. Gillis, "Servants, Sexual Relations, and the Risks of Illegitimacy," 156; Barret-Ducrocq, *Love in the Time of Victoria*, 112; and Shorter, *The Making of the Modern Family*, 148–59. For an overview, see Michael Anderson, *Approaches to the History of the Western Family*, 54–59.

29. Conley, "Rape and Justice," 519–36; and Conley, *The Unwritten Law*, 81–95.

30. Susan Edwards, *Female Sexuality and the Law*, 146–48.

31. *Beazor v. Gooch, Norwich Argus*, Aug. 12, 1871, 7; *Williams v. Thomas, Annual Register* 85 (1843): 391–94, quote from 392; and *Nicholson v. Maclachlan.* Beazor got £250, Williams, £500. Nicholson was nonsuited, but Maclachlan agreed to give her father £75 in a simultaneous seduction suit.

32. Gillis, "Servants, Sexual Relations, and the Risks of Illegitimacy," 156; and Barret-Ducrocq, *Love in the Time of Victoria*, 45–50. For different reactions of rape victims, see Margaret Llewelyn Davies, ed., *Life as We Have Known It*, 33; and Conley, "Rape and Justice," 524–25.

33. *Nicholson v. Maclachlan.*

34. Susan Edwards, "Sex Crimes in the Nineteenth Century," 562; and *Brown v. Friend.* See also Anna Clark, *Women's Silence, Men's Violence,* chapter 3; and Conley, "Rape and Justice," 524. For criminal seduction, see *Vigilance Record: Organ of the National Vigilance Association* 2 (1888): 14, 73; 3 (1889): 15; 6 (1892): 55.

35. *Williams v. Mathias;* and *Roberts v. Hughes* (1876).

36. *Ball v. Spickett;* and *Levens v. Hutton.* See also *Williams v. Hughes.*

37. *Wiedemann v. Walpole,* 2 Law Reports, Queen's Bench Division 534–42 (1891); *The Times,* June 11, 1891, 13; June 12, 1891, 4; June 13, 1891, 18; June 15, 1891, 3; June 16, 1891, 3; June 17, 1891, 3; June 18, 1891, 4.

38. *Hirst v. Waddington;* and *Hairs v. Elliot.*

39. *Harrison v. Sherlock,* ASSI 54/11; *Liverpool Mercury,* Dec. 9, 1892, 7; *Palmer v. Wootten, Illustrated Police News,* Feb. 7, 1880, 2; and *Dales v. McMaster.*

40. *Blum v. Reeve, Oxfordshire, Buckinghamshire and Northamptonshire Telegraph,* July 16, 1873, 3; and *Gore v. Sudley.* See also *Evans v. Jones.*

41. Walkowitz, *Prostitution and Victorian Society,* 171–213; and Backhouse, *Petticoats and Prejudice,* 81–101, 228–59.

42. *Thatcher v. D'Aguilar,* 142, 137; *Irvine v. Vickers,* ASSI 1/65; *Berkshire County Chronicle,* July 17, 1869, 5; and *Gardner v. Thomas.*

43. For these quotes, see *Swift v. Rhodes; Roberts v. Jones;* and *Grave v. Mitchell.* See also *Kelly v. Bell.*

44. Stephen Parker, *Informal Marriage, Cohabitation, and the Law,* 74–95; and Barton, *Cohabitation Contracts,* 13–35. See also Perkin, *Women and Marriage in Nineteenth-Century England,* 161–62; Staves, *Married Women's Separate Property in England,* 164–95; and Davis, "A Poor Man's System of Justice," 309–35, especially 322–23.

45. Gillis, *For Better, For Worse,* 190–228; Perkin, *Women and Marriage in Nineteenth-Century England,* 158–62, 182–84; and Thompson, *The Rise of Respectable Society,* 111–13.

46. *Harworth v. Taylor;* and *Tamikin v. Wilson.*

47. *Maddocks v. Bennett.* For *Day v. Roberts,* see chapter 7.

48. *Elliot v. Stranger;* and *Dixon v. Brearley, The Times,* July 30, 1877, 11. Dixon got £250. See also *Langford v. Tonge.*

49. Amounts were £1 for a baby and 2s. 6d. a week for a child, and the father paid nothing once the child reached thirteen. Shanley, *Feminism, Marriage, and the Law,* 91; and Horn, *The Rise and Fall of the Victorian Servant,* 138.

50. *McCarthy v. Rowbotham,* ASSI 54/9; *Manchester Examiner and Times,* July 18, 1891, 10; *Dean v. Hollins,* ASSI 1/64; *Staffordshire Sentinel and Commercial and General Advertiser,* Mar. 18, 1865, 8; and *Hope v. Speakerman,* ASSI 54/3; *Illustrated Police News,* Jan. 31, 1885, 3. Awards were £200, £400, and £130, respectively. See also *Potter v. Fox.*

51. Dubinsky, *Improper Advances,* 8.

52. Anna Clark, "Rape or Seduction?" 13–27; and Backhouse, "The Tort of Seduction," 45–80.

53. *Williams v. Thomas* (1843), quote from 391.

54. "Unfortunate" also described prostitutes. See Conley, *The Unwritten Law,* 167.

55. *Wheeler v. Jones;* and *Farrow v. Child,* ASSI 32/36; *Norwich Argus,* Mar. 31, 1877, 7.

56. *Roberts v. Hughes* (1876). See also *Dales v. McMaster.*

57. Dubinsky, *Improper Advances,* 132–33.

58. *Richards v. Palmer.*
59. *Wilkinson v. Hampson;* and *Blakeman v. Bowers.*
60. Quoted from Gillis, *For Better, For Worse,* 238.

VII. Four Case Studies, 1846–1916

1. *Smith v. Ferrers, Proceedings upon the Trial of the Action Brought by Mary Elizabeth Smith against the Right Hon. Washington Sewallis Shirley Earl Ferrers for Breach of Promise of Marriage,* London, 1846. See also *Annual Register* 88 (1846): 349–63; *The Times,* Feb. 16, 1846, 7–8; Feb. 17, 1846, 8; Feb. 18, 1846, 7–8; Feb. 19, 1846, 7–8. Smith also wrote a pamphlet after the trial, *Statement of Facts Respecting the Cause of Smith v. Earl Ferrers* (London, 1846).
2. *Proceedings,* 9.
3. *Statement of Facts,* 14–18, 28, quote from 28.
4. *The Times,* Feb. 18, 1846, 8.
5. *Statement of Facts,* 20–23, quote from 22.
6. *Statement of Facts,* 11.
7. Susan Edwards, *Female Sexuality and the Law,* 146–47.
8. *Annual Register* 88 (1846): 361; and Susan Edwards, *Female Sexuality and the Law,* 146–47.
9. *Annual Register* 89 (1847): 157.
10. *Hansard,* 3d series, 198 (1869): 676.
11. *Law Journal* 4 (1869): 180–81, quote from 180; and Atlay, *The Victorian Chancellors,* 2:103–5, quotes from 103–4. 1962 remark quoted from Susan Edwards, *Female Sexuality and the Law,* 147.
12. Atlay, *The Victorian Chancellors,* 2:105.
13. Tudgill, *Madonnas and Magdalenes.* See also Atkins and Hogett, *Women and the Law,* 74–75.
14. *Frost v. Knight,* 7 *Law Reports, Exchequer Cases* 111–18 (1872); *Staffordshire Sentinel,* Mar. 19, 1870, 7.
15. Ibid.
16. *Law Times* 50 (1870–71): 113.
17. *Albany Law Journal* 3 (1871): 134.
18. 120 *English Reports* 695–706 (1859). Pollock's remarks quoted in full in chapter 8 below.
19. *Albany Law Journal* 3 (1871): 134, 136; entire case found on 133–37.
20. *Law Times* 50 (1870–71): 113–14, first quote 113, second quote 114.
21. 7 *Law Reports,* 111–18 (1872), quote from 116.
22. *Law Times* 52 (1872): 287; *Solicitor's Journal and Reporter* 16 (1872): 280; and Cook, "A Point of Law," 75–76.
23. *Frost v. Knight,* Popplestone, "Frost v. Knight," 161–62.
24. Gillis, *For Better, For Worse,* 286–92, quote from 287. See also Cicily Hamilton, *Marriage as a Trade,* 28–29.
25. *Day v. Roberts, Woman,* issue 13 (Mar. 29, 1890): 1; *Birmingham Daily Gazette,* Mar. 25, 1890, 6; Mar. 26, 1890, 3; Mar. 27, 1890, 6.
26. Gillis, *For Better, For Worse,* 210.
27. Ibid., 192–96.

28. Walkowitz, "Jack the Ripper," 558–66; and Walkowitz, *City of Dreadful Delight,* chapter 7.
29. Since Day was penniless, her counsel must have taken her case on spec.
30. Hammerton, "The Limits of Companionate Marriage"; Hammerton, "Victorian Marriage and the Law of Matrimonial Cruelty," 269–92; and Hammerton, *Cruelty and Companionship,* 82–133. See also Dyhouse, *Feminism and the Family in England,* 13. For positive views, see Peterson, *Family, Love, and Work;* and Jalland, *Women, Marriage, and Politics.*
31. Shanley, *Feminism, Marriage, and the Law,* chapters 1, 2, and epilogue. See also Philippa Levine, *Feminist Lives in Victorian England,* chapters 4, 6; Jalland, *Women, Marriage, and Politics,* 221–49; Perkin, *Women and Marriage in Nineteenth-Century England,* 233–316; and Phyllis Rose, *Parallel Lives.*
32. *Quirk v. Thomas,* 1 *Law Reports, King's Bench Division* 516–41 (1915); *The Times,* Feb. 4, 1915, 5; Feb. 6, 1915, 5; Feb. 9, 1915, 3; Feb. 10, 1915, 3; Feb. 16, 1915, 3; Mar. 20, 1915, 3.
33. 1 *Law Reports, King's Bench Division* 527 (1916).
34. Law Reform (Miscellaneous Provisions) Act of 1934.
35. Quoted from Gillis, *For Better, For Worse,* 237.
36. Judicial Statistics, *Parliamentary Papers.* The average per decade: 34 in the 1860s, 59 in the 1870s, 48 in the 1880s, and 67 in the 1890s.
37. *Cock v. Richards,* 32 *English Reports* 911–15 (1805); 34 *English Reports* 1071–72 (1805). See also *Earp v. Tomkinson, Chronicles of Breaches of Promise* (n.d.), 186–88.
38. Savage, "'The Wilful Communication of a Loathsome Disease,'" 45–46.
39. Savage, "The Divorce Court and the Construction of Marital Sexuality"; and Hammerton, *Cruelty and Companionship.*
40. In the 1850s seductions were 9 of 35 cases; 1860s, 24 of 74; 1870s, 45 of 196; 1880s, 61 of 239; and 1890s, 59 of 244. As a percentage, seductions were highest in the 1860s and lowest in the 1890s.
41. For the 1850s and 1860s the defense of unchastity was used in 24 of 69 cases; for the 1870s to 1890s, 94 of 391 cases.
42. Gillis, *For Better, For Worse,* 179–89, 231–47; and David Levine, *Family Formation,* 131–45.
43. The figures for the delays were as follows: 1860s, 8 of 74; 1870s, 48 of 196; 1880s, 45 of 239; and 1890s, 39 of 244. For separations: 1860s, 7 of 74; 1870s, 34 of 196; 1880s, 23 of 239; and 1890s, 33 of 244.
44. Before 1850 the numbers are 14 of 28; 1850s, 12 of 21; 1860s, 24 of 40; 1870s, 62 of 106; 1880s, 70 of 120; and 1890s, 54 of 120.
45. Before 1860 the figures were 7 of 39; 1860s, 8 of 29; 1870s, 20 of 87; 1880s, 26 of 106; and 1890s, 19 of 89.
46. Before 1860 the figures were 11 of 49; 1860s, 7 of 40; 1870s, 19 of 106; 1880s, 28 of 120; and 1890s, 26 of 120.
47. *Addison v. Scoular.*

VIII. Elite Men Debate

1. *Hansard,* 3d series, 245 (1879): 1871.
2. "Breach of Promise Actions," *Law Times* 45 (1868): 299; and MacColla, *Breach of*

Promise, 61–62. See also "Breach of Promise," *Journal of Jurisprudence* 32 (1888): 405.

3. *Hansard,* 3d series, 245 (1879): 1880–81; MacColla, *Breach of Promise,* 44–46; and White, "Breach of Promise of Marriage," 142. See also "The Action for Breach of Promise of Marriage," *The Times,* May 8, 1879, 6.

4. "The Action for Breach of Promise of Marriage," *Law Times* 45 (1868): 340.

5. These terms come from the following: "Parties as Witnesses in Breach of Promise," 389; "The Action for Breach of Promise of Marriage," *Law Times* 45 (1868): 340; "Breach of Promise of Marriage," *Law Times* 78 (1884): 77; and MacColla, *Breach of Promise,* 37.

6. "The Action for Breach of Promise of Marriage," *Solicitor's Journal and Reporter* 25 (1881): 791. See also *Law* 1 (1874–75): 58–59; and "The Action for Breach," 100.

7. *Law Times* 48 (1869–70): 407; and *The Times,* May 8, 1880, 11. *Sans v. Whalley, The Times,* May 6, 1880, 6; May 8, 1880, 6, 11; *Jacobs v. Wolfe, The Times,* May 7, 1880, 4; May 8, 1880, 11. See also *Law Times* 37 (1862): 539–40; 44 (1868): 484; 47 (1869): 296; 48 (1870): 389–90; *Law Notes* 9 (1890): 134; 10 (1891): 102; *Solicitor's Journal and Reporter* 17 (1872): 159; and *Pump Court* 7 (1888): 117.

8. *Law Times* 40 (1865): 194; *Hansard,* 3d series, 245 (1879): 1874; and *Saturday Review* 1–2 (1856): 314–15, quote from 315. See also *Pump Court* 3 (1886): 113.

9. Higginbotham, "The Unmarried Mother and Her Child," 10–12.

10. MacColla, *Breach of Promise,* 57.

11. *Law Times* 45 (1868): 340. See also ibid., 40 (1865): 194; and White, "Breach of Promise of Marriage," 142.

12. Atlay, *The Victorian Chancellors,* 2:453.

13. "Parties as Witnesses in Breach of Promise," 390.

14. Winder, "The Development of Blackmail," 21–50; and Hepworth, *Blackmail,* 32–45. See also Showalter, "Family Secrets and Domestic Subversion," 101–16.

15. MacDonell, "The Fetich of Publicity," 651–52; "Sexual Litigation," 29–30, quote from 30. See also *Hansard,* 3d series, 245 (1879): 1867; and Fleming, *Love and Courtship,* 12.

16. *Hansard,* 3d series, 245 (1879): 1875.

17. The contract *to* marry was not the same as the contract *of* marriage but was considered binding. See Wharton, *An Exposition of the Laws,* 212–13; and Bodichon, *A Brief Summary,* 8.

18. Staves, *Married Women's Separate Property in England,* 116–30, 164–70.

19. *Hansard,* 3d series, 245 (1879): 1884; "Breach of Promise Actions," *Law Times* 45 (1868): 299; and *The Times,* Feb. 14, 1878, 10.

20. "Breach of Promise Actions," *Law Times* 45 (1868): 299; "Cupid at Law," 399–400, quote from 400; Mintz, *A Prison of Expectations,* 133–46; and *Hansard,* 3d series, 245 (1879): 1879.

21. "The Action for Breach of Promise of Marriage," *Solicitor's Journal and Reporter* 25 (1881): 791–92, quote from 792; Mosely, "Breach of Promise Actions," 304–5, quote from 304; *Hansard,* 3d series, 245 (1879): 1875–78, 1882; and "Breach of Promise of Marriage," *Law Times* 78 (1884): 77.

22. *Hansard,* 3d series, 245 (1879): 1879; Earl of Birkenhead, *Law Life and Letters,* 1:125–41, quote from 128. See also *Solicitor's Journal and Reporter* 22 (1878): 297–98; and "Breach of Promise of Marriage," *Law Journal* 14 (1879): 509–10.

23. "The Action for Breach of Promise of Marriage," *Solicitor's Journal and Reporter* 25 (1881): 792; and Dodd's speech from "Breach of Promise," *Pump Court* 10 (1890): 464–65, quote from 464. See also "A Plea for 'Breach of Promise,'" *The Times*, Feb. 22, 1878, 5.

24. Mosely, "Breach of Promise Actions," 162–63, quote from 163; "Breach of Promise Actions," *Law Times* 8 (1878): 304–5. See also "Breach of Promise of Marriage," *Law Times* 78 (1884): 77; and Clephane, *Towards Sex Freedom*, 20.

25. Atiyah, *The Rise and Fall of Freedom of Contract*, 579–80, 729–42.

26. "Familiar Sketches of English Law," 102–5, quote from 105; and Birkenhead, *Law Life and Letters*, 1:132.

27. Sachs and Wilson, *Sexism and the Law*, 53.

28. Atiyah, *The Rise and Fall of Freedom of Contract*, 204.

29. "Breach of Promise of Marriage," *Law* 2 (1875–76): 112; *Law Journal* 25 (1890): 204; 26 (1891): 97, 635; and *Law Times* 40 (1865): 194; 37 (1862): 539–40; 44 (1868): 484; 64 (1878): 287.

30. Hedley, "Keeping Contract in Its Place," 402. See also n. 59 in the same article.

31. Atiyah, *The Rise and Fall of Freedom of Contract*, 401–2, 656.

32. I am indebted to Roderick Phillips for this insight. See also Donisthorpe, *Love and Law*, 8.

33. Atiyah, *The Rise and Fall of Freedom of Contract*, 374–80, quotes from 375, 380.

34. *Law Times* 4 (1865): 71; and *Solicitor's Journal and Reporter* 20 (1876): 790; 18 (1874): 729.

35. For examples of his influence, see *Andrews v. Huff*, *Chronicles of Breaches of Promise* (n.d.), 182–83; *Vineall v. Veness*, 176 *English Reports* 593–94 (1865); *Thomas v. Shirley; Farrow v. Child; Palmer v. Wootten;* and *Wilkinson v. Bainbridge*, ASSI 54/2; *Lancaster Gazette*, July 7, 1880, 2–3.

36. See, for example, *Wilcox v. Godfrey*, ASSI 22/32; *Taunton Courier*, Mar. 27, 1872, 5; *Law Times* 26 (1872): 328–29, 481–82. Bramwell summed up against her, but the jury gave her £600.

37. *Solicitor's Journal and Reporter* 19 (1875): 476. See also ibid., 20 (1876): 790.

38. *Solicitor's Journal and Reporter* 25 (1881): 771; and *Journal of Jurisprudence* 33 (1889): 39–40. See also *Law Notes* 3 (1884): 37.

39. Quote from *Smith v. Mitchell*. See also *Ditcham v. Worrall*, 5 *Law Reports, Common Pleas Division* 410–23 (1880), Coleridge's remarks, 417–23.

40. *Austin v. Harding*, *Law Notes* 12 (1893): 164; *The Times*, May 6, 1893, 18. See also *Smith v. Mitchell;* and *Perry v. Wood*, ASSI 22/36; *Somerset County Gazette and Bristol Express*, July 28, 1877, 11.

41. *Hole v. Harding*.

42. *Berry v. Da Costa*, 1 *Law Reports, Common Pleas Division* 331–36 (1866), quote from 334; and J. R. Lewis, *The Victorian Bar*, 50. For more of his opinions, see *Smith v. Woodfine*, 140 *English Reports* 275–77 (1856); and *Hawkins v. Toogood*, *Bristol Daily Post*, Aug. 15, 1871, 13.

43. For Burchell, see *Mitchell v. Hazeldine*, *The Times*, Mar. 18, 1870, 11; and Brett's summation in *Townsend v. Bennett*, *Solicitor's Journal and Reporter* 19 (1875): 276. For Grantham's opinion, see *Wilkinson v. Hampson*, *Liverpool Daily Post*, June 2, 1886, 3; for Field, see *Hancock v. Davies;* and for Matthew, see *Benson v. Durrant*, *Jurist* 2 (1888): 180.

44. *Hall v. Wright*, 120 *English Reports* 706 (1859). See also Pollock, *Principles of Contract at Law and in Equity*, 343; and Pollock, *A First Book of Jurisprudence*, 93–94, 205–9.

45. For McCardie, see Birkenhead, *Law Life and Letters*, 132–33. For Manisty, see *Lewis v. Molyneux, Liverpool Mercury*, Nov. 6, 1878, 8; and *Pain v. M'Ewin, Illustrated Police News*, Mar. 3, 1888, 3. For Huddleston, see *Owen v. Williams, Caernarvon and Denbigh Herald*, July 19, 1879, 7. See also Tilley, "Is Marriage a Contract?" 26–42.

46. For example, Hedley, "Where Anson Went Wrong"; and "'No Stranger to Myself.'"

47. *Cherry v. Thompson*, 7 *Law Reports, Queen's Bench Division* 573–79 (1872), first quote from 573 n. 1, second quote from 579; *The Times*, Apr. 17, 1872, 11; May 29, 1872, 11.

48. *Franklyn v. Chaplin, Times Law Reports* 17 (1900): 84; *The Times*, Nov. 27, 1900, 14.

49. See *Hadad v. Bruce; Hanson v. Dixon;* and *Kremezi v. Ridgeway*.

50. Shanley, *Feminism, Marriage, and the Law;* and Rubenstein, *Before the Suffragettes*. For contemporary views, see Quilter, *Is Marriage a Failure?*

51. Hammerton, "Victorian Marriage and the Law of Matrimonial Cruelty," 269–92; and Hammerton, *Cruelty and Companionship*, 82–133.

52. Richard Harris, ed., *The Reminiscences of Sir Henry Hawkins*, 2:88. For the efforts of Lockwood and Lethbridge, see *Law Journal* 25 (1890): 204; 26 (1891): 635; 28 (1893): 96.

53. *Law Journal* 15 (1880): 83.

54. Both quoted in *Supplement to the Gloucester Mercury*, Apr. 11, 1863, 1.

55. *Englishwoman's Review* 1 (Jan. 1870): 68–69, quote from 69.

56. Harrison, "The Future of Marriage," 263; and Black, "On Marriage," 593. For more on Black, see Dyhouse, *Feminism and the Family in England*, 128–32. See also De Pomerai, *Marriage, Past, Present, and Future*, 254–72; Carpenter, *Love's Coming of Age*, 109; and Donisthorpe, *Love and Law*, 11.

57. "The Decline of Breach of Promise," *Journal of Jurisprudence* 34 (1890): 62; and *Pump Court* 10 (1890): 94.

58. "Breach of Promise of Marriage," *Law Times* 78 (1884): 77. The split continued into the twentieth century. See Leonard, *Sex and Generation*, 18–19.

59. "A Word for Amelia Roper," *Spectator* 64 (1890): 83; whole article on 83–84. For Coombe's views, see "'The Most Disgusting, Disgraceful, and Inequitous Proceeding,'" 76–79, 87–93. My thanks to David Sugarman for bringing Coombe's work to my attention.

60. "A Word for Amelia Roper," 84. See also "The Action for Breach of Promise of Marriage," *Solicitor's Journal and Reporter* 25 (1881): 791–92.

61. Again, I am grateful to Roderick Phillips for this insight.

62. David Roberts, "The Paterfamilias of the Victorian Governing Classes," 59–81, especially 69–70.

63. Hammerton, *Cruelty and Companionship*.

64. Fourteen of these were brought before 1870, 9 before 1850. Of the remaining 8, 6 occurred in the 1870s, 1 in 1882, and 1 in 1893. Male plaintiffs, always rare, became more so as the century went on.

65. See *Heap v. Morris; Thomas v. Jones, Annual Register* 64 (1822): 139–41; *Currie v. Currie, Lady's Own Paper* 7 (1871): 131; and *Schreiber v. Frazer, Annual Register* 23 (1780): 218–19. The only exception was *Eden v. Ormand*.

66. See *Fordon v. Woolridge, Chronicles of Breaches of Promise* (n.d.), 176–78; *Farrow v. Child; Barrow v. Twist;* and *Bench v. Merrick,* 174 *English Reports* 893–95 (1844); *The Times,* July 18, 1844, 7.

67. For the first reason, see *Chedzoy v. Woodbery; Booth v. Pearce,* ASSI 75/2; *South Wales Daily News,* Mar. 18, 1874, 3; Mar. 19, 1874, 3; *Hanson v. Lad,* ASSI 54/7; *Manchester Examiner and Times,* July 14, 1888, 7; and *Black v. Baucalare,* ASSI 22/42; *Cornish Telegraph,* June 25, 1896, 5. For accusations of fraud, see *Girling v. Allsop; Jenkins v. Edwards,* ASSI 1/68; ASSI 8/2; *Shropshire Guardian and Shrewsbury Herald,* July 12, 1884, 8; and *Haycox v. Bishton.*

68. See *Pump Court* 3 (1886): 113.

69. *Read v. Bennion,* ASSI 57/6; ASSI 59/113; *Chester Record,* Apr. 8, 1865, 5. See also *Evans v. Jones; Davis v. Bomford,* 158 *English Reports* 101–3 (1860); *The Times,* July 19, 1860, 11; and *Nelson v. Crathorne,* ASSI 28/12; *Bristol Evening News,* July 17, 1897, 3.

70. *Roper v. Hills;* and *Roper v. Bagley.* See also *Langley v. Rose, Annual Register* 94 (1852): 203–4; *Hubbert v. Copping;* and *Miller v. Joy.*

IX. Elite Women Debate

1. *Woman's Suffrage Journal* 10 (1879): 100.

2. *Englishwoman's Review* and *Woman's Suffrage Journal* had the most coverage. The primary newspaper of the women's movement, *Women's Penny Paper,* confined itself to reporting cases. See Oct. 5, 1889, 7, or, under the new name, *Woman's Herald* 7 (Feb. 11, 1893): 5. Other feminist publications included *Woman, Journal of the Vigilance Association, Woman's Opinion,* and *Work and Leisure. Lady's Own Paper, Young Woman, Woman at Home, Womanhood, Lady's Realm,* and the *Englishwoman's Domestic Magazine* had little or no feminist content.

3. See Butler, ed., *Woman's Work and Woman's Culture,* xxxi; Cicily Hamilton, *Marriage as a Trade,* 62; and Dyhouse, *Feminism and the Family in England,* 33–39.

4. "Breach of Promise," *Englishwoman's Review* 9 (May 15, 1879): 217–19, quote from 218.

5. Sachs and Wilson, *Sexism and the Law,* 53. See also Rubenstein, *Before the Suffragettes,* 114; and Dyhouse, *Feminism and the Family in England,* 81–88.

6. Shanley, *Feminism, Marriage, and the Law,* chapter 2; and Philippa Levine, *Feminist Lives in Victorian England,* 113–19. See also Dyhouse, *Feminism and the Family in England,* 145–84; Perkin, *Women and Marriage in Nineteenth-Century England,* chapter 11; Jalland, *Women, Marriage, and Politics,* chapter 3; and Davidoff and Hall, *Family Fortunes,* chapters 7–9.

7. Swan, "Should Long Engagements Be Encouraged?" 38–39, quote from 39; and "Inconstancy and Breach of Promise," 102. See also *Woman's Opinion* 1 (1874): 19, 52.

8. Rowbotham, *Good Girls Make Good Wives,* 50.

9. Hawies, "The Engaged Girl," 257; "On 'Falling in Love,'" 128.

10. Romilly, Armytage, Dixon, and Lang, "Symposium on the Desirability of Long or Short Engagements," 450; and "Should Men Break Engagements?" 3:89–91, 224–25, 302, 376, 452; 4:63.

11. Beatrice Lewis, "Should Men Break Engagements?" 90; Blott, "Should Men Break

Engagements?" 224; and Swan, "Love, Courtship, and Marriage," 316. See also Howatt, "The Art and Science of Courtship," 74–75.

12. "Breach of Promise," *Englishwoman's Review* 9 (May 15, 1879): 217–19; and "The Law of Breach of Promise," 51–63, quote from 58. It is interesting that women's publications also described female plaintiffs as mercenary; apparently, the criminal imagery had as much to do with class as gender. See also *Lady's Own Paper* 7 (Apr. 1, 1870): 194.

13. "Breach of Promise," *Lady's Own Paper* 9 (Aug. 10, 1872): 459.

14. For further examples of both views, see *Lady's Own Paper* 7 (Apr. 1, 1871): 194; and *Woman,* issue 164 (1893): 9.

15. *Woman's Herald* 7 (Aug. 6, 1892): 4.

16. *Lady's Own Paper* 2 (Aug. 15, 1868): 100; *Woman's Opinion* 1 (Feb. 7, 1874): 18–19, quote from 19; and "Breach of Promise," *Englishwoman's Review* 9 (May 15, 1879), 219.

17. *Woman's Suffrage Journal* 15 (1881): 41; 9 (1878): 20; and Marshall, "The Marriage Laws of England," 231–35, quote from 234.

18. *Woman's Suffrage Journal* 10 (1879): 99; and *Journal of the Vigilance Association* 4 (1884): 24. See also *Woman's Suffrage Journal* 9 (1878): 20; and, for a male point of view, "Breach of Promise of Marriage," *Law Journal* 14 (1879): 509–10. Walkowitz has shown the antifeminist tendencies of the Vigilance Association in *Prostitution and Victorian Society,* and "Male Vice and Feminist Virtue," 79–93. However, Sheila Jeffreys has identified feminist content in much of the organization in *The Spinster and Her Enemies,* and on the issue of breach of promise (particularly the linking of it with suffrage), the Vigilance Association proved to be moderately feminist.

19. *Woman's Suffrage Journal* 10 (1879): 99–100, quote from 100; and *Journal of the Vigilance Association* 4 (1884): 24.

20. *Woman's Suffrage Journal* 10 (1879): 100; and Marshall, "The Marriage Laws of England," 234.

21. This journal ran from 1890 to 1912 and was founded to express the moderate feminist viewpoint. It later deteriorated into a ladies' fashion magazine. Doughan and Sanchez, *Feminist Periodicals,* 13–14.

22. *Woman,* issue 136 (1892): 1. See also ibid., issue 141 (1892): 4; and Cook, "A Point of Law," 75–76.

23. "The Law of Breach of Promise," 50–63, quote from 55.

24. Ibid., 58, 61.

25. Coombs, "Agency and Partnership," 1–23.

26. Conley, *The Unwritten Law,* 68–95.

27. Vicinus, *Independent Women.*

28. For a similar dynamic at work in the divorce court, see Savage, "'The Wilful Communication of a Loathsome Disease,'" 49.

29. "Breach of Promise of Marriage," *Law* 2 (1875–76): 110–11; and MacColla, *Breach of Promise,* 55.

30. "The Law of Breach of Promise," 62; *Woman's Suffrage Journal* 9 (1878): 20; and *Woman,* issue 70 (1891): 3. For other views on this dilemma, see Rubenstein, *Before the Suffragettes,* 38; and Dyhouse, *Feminism and the Family in England,* 114–17.

31. "Matrimony As It Was—As It Is," 119–21, quote from 121.

32. "The Law and Lovers' Vows," 712–14, quote from 713.

33. See Normanton, *Everyday Law for Women,* 82; Reiss, *Rights and Duties of Englishwomen,* 148; and Earengey, *A Milk-White Lamb,* 29.
34. See, for instance, the remarks of Renée Short in *Hansard,* 5th series, 799 (1969–70): 919.
35. Leonard, *Sex and Generation,* 17–19, quote from 18; and Brophy and Smart, "From Disregard to Disrepute," 207–25, quote from 221. See also Pateman, *The Sexual Contract.*

Conclusion: The End of Breach of Promise?

1. Bromley, *Family Law,* 16.
2. First remarks in *Hansard,* 5th series, 621 (1959–60): 1054; second in *Hansard,* 5th series, 653 (1961–62): 587.
3. Ibid., 653 (1961–62): 587.
4. Ibid., 666 (1962–63): 1126.
5. Law Commission, *Breach of Promise of Marriage.*
6. *Hansard,* 5th series, 799 (1969–70): 913–24.
7. Ibid., 925–37, quotes from 926, 937.
8. Hammerton, *Cruelty and Companionship,* 165.

Bibliography

Abel-Smith, Brian, and Robert Stevens. *Lawyers and the Courts: A Sociological Study of the English Legal System, 1750–1965*. Cambridge, Mass., 1967.

"The Action for Breach." *Pump Court* 1 (1883): 100.

"The Action for Breach of Promise of Marriage." *Law Times* 45 (1888): 340.

"The Action for Breach of Promise of Marriage." *Solicitor's Journal and Reporter* 25 (1881): 791–92.

"The Action for Breach of Promise of Marriage." *The Times,* May 8, 1879, 6.

Amussen, Susan Dwyer. *An Ordered Society: Gender and Class in Early Modern England.* Oxford, 1988.

Anderson, Gregory. *Victorian Clerks.* Manchester, 1976.

Anderson, Michael. *Approaches to the History of the Western Family, 1500–1914.* London, 1980.

———. "The Emergence of the Modern Life Cycle in Britain." *Social History* 10 (1985): 69–87.

———. *Family Structure in Nineteenth-Century Lancashire.* Cambridge, 1971.

Annual Register. 1766, 1768, 1776, 1778–1780.

Ashley, F. W. *My Sixty Years in the Law.* London, 1936.

Atiyah, P. S. *The Rise and Fall of Freedom of Contract.* Oxford, 1979.

Atkins, Susan, and Brenda Hogett. *Women and the Law.* Oxford, 1984.

Atlay, J. B. *The Victorian Chancellors.* 2 vols. London, 1906.

Backhouse, Constance. *Petticoats and Prejudice: Women and Law in Nineteenth-Century Canada.* Toronto, 1991.

———. "The Tort of Seduction: Fathers and Daughters in Nineteenth-Century Canada." *Dalhousie Law Journal* 10 (June 1986): 45–80.

Bacon, Matthew. *A New Abridgement of the Law.* 10 vols. Philadelphia, 1842–44.

Bailey, Peter. "Parasexuality and Glamour: The Victorian Barmaid as Cultural Prototype." *Gender and History* 2 (Summer 1990): 148–72.

Barret-Ducrocq, Francoise. *Love in the Time of Victoria: Sexuality, Class and Gender in Nineteenth-Century London.* London, 1991.

Barrymore, William. *Bardell v. Pickwick.* London, n.d.

Barton, Chris. *Cohabitation Contracts: Extra-Marital Partnerships and Law Reform.* Aldershot, England, 1984.

The Bench and the Bar. 2 vols. London, 1837.

Birkenhead, Earl of. *Law Life and Letters.* 2 vols. New York, 1927.

Black, Clementina. "On Marriage: A Criticism." *Fortnightly Review* 53 (1890): 586–94.

Blott, Mabel J. J. "Should Men Break Engagements?" *Womanhood* 3 (1899–1900): 224.

Bodichon, Barbara L. S. *A Brief Summary, in Plain Language, of the Most Important Laws of England Concerning Women, Together with a Few Observations Thereon.* 3d ed. London, 1869.

Booth, Michael. *Hiss the Villain: Six English and American Melodramas.* New York, 1964.

Bowen-Rowlands, Ernest. *In Court and Out of Court: Some Recollections.* London, 1925.

Braby, Maud Churton. *Modern Marriage and How to Bear It.* London, 1908.

The Breach of Promise. 3 vols. London, 1845.

"A Breach of Promise." *All the Year Round* 28 (1881): 297–302.

"A Breach of Promise." *Bow Bells* 6 (1867): 428–29.

"A Breach of Promise." *Chambers' Journal* 33 (1860): 257–60.

"Breach of Promise." *Englishwoman's Review* 9 (May 15, 1879): 217–19.

"Breach of Promise." *Journal of Jurisprudence* 32 (1888): 405.

"Breach of Promise." *Justice of the Peace* 56 (1892): 563–64, 579–80.

"Breach of Promise." *Lady's Own Paper* 9 (Aug. 10, 1872): 459.

"Breach of Promise." *Law Journal* 6 (1871): 209.

"Breach of Promise." *Pump Court* 10 (1890): 464–65.

"Breach of Promise Actions." *Law Times* 8 (1878): 304–5; 45 (1868): 299.

"Breach of Promise and Marriage Morals." *Saturday Review* 1–2 (1856): 314–15.

"Breach of Promise of Marriage." *Law* 2 (1875–76): 110–12.

"Breach of Promise of Marriage." *Law Journal* 14 (1879): 509–10.

"Breach of Promise of Marriage." *Law Times* 78 (1884): 77.

Bromley, P. M. *Family Law.* 5th ed. London, 1976.

Brooks, Barbara. *Abortion in England, 1900–1967.* London, 1988.

Brooks, Peter. *The Melodramatic Imagination: Balzac, Henry James, Melodrama, and the Mode of Excess.* New Haven, Conn., 1976.

Brophy, Julia, and Carol Smart. "From Disregard to Disrepute: The Position of Women in Family Law." In Elizabeth Whitelegg et al., eds., *The Changing Experience of Women,* Oxford, 1982, 207–25.

Buckstone, J. B. *Breach of Promise; Or Second Thoughts Are Best.* New York, 1832.

Bullock, Charles. *Courtship and Marriage: Sidelights of Home Life.* London, 1900.

Burnett, John, ed. *Destiny Obscure: Autobiographies of Childhood, Education, and Family from the 1820s to the 1920s.* London, 1982.

Butler, Josephine, ed. *Woman's Work and Woman's Culture: A Series of Essays.* London, 1869.

Carpenter, Edward. *Love's Coming of Age: A Series of Papers on the Relations of the Sexes.* London, 1909.

Chinn, Carl. *They Worked All Their Lives: Women of the Urban Poor in England, 1880–1939.* Manchester, 1988.

Chitty, Joseph. *A Practical Treatise on the Law of Contracts Not under Seal.* 7th American ed. Springfield, Mass., 1848.

Christian, E. B. V. *Leaves of the Lower Branch: The Attorney in Life and Letters.* London, 1909, 1–21.

Chronicles of Breaches of Promise. London, n.d.

Clark, Anna. "Queen Caroline and the Sexual Politics of Popular Culture in London, 1820." *Representations* 31 (Summer 1990): 47–68.

———. "Rape or Seduction? A Controversy over Sexual Violence in the Nineteenth Century." In London Feminist History Group, eds., *The Sexual Dynamics of History: Men's Power, Women's Resistance,* London, 1983, 13–27.

———. *Women's Silence, Men's Violence: Sexual Assaults in England, 1770–1845.* London, 1987.

Clark, Norma. "Strenuous Idleness: Thomas Carlyle and the Man of Letters as Hero." In John Tosh and Michael Roper, eds., *Manful Assertions: Masculinities in Britain since 1800,* 25–43.

Clephane, Irene. *Towards Sex Freedom.* London, 1935.

Cleveland, Arthur. *Woman under the English Law.* London, 1896.

Conley, Carolyn A. "Rape and Justice in Victorian England." *Victorian Studies* 29 (1985–86): 519–36.

———. *The Unwritten Law: Criminal Justice in Victorian Kent.* New York, 1991.

Cook, Keningale. "A Point of Law." *Woman,* issue 1 (1872): 75–76.

Coombe, Rosemary J. "'The Most Disgusting, Disgraceful and Inequitous Proceeding in Our Law': The Action for Breach of Promise of Marriage in Nineteenth-Century Ontario." *University of Toronto Law Journal* 38 (1988): 64–108.

Coombs, Mary. "Agency and Partnership: A Study of Breach of Promise Plaintiffs." *Yale Journal of Law and Feminism* 2 (1989): 1–23.

Corr, Helen, and Lynn Jamieson, eds. *Politics of Everyday Life: Continuity and Change in Work and the Family.* New York, 1990.

Crispe, Thomas Edward. *Reminiscences of a K.C.* Boston, 1910.

Crofts, Maud. *Women under English Law.* 2d ed. London, 1928.

Crossick, Geoffrey. *An Artisan Elite in Victorian Society: Kentish London, 1840–1880.* London, 1978.

———. "The Petite Bourgeoisie in Nineteenth-Century Britain: The Urban and Liberal Case." In Geoffrey Crossick and Heinz-Gerhard Haupt, eds., *Shopkeepers and Master Artisans in Nineteenth-Century Europe,* London, 1984: 62–94.

"Cupid at Law." *Chambers' Journal* 56 (June 23, 1883): 399–400.

Davidoff, Leonore. "'Adam Spoke First and Named the Orders of the World': Masculine and Feminine Domains in History and Sociology." In Helen Corr and Lynn Jamieson, eds., *Politics of Everyday Life: Continuity and Change in Work and the Family,* 229–55.

———. *The Best Circles: "Society," Etiquette and the Season.* London, 1973.

———. "The Separation of Home and Work? Landladies and Lodgers in Nineteenth-

and Twentieth-Century England." In Sandra Burman, ed., *Fit Work for Women,* London, 1979, 68–92.

Davidoff, Leonore, and Catherine Hall. *Family Fortunes: Men and Women of the English Middle Class, 1780–1850.* Chicago, 1987.

Davies, Harry. "The Courtship of Ezra." *Quiver* (1900), 969–75.

Davies, Margaret Llewelyn, ed. *Life as We Have Known It by Cooperative Working Women.* London, 1977.

Davis, Jennifer. "A Poor Man's System of Justice: The London Police Courts in the Second Half of the Nineteenth Century." *Historical Journal* 27 (1984): 309–35.

de Bertouch, Beatrice. "Should Men Break Engagements? III." *Womanhood* 3 (1899–1900): 376.

"The Decline of Breach of Promise." *Journal of Jurisprudence* 34 (1890): 62.

De Pomerai, Ralph. *Marriage, Past, Present, and Future: An Outline of the History and Development of Human Sexual Relationships.* London, 1930.

Dickens, Charles. *The Pickwick Papers.* Ed. James Kinsley. Oxford, 1986.

Dodd, G. R. "Breach of Promise." *Pump Court* 10 (1890): 464.

Donisthorpe, Wordsworth. *Love and Law: An Essay on Marriage.* London, 1893.

Doughan, David, and Denise Sanchez. *Feminist Periodicals, 1855–1984: An Annotated Critical Bibliography of British, Irish, Commonwealth and International Titles.* Brighton, England, 1987.

Dubinsky, Karen. *Improper Advances: Rape and Heterosexual Conflict in Ontario, 1880–1929.* Chicago, 1993.

———. "'Maidenly Girls' or 'Designing Women'? The Crime of Seduction in Turn-of-the-Century Ontario." In Franca Iacovetta and Mariana Valverde, eds., *Gender Conflicts: New Essays in Women's History,* Toronto, 1992.

Dubois, Ellen Carol, and Linda Gordon. "Seeking Ecstasy on the Battlefield: Danger and Pleasure in Nineteenth-Century Feminist Sexual Thought." *Feminist Studies* 9 (Spring 1983): 7–25.

Dyhouse, Carol. *Feminism and the Family in England, 1880–1939.* Oxford, 1989.

Earengey, Florence. *A Milk-White Lamb: The Legal and Economic Status of Women.* Revised ed. London, 1953.

Edwards, John William. *The Law of Husband and Wife.* London, 1883.

Edwards, Susan. *Female Sexuality and the Law: A Study of Constructs of Female Sexuality as They Inform Statute and Legal Procedure.* Oxford, 1981.

———. "Sex Crimes in the Nineteenth Century." *New Society* 49 (1979): 562–63.

Emery, George Frederick. *The Law Relating to Husband and Wife.* London, 1929.

Englishwoman's Review. 1 (1870): 68–69.

"The Etiquette of Courtship and Marriage." *Bow Bells* 6 (1867): 114.

The Etiquette of Courtship and Matrimony. London, 1852.

Eversley, William. *The Law of Domestic Relations.* 3d ed. London, 1906.

"Familiar Sketches of English Law: 1. Marriages, Settlements, and Breaches of Promise to Marry." *Chambers' Journal* 57 (Feb. 16, 1884): 102–5.

Fitzgerald, Percy. *The History of Pickwick*. London, 1891.

Fitzgerald, Percy, ed. *Bardell v. Pickwick*. London, 1902.

Fleming, Tom. *Love and Courtship*. Malton, England, 1890.

Gay, Peter. *The Bourgeois Experience: Victoria to Freud*. Vol. 1, *The Education of the Senses;* vol. 2, *The Tender Passion*. New York, 1984, 1986.

Geary, Nevill. *The Law of Marriage and Family Relations: A Manual of Practical Law*. London, 1892.

Gilbert, A. D. *Religion and Society in Industrial England: Church, Chapel, and Social Change*. London, 1976.

Gillis, John. *For Better, For Worse: British Marriages, 1600 to the Present*. Oxford, 1985.

———. "Servants, Sexual Relations, and the Risks of Illegitimacy in London, 1801–1900." *Feminist Studies* 5 (Spring 1979): 142–73.

Gorham, Deborah. "The Ideology of Femininity and Reading for Girls, 1850–1914." In Felicity Hunt, ed., *Lessons for Life: The Schooling of Girls and Women, 1850–1950*, 39–59.

———. *The Victorian Girl and the Feminine Ideal*. Bloomington, Ind., 1982.

Grant, H. B. *Marriage, Separation and Divorce*. London, 1946.

Graveson, R. H., and F. H. Crane, eds. *A Century of Family Law*. London, 1957.

Grossberg, Michael. *Governing the Hearth: Law and the Family in Nineteenth-Century America*. Chapel Hill, N. C., 1985.

Hall, Catherine. *White, Male, and Middle-Class: Explorations in Feminism and History*. Cambridge, 1992.

Hamilton, Cicily. *Marriage as a Trade*. London, 1981.

Hamilton, Cosmo, and Frank C. Reilly. *Pickwick: A Play in Three Acts*. London, 1927.

Hammerton, A. James. *Cruelty and Companionship: Conflict in Nineteenth-Century Married Life*. London, 1992.

———. "The Limits of Companionate Marriage." Unpublished paper, 1990.

———. "Manliness and Marriage: Resisting the 'Flight from Domesticity' in Late Nineteenth-Century England and Australia." Unpublished paper, 1994.

———. "Victorian Marriage and the Law of Matrimonial Cruelty." *Victorian Studies* 33 (Winter 1990): 269–92.

Hansard's Parliamentary Debates.

Hardwick, Elizabeth. *Seduction and Betrayal: Women and Literature*. New York, 1974.

Harris, Richard, ed. *The Reminiscences of Sir Henry Hawkins*. 2 vols. London, 1904.

Harris, Ruth. "Melodrama, Hysteria and Feminine Crimes of Passion in the Fin-de-Siècle." *History Workshop Journal* 25 (Spring 1988): 31–63.

Harrison, Frederic. "The Future of Marriage." *Fortnightly Review* 59 (1892): 258–71.

Hawies, Rev. H. R. "The Engaged Girl." *Young Woman* 5 (1896–97): 257.

Head, Edmund. *Report on the Law of Bastardy with a Supplementary Report on a Cheap Civil Remedy for Seduction*. London, 1840.

Hedley, Stephen. "Keeping Contract in Its Place—*Balfour v. Balfour* and the Enforceability of Informal Agreements." *Oxford Journal of Legal Studies* 5 (1985): 391–415.

————. "'No Stranger to Myself'? The Judge as Unemployed Barrister." Unpublished paper, 1989.

————. "Where Anson Went Wrong (and Why We All Followed Him)." Unpublished paper, 1986.

Henriques, Ursula. "Bastardy and the New Poor Law." *Past and Present* 37 (1967): 103–29.

Hepworth, Mike. *Blackmail: Publicity and Secrecy in Everyday Life.* London, 1975.

Higginbotham, Ann Rowell. "'Sin of the Age': Infanticide and Illegitimacy in Victorian London." *Victorian Studies* 32 (1989): 319–37.

————. "The Unmarried Mother and Her Child in Victorian London, 1834–1914." Unpublished dissertation, Indiana University, 1985.

Hill, Bridget. *Eighteenth-Century Women: An Anthology.* London, 1984.

————. *Women, Work, and Sexual Politics in Eighteenth-Century England.* Oxford, 1989.

Hollingshead, J. *Bardell v. Pickwick.* London, 1871.

Holmes, Eleanor. *A Breach of Promise.* London, 1907.

Horn, Pamela. *The Rise and Fall of the Victorian Servant.* Dublin, 1975.

Houlbrooke, Ralph. *Church Courts and the People During the English Reformation, 1520–1570.* Oxford, 1979.

Howatt, J. Reid. "The Art and Science of Courtship, I, II, and III." *Young Woman* 5 (1896–97): 74–75, 112–13, 150–51.

Hunt, Felicity, ed. *Lessons for Life: The Schooling of Girls and Women, 1850–1950.* New York, 1987.

"Inconstancy and Breach of Promise." *Lady's Own Paper* 6 (Aug. 13, 1870): 102.

Ingram, Martin. *Church Courts, Sex, and Marriage in England, 1570–1640.* Cambridge, 1987.

Jalland, Pat. *Women, Marriage, and Politics, 1860–1914.* Oxford, 1986.

Jeffreys, Sheila. *The Spinster and Her Enemies: Feminism and Sexuality, 1880–1930.* London, 1985.

Jenks, Edward. *The Book of English Law.* 6th ed. Athens, Ohio, 1967.

————. *Husband and Wife in the Law.* London, 1909.

————. *A Short History of English Law from Earliest Times to the End of the Year 1911.* London, 1912.

Johnson, E. L. *Family Law.* 2d ed. London, 1965.

Journal of Jurisprudence. Vols. 14–34 (1870–90).

Journal of the Vigilance Association. 4 (1884): 24.

Joyce, Patrick. *Visions of the People: Industrial England and the Question of Class, 1848–1914.* Cambridge, 1991.

————. *Work, Society and Politics: The Culture of the Factory in Later Victorian England.* New Brunswick, N. J., 1980.

Joyce, Patrick, ed. *The Historical Meanings of Work.* Cambridge, 1987.

Judicial Statistics. Parliamentary Papers. 1859–1922.

Jurist. Vols. 1–4 (1882–90).

Jurist: A Journal for Law Students and the Profession. 1 (1887): 163–64.

Justice of the Peace. Vols. 15–56 (1840–1892).

Kent, Christopher. "Image and Reality: The Actress and Society." In Martha Vicinus, ed., *A Widening Sphere: Changing Roles of Victorian Women,* 94–116.

Kuehn, Thomas. "Reading Microhistory: The Example of *Giovanni and Lusanna.*" *Journal of Modern History* 61 (1989): 512–34.

Lady's Own Paper. 2 (Aug. 15, 1868): 100; 7 (Apr. 1, 1871): 194.

Law. Vols. 1–2 (1874–76).

"The Law and Lovers' Vows." *Spectator* 71 (1893): 712–14.

Law Commission. *Breach of Promise of Marriage.* Law Commission no. 26. London, 1969.

"Law for Ladies." *Punch* 71 (1876): 123.

Law Journal. Vols. 4–28 (1869–93).

Law Notes. Vols. 3–15 (1884–96).

"The Law of Breach of Promise." *The Woman Question: Papers Reprinted from the "Examiner."* London, 1872. Reprinted in *Women's Suffrage Pamphlets, 1869–1872,* 51–63.

Law Times. Vols. 37–78 (1862–84).

Leffingwell, Albert. *Illegitimacy and the Influence of Seasons upon Conduct.* 2d ed. London, 1892.

Leonard, Diana. *Sex and Generation: A Study of Courtship and Weddings.* London, 1980.

Levine, David. *Family Formation in the Age of Nascent Capitalism.* New York, 1977.

Levine, Philippa. *Feminist Lives in Victorian England: Private Roles and Public Commitment.* Oxford, 1990.

Lewis, Beatrice. "Should Men Break Engagements?" *Womanhood* 3 (1899–1900): 89–91.

Lewis, J. R. *The Victorian Bar.* London, 1982.

Lewis, Jane. *Women in England, 1870–1950: Sexual Divisions and Social Change.* Bloomington, Ind., 1984.

Lockwood, Frank. *The Law and Lawyers of Pickwick.* London, 1894.

Lovett, William. *The Life and Struggles of William Lovett.* London, 1967.

Lystra, Karen. *Searching the Heart: Women, Men, and Romantic Love in Nineteenth-Century America.* New York, 1989.

McClelland, Keith. "Masculinity and the 'Representative Artisan' in Britain, 1850–1880." In John Tosh and Michael Roper, eds., *Manful Assertions: Masculinities in Britain since 1800,* 74–91.

———. "Time to Work, Time to Live: Some Aspects of Work and the Reformation of Class in Britain, 1850–1880." In Patrick Joyce, ed., *The Historical Meanings of Work,* 180–209.

MacColla, Charles. *Breach of Promise: Its History and Social Considerations.* London, 1879.

MacDonell, John. "The Fetich of Publicity." *Nineteenth Century* 39 (1876): 647–54.

MacKenzie, John. "The Imperial Pioneer and Hunter and the British Masculine Stereotype in Late Victorian and Edwardian Times." In J. A. Mangan and James Walvin, eds., *Manliness and Morality: Middle-Class Masculinity in Britain and America, 1800–1940*, 176–98.

McLaren, Angus. *Birth Control in Nineteenth-Century England.* New York, 1978.

MacQueen, John Fraser. *The Rights and Liabilities of Husband and Wife.* 2d ed. London, 1872.

Magnus, Philip. *Gladstone: A Biography.* London, 1954.

Mangan, J. A., and James Walvin, eds. *Manliness and Morality: Middle-Class Masculinity in Britain and America, 1800–1940.* Manchester, England, 1987.

Marshall, Edward H. "The Marriage Laws of England." *Work and Leisure* 2 (1881): 231–35.

"Matrimony As It Was—As It Is." *Englishwoman's Domestic Magazine* 7 (1869): 119–21.

Milsom, S. F. C. *Historical Foundations of the Common Law.* London, 1969.

Mintz, Steven. *A Prison of Expectations: The Family in Victorian Culture.* New York, 1983.

Mitchell, Sally. "The Forgotten Woman of the Period: Penny Weekly Family Magazines of the 1840s and 1850s." In Martha Vicinus, ed., *A Widening Sphere: Changing Roles of Victorian Women*, 29–51.

Morris, Harold. *The Barrister.* London, 1930.

Mosely, B. L. "Breach of Promise Actions." *Law Journal* 8 (1878): 162–63, 304–5.

Nicholson, Norman. *Wednesday Early Closing.* London, 1975.

Nokes, G. D. "Evidence." In R. H. Graveson and F. R. Crane, eds., *A Century of Family Law*, 143–64.

Normanton, Helena. *Everyday Law for Women.* London, 1932.

Odgers, W. Blake. *A Century of Law Reform.* London, 1901.

"On 'Falling in Love.'" *Young Woman* 2 (1893–94): 128.

"Our Engagement." *Temple Bar* 9 (1863): 132–40.

Parker, Mrs. Joseph. "Should Long Engagements Be Encouraged?" *Woman at Home* 2 (1895): 39–40.

Parker, Stephen. *Informal Marriage, Cohabitation, and the Law, 1750–1989.* London, 1990.

Parry, Edward Albert. *The Law and the Woman.* London, 1916.

"Parties as Witnesses in Breach of Promise." *Law Times* 48 (1870): 389–90.

"Parties as Witnesses in Breach of Promise Cases." *Journal of Jurisprudence* 14 (1870): 271.

Pateman, Caroline. *The Sexual Contract.* Stanford, 1988.

Pearsall, Ronald. *The Worm in the Bud: The World of Victorian Sexuality.* London, 1969.

Penn, Margaret. *Manchester Fourteen Miles.* Firle, England, 1979.

"The Perils of Paying Attention." *Modern Women and What Is Said of Them.* New York, 1868, 118–27.

Perkin, Joan. *Women and Marriage in Nineteenth-Century England.* London, 1988.

Peterson, M. Jeanne. *Family, Love, and Work in the Lives of Victorian Gentlewomen.* Bloomington, Ind., 1989.

"A Plea for 'Breach of Promise.'" *The Times,* Feb. 22, 1878, 5.

Pollock, Frederick. *A First Book of Jurisprudence for Students of the Common Law.* 5th ed. London, 1923.

———. *Principles of Contract at Law and in Equity.* London, 1876.

Polson, A. *Law and Lawyers: Or Sketches and Illustrations of Legal History and Biography.* 2 vols. London, 1840.

Pooth-Clibborn, Catherine. *Love and Courtship.* 2nd ed. London, 1927.

Poovey, Mary. *Uneven Developments: The Ideological Work of Gender in Mid-Victorian England.* Chicago, 1988.

"Proposed Mode of Redress for the Poor in Cases of Seduction, under Breach of Promise of Marriage." *Justice of the Peace* 15 (1840): 233–34.

Pump Court. Vols. 1–11 (1883–91).

Quilter, Harry. *Is Marriage a Failure? A Modern Symposium.* Chicago, 1889.

Reiss, Erna. *Rights and Duties of Englishwomen: A Study in Law and Public Opinion.* Manchester, England, 1934.

Roberts, David. "The Paterfamilias of the Victorian Governing Classes." In Anthony S. Wohl, ed., *The Victorian Family: Structure and Stresses,* London, 1978, 59–81.

Roberts, Elizabeth. *A Woman's Place: An Oral History of Working-Class Women, 1890–1940.* Oxford, 1984.

Robin, Jean. *Elmson: Continuity and Change in a Northwest Essex Village, 1861–1964.* Cambridge, 1980.

Robinson, Jerome, ed. *Trial by Jury.* In *The Complete Plays of Gilbert and Sullivan,* New York, 1938, 42–57.

Romilly, Arabella, Mrs. Armytage, Ella Hepworth Dixon, and Evelyn M. Lang. "Symposium on the Desirability of Long or Short Engagements." *Lady's Realm* (May 1899), 445–50.

Rose, Phyllis. *Parallel Lives: Five Victorian Marriages.* New York, 1984.

Rose, Sonya. *Limited Livelihoods: Gender and Class in Nineteenth-Century England.* Berkeley, Calif., 1992.

Rosenthal, Michael. *The Character Factory: Baden-Powell and the Origins of the Boy Scout Movement.* London, 1986.

Ross, Ellen. "'Fierce Questions and Taunts': Married Life in Working-Class London, 1870–1914." *Feminist Studies* 8 (Fall 1982): 575–602.

———. *Love and Toil: Motherhood in Outcast London, 1870–1918.* Oxford, 1993.

———. "'Not the Sort That Would Sit on the Doorstep': Respectability in Pre–World War I London Neighborhoods." *International Labor and Working Class History* 29 (Spring 1985): 39–59.

———. "Survival Networks: Women's Neighborhood Sharing in London before World War I." *History Workshop Journal* 15 (Spring 1983): 4–27.

Rothman, Ellen K. *Hands and Hearts: A History of Courtship in America.* New York, 1984.

Rowbotham, Judith. *Good Girls Make Good Wives: Guidance for Girls in Victorian Fiction.* Oxford, 1989.

Rubenst in, David. *Before the Suffragettes: Women's Emancipation in the 1890s.* Brighton, England, 1986.

Ryan, Michael. *The Philosophy of Marriage in Its Social, Moral, and Physical Relations.* London, 1839.

Sachs, Albie, and Joan Hoff Wilson. *Sexism and the Law: A Study of Male Beliefs and Legal Bias in Britain and the United States.* New York, 1979.

Savage, Gail. "The Divorce Court and the Construction of Marital Sexuality in England." Unpublished paper, 1992.

————. "'The Wilful Communication of a Loathsome Disease': Marital Conflict and Venereal Disease in Victorian England." *Victorian Studies* 34 (Autumn 1990): 35–54.

Scott, Joan Wallach. *Gender and the Politics of History.* New York, 1988.

"Sexual Litigation." *Law Journal* 12 (1877): 29–30.

Shanley, Mary Lyndon. *Feminism, Marriage, and the Law in Victorian England, 1850–1895.* Princeton, N. J., 1989.

Shorter, Edward. *The Making of the Modern Family.* New York, 1975.

"Should Men Break Engagements?" *Womanhood* 3 (1899–1900): 89–91, 224–25, 302, 376, 452; 4 (1900): 63.

Showalter, Elaine. "Family Secrets and Domestic Subversion: Rebellion in the Novels of the 1860s." In Anthony S. Wohl, ed., *The Victorian Family: Structure and Stresses,* London, 1978, 101–16.

Smith, F. Barry. "Sexuality in Britain, 1800–1900: Some Suggested Revisions." In Martha Vicinus, ed., *A Widening Sphere: Changing Roles of Victorian Women,* 182–98.

Solicitor's Journal and Reporter. Vols. 17–25 (1872–81).

"Some Early Breach of Promise Cases." *Pump Court* 11 (1891): 592–93.

Springhall, John. "Building Character in the British Boy: The Attempt to Extend Christian Manliness to Working-Class Adolescents, 1880–1914." In J. A. Mangan and James Walvin, eds., *Manliness and Morality: Middle-Class Masculinity in Britain and America, 1800–1940,* 54–74.

————. *Youth, Empire and Society: British Youth Movements, 1883 to 1940.* London, 1977.

Stansell, Christine. *City of Women: Sex and Class in New York, 1789–1860.* New York, 1986.

Staves, Susan. *Married Women's Separate Property in England, 1660–1833.* Cambridge, Mass., 1990.

Stearns, Peter. *Be a Man! Males in Modern Society.* New York, 1979.

Stone, Lawrence. *The Family, Sex and Marriage in England, 1500–1800.* New York, 1977.

————. *Road to Divorce: England, 1530–1987.* Oxford, 1990.

Stone, Olive. *Family Law.* London, 1987.

A Strange Case of Breach of Promise of Marriage. Wenbridge, 1890?

"Summary of Proceedings." *Transactions of the Society for the Promotion of Social Science.* London, 1866.

Sutthery, Frank P. "Letter." *Law Times* 64 (1878): 287.

Swan, Annie. "Love, Courtship, and Marriage." *Woman at Home* 2 (1895): 155, 237, 316, 472.

Swan, Annie, and Lady Gilzean Reid. "Should Long Engagements Be Encouraged?" *Woman at Home* 2 (1895): 38–39.

Thicknesse, Ralph. *The Rights and Wrongs of Women.* London, 1905.

Thompson, F. M. L. *The Rise of Respectable Society: A Social History of Victorian Britain, 1830–1900.* London, 1988.

Tilley, Arthur. "Is Marriage a Contract?" *Law Magazine and Review* (4th series) 5 (1879–80): 26–42.

The Times (London). 1801–1970.

Tosh, John. "Domesticity and Manliness in the Victorian Middle Class: The Family of Edward White Benson." In John Tosh and Michael Roper, eds., *Manful Assertions: Masculinities in Britain since 1800,* 44–73.

Tosh, John, and Michael Roper, eds. *Manful Assertions: Masculinities in Britain since 1800.* London, 1990.

Travers, R. L. *Husband and Wife in English Law.* London, 1956.

Tudgill, Eric. *Madonnas and Magdalenes: The Origins and Development of Victorian Sexual Attitudes.* New York, 1976.

Turner, E. S. *A History of Courting.* London, 1954.

Vance, Norman. *Sinews of the Spirit: The Ideal of Christian Manliness in Victorian Literature and Religious Thought.* Cambridge, 1985.

Vicinus, Martha. *Independent Women: Work and Community for Single Women, 1850–1920.* Chicago, 1985.

Vicinus, Martha, ed. *A Widening Sphere: Changing Roles of Victorian Women.* Bloomington, Ind., 1977.

Vigilance Record: Organ of the National Vigilance Association. 2 (1888): 14, 73; 3 (1889): 15; 6 (1892): 55.

Vincent, David. *Bread, Knowledge and Freedom: A Study of Nineteenth-Century Working-Class Autobiography.* London, 1981.

Waddilove, Arthur. "The Law of Evidence." *Transactions of the Society for the Promotion of Social Science,* London, 1866, 133–42.

Walker, Pamela. "'I Live but Not Yet I for Christ Liveth in Me': Men and Masculinity in the Salvation Army, 1865–1890." In John Tosh and Michael Roper, eds., *Manful Assertions: Masculinities in Britain since 1800,* 92–112.

Walkowitz, Judith. *City of Dreadful Delight: Narratives of Sexual Danger in Mid-Victorian London.* Chicago, 1992.

———. "Jack the Ripper and the Myth of Male Violence." *Feminist Studies* 8 (Fall 1982): 542–74.

———. "Male Vice and Feminist Virtue: Feminism and the Politics of Prostitution in Nineteenth-Century Britain." *History Workshop Journal* 13 (Spring 1982): 79–93.

———. *Prostitution and Victorian Society: Women, Class and the State.* Cambridge, 1980.

Walton, Robert. *Random Recollections of the Midland Circuit.* 2 vols. London, 1869.

Warren, Allen. "Popular Manliness: Baden-Powell, Scouting, and the Development of Manly Character." In J. A. Mangan and James Walvin, eds., *Manliness and Morality: Middle-Class Masculinity in Britain and America, 1800–1940*, 199–216.

Weeks, Jeffrey. *Sex, Politics, and Society: The Regulation of Sexuality since 1800*. 2d ed. London, 1989.

Wharton, J. J. S. *An Exposition of the Laws Relating to the Women of England Showing Their Rights, Remedies, and Responsibilities in Every Position of Life*. London, 1853.

Wheeler, Maud. *Whom to Marry or All about Love and Matrimony*. London, 1894.

White, J. Dundas. "Breach of Promise of Marriage." *Law Quarterly Review* 10 (1894): 135–42.

Winder, W. H. D. "The Development of Blackmail." *Modern Law Review* (July 1941), 21–50.

Woman. Issue 10 (Mar. 8, 1890): 1; issue 17 (Apr. 26, 1890): 1; issue 70 (1891): 3; issue 136 (1892): 1; issue 141 (1892): 4; issue 164 (1893): 9.

Woman's Herald. 7 (1892–93): 4–5.

Woman's Opinion. 1 (1874): 18–19, 52.

Woman's Suffrage Journal. 9 (1878): 20; 10 (1879): 99–100; 15 (1881): 41.

Women's Penny Paper. Oct. 5, 1889, 7.

"A Word for Amelia Roper." *Spectator* 64 (1890): 83–84.

Young, Stanley. *Mr. Pickwick: A Comedy Freely Drawn from Charles Dickens'* The Pickwick Papers. New York, 1952.

List of Cases

Abbot v. Harrison, Manchester Examiner and Times, July 13, 1889, 8.

Ackerman v. Saunders, Law Notes 11 (1892): 69; *The Times,* Jan. 27, 1892, 14.

Adams v. Ireland, Cornish Telegraph, Mar. 10, 1892, 2.

Adams v. Jeeves, ASSI 32/34; *Bedfordshire Times and Independent,* July 25, 1874, 6–7.

Adams v. Leach, ASSI 22/42; *Taunton Courier,* Jan. 23, 1895, 6.

Addison v. Scoular, Norwich Argus, Aug. 12, 1871, 7.

Aggett v. Elliott, ASSI 22/33; *The Times,* July 29, 1872, 11.

Alderton v. Hunt, ASSI 1/67; *Oxford Chronicle and Berks and Bucks Gazette,* July 10, 1880, 7.

Allen v. Hutchings, The Times, Mar. 22, 1878, 10.

Allit v. Bradley, ASSI 1/66; ASSI 8/1; *Oxford Times,* July 7, 1877, 2.

Allmand v. Forrester, ASSI 1/67; *Shrewsbury Chronicle,* Feb. 3, 1882, 6.

Amm v. Hill, ASSI 22/42; *Devon Weekly Times,* Feb. 1, 1895, 6.

Andrews v. Huff, Chronicles of Breaches of Promise (London, n.d.), 182–83.

Appleton v. Morse, Chronicles of Breaches of Promise (London, n.d.), 152–55.

Appleton v. Scotter, ASSI 54/5; *Liverpool Daily Post,* July 30, 1886, 3.

Armstrong v. Gray, ASSI 1/66; ASSI 8/1 (1876).

Ashton v. Scholes, ASSI 54/14; *Manchester Evening Mail,* Dec. 9, 1895, 3.

Atchinson v. Baker, 170 *English Reports* 217, 209 (1796).

Austin v. Harding, Law Notes 12 (1893): 164; *The Times,* May 6, 1893, 18.

B. v. R., Greater London Record Office, Foundling Hospital Petitions, A/FH/A8/1, Rejected Petition 1 (1841).

Bailey v. Rolph, ASSI 32/36; *Suffolk Chronicle,* Aug. 4, 1877, 10.

Baker v. Cartwright, 142 *English Reports* 397–98 (1861).

Ball v. Spickett, South Wales Daily News, July 14, 1893, 4.

Bardens v. Amey, ASSI 22/41; ASSI 28/8, Correspondence, Letters 1–9; *Western Times,* Mar. 9, 1893, 3.

Barker v. Birkett, ASSI 54/4; *Liverpool Daily Post,* Feb. 10, 1886, 7.

Barrow v. Twist, ASSI 54/5; *Manchester Examiner and Times,* July 17, 1886, 3.

Barter v. Lawrence, ASSI 22/37; *Western Times,* Jan. 26, 1880, 3–4.

Bath v. Williams, South Wales Daily News, Apr. 7, 1876, 6.

Beazor v. Gooch, Norwich Argus, Aug. 12, 1871, 7.

Bebbington v. Hitchen, ASSI 57/7; ASSI 59/130; Chester Chronicle, Aug. 9, 1873, 3.

Bell v. Jackson, Chronicles of Breaches of Promise (London, n.d.), 131–33.

Bench v. Merrick, 174 English Reports 893–95 (1844); The Times, July 18, 1844, 7.

Bennett v. Smith, ASSI 54/12; Manchester Evening Mail, July 24, 1894, 2.

Benson v. Durrant, Jurist 2 (1888): 180; The Times, June 6, 1888, 4.

Berry v. Da Costa, 1 Law Reports, Common Pleas Division 331–36 (1865–66); The Times, Jan. 15, 1866, 11; Jan. 26, 1866, 11.

Berry v. Dunn, Manchester Evening Mail, Feb. 2, 1898, 2.

Berry v. Hurst, ASSI 54/1; Manchester Evening News, Jan. 21, 1872, 2.

Bessela v. Stern, 2 Law Reports, Common Pleas Division 265–72 (1877); The Times, Feb. 8, 1877, 10.

Beyers v. Green, 1 All England Law Reports 613–15 (1936).

Bingley v. Barnes, ASSI 54/11; Manchester Examiner and Times, Mar. 8, 1893, 7; Mar. 9, 1893, 7.

Black v. Baucalare, ASSI 22/42; Cornish Telegraph, June 25, 1896, 5.

Black v. Sparling, ASSI 54/16; Liverpool Daily Post, Feb. 16, 1898, 3.

Blackburn v. Kershaw, Somerset County Gazette and Bristol Express, Aug. 10, 1872, 5.

Blackham v. Pratt, The Times, Mar. 7, 1864, 11; Law Times 39 (1864): 217–18.

Blackham v. Simpson, ASSI 1/68; Staffordshire Advertiser, Feb. 19, 1887, 6.

Blakeman v. Bowers, ASSI 1/68; Staffordshire Advertiser, Aug. 2, 1881, 6.

Blinkinsop v. Chapman, ASSI 32/37; Norwich Argus, Aug. 11, 1883, 8.

Blum v. Reeve, Oxfordshire, Buckinghamshire and Northamptonshire Telegraph, July 16, 1873, 3.

Booth v. Pearce, ASSI 75/2; South Wales Daily News, Mar. 18, 1874, 3; Mar. 19, 1874, 3.

Bowden v. Tucker, ASSI 22/40; Western Times, July 23, 1889, 5.

Brett v. Stone, Annual Register 85 (1843): 180–81.

Brewett v. Humber, ASSI 75/3; Swansea and Glamorgan Herald and the Herald of Wales, June 29, 1895, 3.

Brice v. Pemberton, ASSI 54/11; Manchester Examiner and Times, Mar. 1, 1893, 3.

Brookes v. Cox, Chronicles of Breaches of Promise (London, n.d.), 173–76.

Brookfield v. Wilcock, Lady's Own Paper 8 (Aug. 19, 1871): 125.

Brown v. Barnfather, ASSI 54/4; Carlisle Express and Examiner, Jan. 23, 1883, 8.

Brown v. Friend, ASSI 39/27; Norwich Argus, Mar. 29, 1873, 7.

Buhrer v. Holloway, Pump Court 1 (1883): 98; The Times, Nov. 8, 1883, 3.

Bull v. Robinson, ASSI 32/31; Cambridge Independent Press, Aug. 6, 1870, 6–7.

Burgoyne v. Oldrieve, ASSI 22/33; Western Times, Mar. 18, 1873, 5.

Burrow v. Lovell, ASSI 22/41; Western Times, Mar. 9, 1893, 3.

Burton v. Howlett, ASSI 32/37; Supplement to the Norwich Argus, Feb. 18, 1882, 1.

Callan v. Price, ASSI 54/2; Liverpool Daily Post, Feb. 9, 1880, 6.

Capron v. Denning, ASSI 22/28; *Exeter and Plymouth Gazette*, July 27, 1866, 6.

Carter v. Stowe, ASSI 54/9; *Liverpool Mercury*, Mar. 24, 1891, 7.

Chamberlain v. Weston, Chronicles of Breaches of Promise (London, n.d.), 159–61.

Chamberlaine v. Cave, ASSI 32/39; ASSI 37/7 (1888).

Chana v. Chana, The Times, May 20, 1969, 2.

Chapman v. Rushman, ASSI 32/29; *The Times*, Mar. 27, 1862, 11.

Chedzoy v. Woodbery, ASSI 22/33; *Somerset County Gazette and Bristol Express*, Aug. 10, 1872, 7–8.

Cherry v. Thompson, 7 *Law Reports, Queen's Bench Division* 573–79 (1872); *The Times*, Apr. 17, 1872, 11; May 29, 1872, 11.

Chilton v. Hawkes, ASSI 1/68; *Shrewsbury Chronicle*, Mar. 15, 1889, 6.

Clark v. Daintith, ASSI 59/14; *Chester Chronicle*, Mar. 14, 1891, 2.

Clough v. Southern, ASSI 54/11; *Liverpool Mercury*, Apr. 14, 1892, 7.

Cock v. Richards, 32 *English Reports* 911–15 (1805); 34 *English Reports* 1071–72 (1805).

Cooper v. Hyatt, ASSI 22/42; *Bristol Mercury and Daily Post*, July 4, 1895, 2.

Copeland v. Hopkins, ASSI 54/13; *Manchester Evening Mail*, Nov. 2, 1894, 2.

Copley v. Ottley, Lady's Own Paper 8 (Oct. 14, 1871): 253.

Corbett v. Palmer and Another, ASSI 1/63; *Supplement to the Gloucester Mercury*, Apr. 11, 1863, 1.

Corio v. Salmon, ASSI 32/38; ASSI 37/7 (1886).

Cork v. Baker, 1 *Strange's Reports* 34 (1717).

Cottam v. Scott, ASSI 54/4; *Manchester Evening Mail*, Apr. 17, 1885, 3.

Cowper v. Holden, ASSI 54/7; *Manchester Examiner and Times*, Mar. 6, 1889, 3.

Coxhead v. Mullis, 3 *Law Reports, Common Pleas Division* 439 (1878); *The Times*, Mar. 19, 1878, 6.

Crookshank v. Farrow, ASSI 54/7; *Manchester Examiner and Times*, Feb. 28, 1889, 3.

Crosswell v. Hearn, The Times, Nov. 13, 1893, 3; Nov. 14, 1893, 13.

Currie v. Currie, Lady's Own Paper 7 (Mar. 4, 1871): 131.

Curtis v. Olden, ASSI 22/39; *Hampshire Chronicle*, Aug. 8, 1885, 8.

Dainty v. Brown, ASSI 32/31; *Northampton Mercury*, July 23, 1870, 7.

Dales v. McMaster, ASSI 54/3; *Liverpool Mercury*, May 22, 1884, 6; May 23, 1884, 5, 8.

Daniel v. Bowles, The Times, Dec. 19, 1826, 3.

Davies v. Harris, ASSI 1/63; *Hereford Journal*, Mar. 26, 1864, 3.

Davies v. Jenkins, ASSI 75/2; *Cardiff Times*, July 24, 1869, 8.

Davies v. Jenkins, ASSI 75/2; *Swansea and Glamorgan Herald*, July 31, 1878, 8.

Davies v. Jones, ASSI 75/2; *Brecon County Times*, Aug. 2, 1873, 7; *The Times*, Aug. 2, 1873, 11.

Davies v. Williams, ASSI 57/6; *Caernarvon and Denbigh Herald*, Aug. 3, 1867, 6.

Davis v. Bomford, 158 *English Reports* 101–3 (1860); *The Times*, July 19, 1860, 11.

Davis v. Goddard, ASSI 22/35; *Somerset County Gazette and Bristol Express,* Mar. 17, 1877, 6.

Davis v. Latham, ASSI 1/63; *The Times,* July 13, 1863, 11.

Day v. Roberts, Woman, issue 13 (Mar. 29, 1890): 1; *Birmingham Daily Gazette,* Mar. 25, 1890, 6; Mar. 26, 1890, 3; Mar. 27, 1890, 6.

Dean v. Hollins, ASSI 1/64; *Staffordshire Sentinel and Commercial and General Advertiser,* Mar. 18, 1865, 8.

Dennis v. McKenzie, ASSI 32/32; ASSI 39/27; *Law Times* 24 (1871): 363; *Cambridge Independent Press,* Mar. 25, 1871, 6–7.

Desforges v. Hibbert, The Times, July 30, 1877, 11.

Dickison v. Holcroft, Carthew's Reports, 233 (1674).

Ditcham v. Worrall, 5 *Law Reports, Common Pleas Division* 410–23 (1880); *The Times,* Mar. 12, 1880, 4; May 10, 1880, 6; June 24, 1880, 6.

Dixon v. Brearley, The Times, July 30, 1877, 11.

Dods v. Woollett, Liverpool Daily Post, May 15, 1882, 7; *Liverpool Mercury,* May 15, 1882, 8.

Drake v. Blake, ASSI 22/32; *Winchester Herald,* Mar. 9, 1872, 3.

Drinkwater v. Woodhead, ASSI 15/8; *Nottingham and Midland Counties Daily Express,* Mar. 11, 1864, 3.

Duxbury v. Smith, ASSI 54/9; *Manchester Examiner and Times,* Apr. 29, 1891, 3.

Dyer v. Hare, ASSI 22/41; *Bristol Evening News,* Apr. 6, 1892, 4.

Earp v. Tomkinson, Chronicles of Breaches of Promise (London, n.d.), 186–88.

Eden v. Ormand, ASSI 32/31; *Buckinghamshire Herald,* Mar. 20, 1869, 3.

Edwards v. Roberts, ASSI 59/151; *Caernarvon and Denbigh Herald,* Feb. 2, 1884, 6.

Elder v. Brearley, Illustrated Police News, Feb. 20, 1897, 6.

Eldridge v. Rees, ASSI 22/42; *Bristol Mercury,* July 1, 1895, 6.

Elliot v. Stranger, Bristol Mercury and Daily Post, Apr. 15, 1878, 3.

Ellis v. Cock, Annual Register 19 (1776): 200–201.

Evans v. Jones, ASSI 59/21; *Caernarvon and Denbigh Herald,* June 8, 1894, 8.

Farrow v. Child, ASSI 32/36; *Norwich Argus,* Mar. 31, 1877, 7.

Fawkes v. Harding, ASSI 54/11; *Carlisle Journal,* Feb. 20, 1893, 3.

Fender v. St. John-Mildmay, 1 *Appeal Cases before the House of Lords* 1–56 (1938).

Finney v. Garmoyle, Horace Wyndham, "Case of Viscount Garmoyle," *Blotted 'Scutcheons: Some Society Cause Célèbres,* London, 1926, 127–48; *The Times,* Nov. 21, 1884, 4.

Fishwick v. Barrow, ASSI 54/14; *Liverpool Mercury,* July 29, 1896, 7.

Fitzpatrick v. Curling, Illustrated Police News, Feb. 6, 1897, 2.

Fleming v. Thompson, Lady's Own Paper 4 (Aug. 28, 1869): 98.

Foote v. Hayne, 171 *English Reports* 1310–11 (1824); *The Times,* Dec. 22, 1824, 1–4; Dec. 23, 1824, 2; Dec. 27, 1824, 3.

Ford v. Strongitharm, ASSI 54/14; *Manchester Evening Mail,* Mar. 5, 1896, 2.

Fordon v. Woolridge, Chronicles of Breaches of Promise (London, n.d.), 176–78.

Foster v. Mellish, Annual Register 44 (1802): 371.

Frampton v. Veeley, ASSI 28/12 (1897).

Franklyn v. Chaplin, Times Law Reports 17 (1900): 84; *The Times,* Nov. 27, 1900, 14.

Frost v. Knight, 7 *Law Reports, Exchequer Cases* 111–18 (1872); *Staffordshire Sentinel,* Mar. 19, 1870, 7; *Albany Law Journal* 3 (1871): 133–37; 5 (1872): 152–53; *Law Times* 50 (1870–71): 113–14; 52 (1872): 287; *Solicitor's Journal and Reporter* 16 (1872): 280; Keningale Cook, "A Point of Law," *Woman,* issue 1 (1872): 75–76; John Popplestone, "Frost v. Knight," *Green Bag* 1 (1889): 161–62; *The Times,* June 22, 1871, 11.

Fuller v. Sheppard, Lambeth Palace Library, Court of Arches Depositions, D797, Case 3544, 105–341 (fiches 4400–4408; 1750).

Gardner v. Thomas, ASSI 22/27; *Bristol Mercury,* Aug. 23, 1873, 3.

Gee v. Entwistle, ASSI 54/2; *Liverpool Mercury,* July 27, 1878, 8; July 29, 1878, 6.

Gibson v. Moore, ASSI 59/3 (1885).

Girdwood v. Holme, ASSI 54/7; *Lancaster Gazette,* July 13, 1889, 6.

Girling v. Allsop, ASSI 32/29; *Suffolk Chronicle,* Aug. 3, 1861, 7.

Gordon v. Woolridge, Chronicles of Breaches of Promise (London, n.d.), 176–78.

Gore v. Sudley, Cardiff Times, June 13, 1896, 6.

Gould v. Ingram, Woman, issue 10 (Mar. 8, 1890): 1.

Grafton v. King, Chronicles of Breaches of Promise (London, n.d.), 161–63.

Grave v. Mitchell, ASSI 54/2; *Supplement to the Carlisle Patriot,* Jan. 21, 1881, 1.

Graves v. Cutforth, Illustrated Police News, Jan. 25, 1896, 2.

Green v. Patey, Jurist 1 (1887): 324; *The Times,* Oct. 12, 1887, 7.

Green v. Ramwell, The Times, Apr. 2, 1866, 11.

Gregory v. Beach, ASSI 22/33; *Dorset County Chronicle,* Mar. 13, 1873, 8.

Hadad v. Bruce, Times Law Reports 8 (1891–92): 409–10; *Cornish Telegraph,* Mar. 10, 1892, 2.

Hagger v. Bush, Chronicles of Breaches of Promise (London, n.d.), 169–73.

Haines v. Lawrence, ASSI 1/66; ASSI 8/2; *Gloucester Mercury,* Apr. 10, 1875, 4.

Hairs v. Elliot, Woman, issue 17 (Apr. 26, 1890): 1; *The Times,* Apr. 18, 1890, 3; Apr. 19, 1890, 5–6; Apr. 22, 1890, 10.

Hall v. Taylor, ASSI 1/65; *Oxford Chronicle and Berks and Bucks Gazette,* Mar. 1, 1873, 5.

Hall v. Wright, 120 *English Reports* 695–706 (1859).

Halliwell v. Rigby, ASSI 54/3; *Manchester Evening News,* Feb. 3, 1885, 3.

Hamer v. Jennings, Liverpool Mercury, Aug. 1, 1885, 3.

Hamilton v. Jacobs, Illustrated Police News, Jan. 16, 1897, 8.

Hampton v. Boalsh, Chronicles of Breaches of Promise (London, n.d.), 183–84.

Hancock v. Clifford, ASSI 22/39; *Bristol Mercury,* Feb. 6, 1886, 6.

Hancock v. Davies, ASSI 73/3; *Swansea Herald and Neath Gazette,* Aug. 7, 1889, 3.

Hancock v. Thomas, Newgate Calendar and Divorce Court Chronicle, issue 3 (May 20, 1872): 45–46.

Handley v. Smith, ASSI 1/63; *Staffordshire Sentinel,* Mar. 23, 1861, 7.

Hanson v. Dixon, Law Times 96 (1907): 32–34.

Hanson v. Lad, ASSI 54/7; *Manchester Examiner and Times,* July 14, 1888, 7.

Harbert v. Edginton, Law Times 3 (1844): 51; *The Times,* Apr. 1, 1844, 6; Apr. 20, 1844, 8.

Harrison v. Cage et uxor, Carthew's Reports, 469; 5 *Modern Reports* 411; 1 *Salkeld's Reports* 24 (1698).

Harrison v. Sherlock, ASSI 54/11; *Liverpool Mercury,* Dec. 9, 1892, 7.

Hart v. Clinker, Staffordshire Times and Newcastle Pioneer, Mar. 23, 1861, 3.

Harvey v. Foard, ASSI 1/65; *Gloucestershire Chronicle,* Apr. 5, 1873, 5.

Harworth v. Taylor, ASSI 54/4; *Manchester Examiner and Times,* Feb. 4, 1886, 8.

Haun v. Bradford, The Times, July 29, 1872, 11; July 31, 1872, 11.

Hawkins v. Toogood, Bristol Daily Post, Aug. 15, 1871, 13.

Hawkridge v. Dommet, ASSI 22/42; *Devon and Exeter Gazette,* June 29, 1897, 3.

Haycox v. Bishton, ASSI 1/65; *Staffordshire Sentinel and Commercial and General Advertiser,* Mar. 19, 1870, 8.

Hayes v. Cox, ASSI 54/12; *Liverpool Mercury,* Mar. 15, 1893, 7.

Haynes v. Haynes, Chronicles of Breaches of Promise (London, n.d.), 178–80.

Hazeldine v. Hampton and Wife, Chronicles of Breaches of Promise (London, n.d.), 143.

Heal v. Nicholls, ASSI 22/42; *Bristol Mercury,* July 17, 1897, 6.

Heap v. Morris, The Times, Mar. 8, 1878, 11.

Herron v. Mort, ASSI 54/8; *Liverpool Mercury,* July 28, 1890, 7.

Hettena v. Joseph, ASSI 54/11; *Manchester Examiner and Times,* Dec. 5, 1892, 6; Dec. 6, 1892, 7.

Hewitt v. Mowis, Lady's Own Paper 1 (Apr. 6, 1867): 317; *The Times,* Mar. 28, 1867, 11.

Heywood v. Yeomans, ASSI 54/12; *Manchester Examiner and Times,* Dec. 9, 1893, 5.

Hickey v. Campion, Weekly Reporter 20 (1872): 752–54.

Higgs v. Trow, ASSI 32/33; *Leicester Advertiser,* Mar. 2, 1872, 8.

Hill v. Proctor, ASSI 32/34; *Norwich Argus,* Aug. 9, 1873, 7.

Hirst v. Waddington, ASSI 54/7; *Manchester Guardian,* July 13, 1889, 11.

Hole v. Harding, ASSI 22/38; ASSI 28/6; *Exeter and Plymouth Gazette Daily Telegram,* Jan. 30, 1882, 3.

Holmes v. Brierly, Law Times 59 (1888): 70–72; *Pump Court* 7 (1888): 117; 8 (1889): 32.

Holmes v. Preston, Illustrated Police News, May 23, 1896, 8.

Holt v. Hamer, ASSI 54/2; *Manchester Evening News,* July 22, 1881, 3.

Hooper v. Stokes, Cornish Telegraph, Feb. 16, 1882, 3.

Hope v. Speakerman, ASSI 54/3; *Illustrated Police News,* Jan. 31, 1885, 3.

Hope v. Watson, The Times, July 22, 1872, 13.

Hopley v. Hurst, ASSI 57/6; *Chester Chronicle,* Apr. 5, 1862, 2–3.

Horam v. Humphreys, 98 *English Reports* 543 (1772).

Houghton v. Thompson, ASSI 54/14; *Manchester Guardian,* Apr. 14, 1896, 9.

Hounsell v. Parkin, ASSI 22/39; *Hampshire Chronicle,* Feb. 14, 1885, 3.

Hubbert v. Copping, Bristol Daily Post, Aug. 15, 1871, 13.

Humphries v. Gain, ASSI 22/39; *Hampshire Chronicle,* Aug. 9, 1884, 7.

Hutley v. Master, Illustrated Police News, Feb. 1, 1896, 7.

Ibbetson v. Strickland, ASSI 22/40; *Western Times,* Mar. 5, 1889, 3.

Irvine v. Vickers, ASSI 1/65; *Berkshire County Chronicle,* July 17, 1869, 5.

Jacobs v. Wolfe, The Times, May 7, 1880, 4; May 8, 1880, 11.

James v. Phillips, ASSI 75/3; *Cardigan and Tivy-Side Advertiser,* Mar. 1, 1889, 4.

Jardenes v. Oppler, Illustrated Police News, June 25, 1898, 8.

Jenkins v. Edwards, ASSI 1/68; ASSI 8/2; *Shropshire Guardian and Shrewsbury Herald,* July 12, 1884, 8.

Jillard v. Ryder, ASSI 22/43; *Western Times,* June 21, 1899, 2.

Jones v. Boumphrey, Gloucester Mercury, Apr. 11, 1863, 5.

Jones v. Chapman, ASSI 22/40; *Cornish Telegraph,* Mar. 7, 1889, 6.

Jones v. Griffiths, ASSI 59/144; *Chester Chronicle,* July 31, 1880, 5.

Jones v. James, ASSI 75/2; *Carmarthen Journal,* Mar. 6, 1868, 2.

Jones v. Jeffries, ASSI 1/63; *Staffordshire Sentinel,* July 25, 1863, 7.

Jones v. Lloyd, ASSI 59/14; *Chester Chronicle,* Mar. 14, 1891, 2.

Jones v. Southworth, ASSI 54/2; *Lancaster Observer and Morecambe Chronicle,* Jan. 21, 1881, 6.

Jones v. Williams, ASSI 75/3; *Swansea and Glamorgan Herald and the Herald of Wales,* Nov. 28, 1896, 1.

Jukes v. Lloyd, ASSI 1/67; *Shrewsbury Chronicle,* July 28, 1882 (Second Sheet), 9.

Kelly v. Bell, ASSI 54/2; *Carlisle Express and Examiner,* July 3, 1880, 8.

Kelly v. Routledge, Liverpool Daily Post, Dec. 11, 1897, 3.

Kennedy v. McCann, ASSI 54/13; *Manchester Evening Mail,* Apr. 17, 1895, 3; Apr. 18, 1895, 2; Feb. 14, 1896, 2.

Kennerley v. Boulton, ASSI 54/14; *Liverpool Mercury,* July 28, 1896, 6.

Kerfoot v. Marsden, 175 *English Reports* 1005 (1860); *The Times,* Aug. 25, 1860, 12.

Killick v. Wilkinson, Chronicles of Breaches of Promise (London, n.d.), 149–52.

Kitteridge v. Crowe, ASSI 32/29; *Cambridge Independent Press,* Mar. 24, 1860, 6.

Knowles v. Duncan, ASSI 32/39; *The Times,* Aug. 13, 1890, 8; Horace Wyndham, "Romance that Failed," *Dramas of the Law* (London, 1936), 169–205.

Kremezi v. Ridgeway, Solicitor's Journal and Reporter 93 (1949): 287–88.

Lacy v. Frankeiss, ASSI 22/36; *Winchester Observer and County News,* July 6, 1878, 8.

Lamb v. Fryer, Liverpool Daily Post, Aug. 9, 1881, 7.

Langford v. Tonge, ASSI 54/5; *Manchester Examiner and Times,* Jan. 28, 1887, 3.

Langley v. Rose, Annual Register 94 (1852): 203–4.

Langley v. Trickett, ASSI 54/2; *Manchester Evening News,* Feb. 3, 1880, 4.

Leathers v. Marshall, Lady's Own Paper 8 (Sept. 16, 1871): 187.

Lee v. Wright, ASSI 32/37; *Supplement to the Norwich Argus,* Feb. 16, 1884, 1.

Levens v. Hutton, ASSI 54/3; *Manchester Evening News*, Apr. 29, 1884, 3; *Manchester Evening Mail*, Apr. 29, 1884, 3; Apr. 30, 1884, 3.

Lever v. Dobson, ASSI 54/7; *Liverpool Mercury*, May 21, 1889, 8.

Lewis v. Davies, ASSI 1/62; *Star of Gwent*, Aug. 11, 1860, 7.

Lewis v. Franklin, ASSI 75/2; *South Wales Daily News*, Mar. 28, 1878, 3.

Lewis v. Jenkins, ASSI 75/4; *Swansea Herald and Herald of Wales*, Aug. 13, 1898, 2.

Lewis v. Molyneux, ASSI 54/2; *Liverpool Mercury*, Nov. 6, 1878, 8; Nov. 7, 1878, 8.

McCarthy v. Rowbotham, ASSI 54/9; *Manchester Examiner and Times*, July 18, 1891, 10.

McGrath v. De Valve, ASSI 54/8; *Liverpool Mercury*, July 29, 1890, 7.

MacLaren v. England, ASSI 34/39; ASSI 37/3; *Kent Messenger and Maidstone Telegraph*, Mar. 2, 1889, 4.

McLeod v. Horrocks, *Illustrated Police News*, Mar. 30, 1872, 3.

Maddocks v. Bennett, ASSI 59/14; *Chester Chronicle*, Mar. 14, 1891, 2.

Mallett v. Sutton, *Illustrated Police News*, Apr. 1, 1871, 4.

Martin v. Secker, ASSI 22/41; *Western Times*, July 26, 1892, 7.

Mason v. Mason, ASSI 54/2; *Westmorland Gazette*, July 27, 1878, 7.

Mather v. Royston, ASSI 54/17; *Liverpool Mercury*, Aug. 7, 1899, 7.

Matthews v. Miller, *Cornish Telegraph*, Feb. 16, 1882, 3.

May v. Rotton, ASSI 22/36; *Somerset County Gazette*, Apr. 13, 1878, 7.

Micklewright v. Bryning, ASSI 54/3; *Liverpool Mercury*, Feb. 11, 1882, 8.

Miller v. Joy, *The Times*, Jan. 25, 1884, 3.

Mitchell v. Hazeldine, *Lady's Own Paper* 5 (Mar. 12, 1870): 146; *The Times*, Mar. 4, 1870, 11.

Modestou v. Yeannopoulis, *The Times*, Mar. 31, 1954, 11.

Morris v. Bonville, ASSI 75/2; *Carmarthen Weekly Reporter*, July 21, 1876, 3.

Morris v. Leigh, ASSI 54/11; *Manchester Examiner and Times*, Mar. 2, 1893, 7.

Morris v. Perkin, *Staffordshire Times*, Apr. 3, 1875, 6.

Nangle v. Bamford, ASSI 54/12; *Manchester Examiner and Times*, July 13, 1893, 8.

Nates v. Heap, ASSI 54/9; *Manchester Examiner and Times*, Nov. 30, 1891, 6.

Nelson v. Crathorne, ASSI 28/12; *Bristol Evening News*, July 17, 1897, 3.

Nelson v. Taylforth, ASSI 54/16; *Westmorland Gazette*, Jan. 21, 1899, 6.

Nicholson v. Maclachlan, ASSI 75/3; *Haverfordwest and Milford Haven Telegraph*, Jan. 22, 1896, 4.

Nightengale v. Perry, *The Times*, Apr. 20, 1875, 11.

Nixon v. Moss, ASSI 1/63; *Staffordshire Sentinel*, July 25, 1863, 7.

Norman v. Baker, ASSI 22/43; ASSI 28/13; *Western Times*, Feb. 7, 1899, 5.

Norris v. Burnett, *Somerset County Gazette and Bristol Express*, Aug. 10, 1872, 7–8.

Northcote v. Doughty, 4 *Law Reports, Common Pleas Division* 385–91 (1879).

Orford v. Cole, 171 *English Reports* 670–71 (1818); *The Times*, Apr. 6, 1818, 3.

Orman v. James, ASSI 22/43; ASSI 28/13 (1898).

Otte v. Grant, The Times, Nov. 27, 1868, 11.

Owen v. Jones, ASSI 59/23; *Caernarvon and Denbigh Herald,* June 14, 1895, 7.

Owen v. Lawley, ASSI 1/68; *Shrewsbury Chronicle,* Mar. 9, 1888, 7.

Owen v. Moberly, Justice of the Peace 64 (1900): 88.

Owen v. Williams, ASSI 59/142; *Caernarvon and Denbigh Herald,* July 19, 1879, 7.

Owens v. Horton, Birmingham Daily Gazette, Mar. 22, 1890, 6.

Pain v. M'Ewin, Illustrated Police News, Mar. 3, 1888, 3.

Palmer v. Wilder, 2 *Croke's Reports* 66 (n.d.).

Palmer v. Wootten, Illustrated Police News, Feb. 7, 1880, 2.

Paris v. Jackson, The Times, May 7, 1879, 6; May 10, 1879, 6; May 12, 1879, 11.

Parker v. Jackson, ASSI 22/28; ASSI 28/3; *Supplement to the Hampshire Chronicle,* July 20, 1867, 2.

Parker v. Stockwell, ASSI 54/17; *Manchester Guardian,* Apr. 26, 1899, 10.

Parker v. Wilkins, ASSI 32/38; *Norwich Argus,* July 25, 1885, 8.

Parnell v. Hancock, ASSI 22/42; *Western Times,* Aug. 2, 1893, 3.

Pattinson v. Heslop, ASSI 54/14; *Carlisle Express and Examiner,* July 4, 1896, 6.

Pearce v. Boardman, ASSI 22/27; *Bristol Daily Post,* Aug. 16, 1867, 3.

Pendlebury v. Doody, ASSI 54/9; *Manchester Examiner and Times,* July 16, 1891, 3.

Penny v. Rees, ASSI 22/32; *Western Times,* Mar. 18, 1872, 3–4; Mar. 19, 1872, 5.

Pepperell v. Grills, ASSI 22/33; *Devon Weekly Times,* Aug. 1, 1878, 8.

Perry v. Wood, ASSI 22/36; *Somerset County Gazette and Bristol Express,* July 28, 1877, 11.

Pettit v. Tough, ASSI 54/16; *Lancaster Gazette,* July 9, 1898, 6.

Pierce v. Smith, Newgate Calendar and Divorce Court Chronicle, issue 9 (July 8, 1872): 146.

Pope v. Staples, ASSI 32/31; *Ipswich Express and Essex and Suffolk Mercury,* Mar. 29, 1870, 7.

Potter v. Fox, ASSI 54/4; *Manchester Evening News,* July 17, 1885, 3.

Powers v. Battersby, ASSI 54/17; *Manchester Evening News,* Feb. 5, 1900, 4.

Prevost v. Wood, Times Law Reports 21 (1905): 684–85.

Price v. Brooks, ASSI 1/66; ASSI 8/3; *Worcester Chronicle,* Mar. 16, 1878, 8.

Pryke v. Smith, ASSI 32/32; *Norwich Argus,* Aug. 12, 1871, 7.

Pullock v. Allard, ASSI 1/64; *Gloucester Mercury,* Apr. 6, 1867, 2.

Quirk v. Thomas, 1 *Law Reports, King's Bench Division* 516–41 (1915); *The Times,* Feb. 4, 1915, 5; Feb. 6, 1915, 5; Feb. 9, 1915, 3; Feb. 10, 1915, 3; Feb. 16, 1915, 3; Mar. 20, 1915, 3.

Railton v. Wilcox, Manchester Evening News, Apr. 12, 1880, 3.

Read v. Bennion, ASSI 57/6; ASSI 59/113; *Chester Record,* Apr. 8, 1865, 5.

Readhead v. Hyatt, ASSI 22/38; *Hampshire Chronicle,* July 15, 1882, 3.

Redfern v. White, ASSI 1/68; *Staffordshire Advertiser,* Aug. 1, 1885, 5.

Redhead v. Huddleston, Law Journal 8 (1873): 674–75; *The Times,* Aug. 2, 1873, 11.

Redshaw v. Wilman, Annual Register 85 (1843): 87–88.

Rees v. Powell, ASSI 75/3; *South Wales Daily News,* Mar. 13, 1888, 2.

Reeves v. Powell, ASSI 32/34; *Buckinghamshire Herald,* Mar. 15, 1873, 6–7.

Rice v. Hall, ASSI 75/2; *Brecon County Times,* Jan. 31, 1880, 2.

Richards v. Palmer, ASSI 22/40; *Taunton Courier,* Feb. 22, 1888, 7.

Richardson v. Anderson, ASSI 54/12; *Manchester Examiner and Times,* May 2, 1893, 7.

Roberts v. Denham, Law Times 4 (1844): 118.

Roberts v. Hughes, ASSI 57/7; ASSI 59/135; *Caernarvon and Denbigh Herald,* Mar. 25, 1876, 8.

Roberts v. Hughes, ASSI 75/2; *Cardiff Times,* Feb. 25, 1882, 2.

Roberts v. Jones, ASSI 59/142; *Caernarvon and Denbigh Herald,* July 19, 1879, 7.

Roberts v. Williams, ASSI 59/3; *Caernarvon and Denbigh Herald,* July 25, 1885, 8.

Roberts v. Williams, ASSI 59/29; *Chester Observer,* July 30, 1898, 6.

Robinson v. Atkinson, ASSI 54/3; *Carlisle Express and Examiner,* July 19, 1884, 6.

Robinson v. Cumming, 26 *English Reports* 646–48 (1742).

Roper v. Bagley, ASSI 32/36; *The Times,* Aug. 2, 1880, 11.

Roper v. Hills, ASSI 32/32; *Suffolk Chronicle,* Apr. 1, 1871, 7; *The Times,* Mar. 31, 1871, 11.

Sans v. Whalley, The Times, May 6, 1880, 6; May 8, 1880, 6, 11.

Schreiber v. Frazer, Annual Register 23 (1780): 218–19.

Scrine v. M'Kay, Illustrated Police News, Feb. 28, 1880, 2.

Searing v. Newton, ASSI 32/36; ASSI 37/1, Correspondence, Letters 1–9; ASSI 39/1 (1878).

Seed v. Caldwell, ASSI 54/12; *Manchester Examiner,* Mar. 7, 1894, 2.

Seymour v. Gartside, The Times, Aug. 19, 1822, 3.

Shaw v. Shaw and Another, 2 *Law Reports, Queen's Bench Division* 429–43 (1954).

Sheppard v. Forder, ASSI 22/36; *Exeter and Plymouth Gazette Daily Telegram,* July 22, 1878, 3.

Sherratt v. Webster, Law Times 8 (1863): 254–55; *Jurist* 9 (1863): 629.

Shickell v. Warren, ASSI 32/39; *Norwich Argus,* July 26, 1890, 4.

Siveyer v. Allison, 2 *Law Reports, King's Bench Division* 403–8 (1935).

Skipp v. Kelly, Times Law Reports 42 (1926): 258–59.

Slack v. Bradley, ASSI 54/7; *Manchester Examiner and Times,* July 16, 1888, 6.

Smith v. Ferrers, Annual Register 88 (1846): 349–63; *The Times,* Feb. 16, 1846, 7–8; Feb. 17, 1846, 8; Feb. 18, 1846, 7–8; Feb. 19, 1846, 7–8; *Proceedings upon the Trial of the Action Brought by Mary Elizabeth Smith against the Right Hon. Washington Sewallis Shirley Earl Ferrers for Breach of Promise of Marriage* (London, 1846); Mary Smith, *Statement of Facts Respecting the Cause of Smith v. Earl Ferrers* (London, 1846).

Smith v. Mitchell, ASSI 54/9; *Manchester Examiner and Times,* Mar. 17, 1892, 7.

Smith v. Strickland, ASSI 54/1; *Liverpool Mercury,* Aug. 8, 1877, 8.

Smith v. Woodfine, 140 *English Reports* 272–77 (1856); *The Times,* July 8, 1856, 11.

Softley v. Thompson, The Times, Feb. 19, 1883, 10.

Southwood v. Arscott, ASSI 22/42; *Devon Weekly Times,* Feb. 1, 1895, 6.

Spender v. Orchard, ASSI 22/36; *Hampshire Chronicle*, Mar. 9, 1878, 7.

Spink v. Lord, ASSI 32/33; *Suffolk Chronicle*, Aug. 3, 1872, 7.

Spooner v. Godfrey, The Times, May 6, 1908, 17–18.

Stanton v. Paton and Wife, Annual Register 85 (1843): 383–88.

Stringer v. Oldham, ASSI 54/17; *Manchester Evening Mail*, July 12, 1900, 4.

Sutton v. Aronsberg, ASSI 54/12; *Manchester Examiner and Times*, July 18, 1893, 5; July 19, 1893, 5.

Swain v. Brinn, Newgate Calendar and Divorce Court Chronicle, issue 9 (July 8, 1872): 138–40.

Swift v. Rhodes, ASSI 54/2; *Liverpool Mercury*, Aug. 5, 1878, 3.

Tamikin v. Wilson, ASSI 54/7; *Carlisle Express and Examiner*, July 6, 1889, 8.

Taylor v. Entwistle, ASSI 54/17; *Manchester Evening Mail*, Apr. 24, 1899, 4.

Taylor v. Hardman, ASSI 54/5; *Manchester Examiner and Times*, Jan. 31, 1887, 3.

Thatcher v. D'Aguilar, Chronicles of Breaches of Promise (London, n.d.), 137–42.

Theophilus v. Howard, ASSI 75/2; *Cardiff Times*, Aug. 1, 1874, 6.

Thomas v. Edwards, Manchester Evening Mail, Apr. 21, 1898, 2.

Thomas v. Jones, Annual Register 64 (1822): 139–41.

Thomas v. Shirley, Weekly Reporter 11 (1862): 21; *The Times*, Nov. 6, 1862, 8; Nov. 7, 1862, 9.

Tilliott v. Wrightup, ASSI 32/31; *Norwich Argus*, Mar. 27, 1869, 1.

Tittle v. Hooper, ASSI 75/2; *South Wales Daily News*, Feb. 14, 1883, 4.

Townsend v. Bennett, Solicitor's Journal and Reporter 19 (1875): 276; *The Times*, Apr. 20, 1875, 11.

Trainor v. Radcliffe, ASSI 54/14; *Liverpool Mercury*, Nov. 23, 1895, 6.

Turner v. Jackson, ASSI 54/16; *Manchester Evening Mail*, Apr. 26, 1898, 4.

Vaughan v. Robinson, ASSI 54/15; *Liverpool Mercury*, May 19, 1897, 10.

Vibert v. Hampton, ASSI 22/35; *Cornish Telegraph*, Mar. 13, 1877, 4.

Vickery v. Strawbridge, ASSI 22/42; *Devon Weekly Times*, Feb. 1, 1895, 6.

Vineall v. Veness, 176 *English Reports* 593–94 (1865).

Wade v. Radford, Chronicles of Breaches of Promise (London, n.d.), 144.

Wade v. Rae, ASSI 32/34; ASSI 39/27; *Norwich Argus*, Aug. 9, 1873, 7.

Walker v. Boocock, ASSI 54/14; *Manchester Evening Mail*, July 16, 1896, 3.

Walker v. Owen, ASSI 54/9; *Liverpool Mercury*, May 5, 1891, 7.

Warwick v. Pownall, ASSI 54/3; *Liverpool Mercury*, May 24, 1884, 8; *The Times*, May 26, 1884, 14.

Watkins v. Davies, ASSI 57/7; *Caernarvon and Denbigh Herald*, Mar. 30, 1872, 3; *The Times*, Apr. 20, 1872, 11; *Weekly Notes*, Pt. 1 (1872): 146.

Watkins v. Marjoribanks, Illustrated Police News, Jan. 25, 1896, 8; Feb. 15, 1896, 3.

Weir v. Costello, ASSI 54/9; *Liverpool Mercury*, Dec. 7, 1891, 6.

West v. Sales, ASSI 32/37; *Kent Messenger and Maidstone Telegraph*, July 21, 1883, 5.

Wharton v. Lewis, 171 *English Reports* 1303–4 (1824); *The Times*, Dec. 7, 1824, 2–3.

Wheeler v. Jones, ASSI 57/7; *Chester Chronicle*, Aug. 21, 1869, 7.

White v. Aird, *Newgate Calendar and Divorce Court Chronicle*, issue 3 (May 20, 1872): 46.

White v. Allen, ASSI 22/42; *Bristol Mercury*, July 4, 1896, 3.

Whitehead v. Hall, ASSI 54/5; *Solicitor's Journal and Reporter* 31 (1886–87): 445; *Manchester Examiner and Times*, Apr. 29, 1887, 8; *Jurist* 1 (1882): 164.

Whittaker v. Haythornethwaite, ASSI 54/17; *Manchester Guardian*, July 21, 1899, 3.

Wiedemann v. Walpole, 2 *Law Reports, Queen's Bench Division* 534–42 (1891); *The Times*, June 11, 1891, 13; June 12, 1891, 4; June 13, 1891, 18; June 15, 1891, 3; June 16, 1891, 3; June 17, 1891, 3; June 18, 1891, 4.

Wilcox v. Godfrey, ASSI 22/32; *Taunton Courier*, Mar. 27, 1872, 5; *Law Times* 26 (1872): 328–29, 481–82.

Wilkinson v. Bainbridge, ASSI 54/2; *Lancaster Gazette*, July 7, 1880, 2–3.

Wilkinson v. Hampson, ASSI 54/5; *Liverpool Daily Post*, June 2, 1886, 3.

Wilkinson v. Kelsall, ASSI 57/7; ASSI 59/128; *Chester Chronicle*, Aug. 17, 1872, 7.

Wilkinson v. Rylands, ASSI 54/3; *Liverpool Mercury*, May 4, 1882, 8; *Liverpool Daily Post*, May 4, 1882, 6.

Williams v. Dodd, ASSI 54/16; *Manchester Evening Mail*, Apr. 25, 1898, 4.

Williams v. Haines, ASSI 1/66; *Monmouthshire Merlin*, Apr. 2, 1875, 2.

Williams v. Harman, ASSI 75/3; *Swansea and Glamorgan Herald*, Nov. 28, 1896, 1.

Williams v. Hughes, ASSI 59/146; *Chester Chronicle*, July 30, 1881, 6.

Williams v. Jones, ASSI 75/2; *South Wales Daily News*, July 14, 1883, 4.

Williams v. Mathias, ASSI 75/3; *South Wales Daily News*, June 25, 1894, 7.

Williams v. Roberts, ASSI 54/12; *Liverpool Daily Post*, Mar. 18, 1894, 3.

Williams v. Roberts, ASSI 59/9; *Caernarvon and Denbigh Herald*, July 20, 1888, 8.

Williams v. Thomas, *Annual Register* 85 (1843): 391–94.

Williams v. Thomas, ASSI 75/4; *Brecon County Times*, Mar. 11, 1898, 8.

Windeatt v. Slocombe, ASSI 22/32; *Western Times*, Mar. 15, 1872, 6.

Wood v. Humphreys, ASSI 1/68; *Gloucester Mercury*, Aug. 11, 1883, 3.

Wood v. Hurd, 132 *English Reports* 65–66, 326 (1835); *The Times*, May 7, 1835, 6; May 12, 1835, 6; June 17, 1835, 3.

Wood v. Irving, ASSI 54/9; *Carlisle Express and Examiner*, July 11, 1891, 6.

Woodward v. Clarke, *The Times*, Feb. 7, 1865, 11; Feb. 14, 1865, 9.

Wright v. Lenaker, ASSI 54/2; *Liverpool Daily Post*, Aug. 9, 1881, 7.

Wynn v. Hurst, ASSI 1/66; *Shrewsbury Chronicle*, Mar. 26, 1875, 7.

Index

VICTORIAN LITERATURE AND CULTURE SERIES
Karen Chase, Jerome J. McGann, *and* Herbert Tucker, *General Editors*